Thinking to Transform

Facilitating Reflection in Leadership Learning (Companion Manual)

A Volume in
Contemporary Perspectives on Leadership Learning

Series Editor:
Kathy L. Guthrie,
Florida State University

Contemporary Perspectives on Leadership Learning
Kathy L. Guthrie, Series Editor

Thinking to Transform

Facilitating Reflection in Leadership Learning (Companion Manual)

By

Jillian M. Volpe White, Kathy L. Guthrie, Maritza Torres, and Associates

Information Age Publishing, Inc.
Charlotte, North Carolina • www.infoagepub.com

Library of Congress Cataloging-in-Publication Data

CIP data for this book can be found on the Library of Congress website:
http://www.loc.gov/index.html

Paperback: 978-1-64113-894-9
Hardcover: 978-1-64113-895-6
E-Book: 978-1-64113-896-3

*For all the people who create
and hold space for reflection in leadership learning*

CONTENTS

Acknowledgments

When we imagined a companion manual of reflection activities, we knew it had to be a community effort. This could not exist without the contributions of 52 colleagues and friends. Each activity is a glimpse into the work of a reflective practitioner. We live in a time of uncertainty and chaos, but knowing these colleagues serve as educators gives us hope for our collective future. We are also grateful for Carlo Morante whose feedback in the nascent stages of this endeavor was influential in the direction of this manual. We are especially grateful to Julie LeBlanc without whose intelligence, organization, diligence, and commitment this book would not exist.

CHAPTER 1

Enhancing Your Skills for Facilitating Reflection

Reflection is an iterative process of making meaning of experience. Leadership is a relational process that focuses on creating change. Together, these processes are greater than the sum of their parts: reflection enables leaders to learn from experience, evaluate assumptions and beliefs, and integrate critical perspectives into change processes (Volpe White, Guthrie, & Torres, 2019). Leadership has the potential to amplify reflection, shifting it from an individual exercise to a collective process that results in positive social change (Volpe White et al., 2019). In order for reflection in leadership learning to take root, educators should incorporate this important practice into curricular and co-curricular leadership learning.

As a companion to *Thinking to Transform: Reflection in Leadership Learning* (Volpe White et al., 2019) this companion manual includes more than 50 activities from 52 contributors. The contributors include a diverse group of experiential leadership educators who draw from a wide array of disciplinary backgrounds and influences. This manual is for both novice and seasoned facilitators. If you are new to facilitating reflection in leadership learning, we hope this can be a valuable resource for developing facilitation skills and learning how to guide groups through the process of reflection. If you have are an experienced facilitator, we hope this manual helps you enhance your practice or provides ideas for engaging groups in making meaning of experiences.

FORMAT OF ACTIVITIES

For the purposes of this manual, we organized reflection activities into six methods: contemplative, creative, digital, discussion, narrative, and written. Each chapter includes an introductory overview of the method followed by activities. At the beginning of each activity, there is a recommended time frame and group size. These are suggested, and the time required may vary based upon your specific context and group size. Activities range from a few minutes to several semes-

ters in duration, and include both small and large group activities. Next, there are learning goals to frame the potential outcomes for the activity. Some activities do not require any materials, some require only paper and pencil, and others require technology or artistic materials you may need to gather in advance. The process outlines the activity step by step and includes facilitator notes. For some activities, there are sections that could be read to participants as directions. In the cases where a facilitator could read instructions or framing information verbatim, the tex*t is italicized.* Activities conclude with debriefing questions. These are suggestions for where to begin, and you may have other questions that emerge as you facilitate activities. Finally, activities may include references to materials cited in text, resources, or both.

STRATEGY FOR REFLECTION

When it comes to selecting activities for reflection, there are countless options and variations from which to choose, and educators are consistently developing new and creative ways to engage participants in reflection. However, choosing activities is only part of the process. Reflection that is planned and sequenced can be more effective than reflection that is disorganized or occurs sporadically (Eyler, 2001). Ash and Clayton (2009) described the importance of developing a reflection strategy that begins by identifying learning goals. A taxonomy of learning objectives can provide guidance for this process (Suskie, 2018). Once learning goals are established, educators should select reflection activities that align with the goals (Ash & Clayton, 2009). Finally, educators should include assessment throughout and at the conclusion of an experience to evaluate learning. Eyler (2001) encouraged educators to develop a "reflection map" that included two dimensions: reflection before, during, and after experiential learning as well as reflection individually, in the classroom, and in the community. Although this suggestion is framed around service-

Thinking to Transform: Facilitating Reflection in Leadership Learning (Companion Manual), pp. 1–9

learning, it translates well to leadership learning where reflection may occur in groups or communities.

In this manual, we placed each activity in one method, but we acknowledge there is significant overlap. To that end, we provided a table of activities that shows some of the potential cross listings for activities. One activity may be creative and include narrative or writing. Another activity may be digital and include discussion. Some of these activities may be used in combination: a contemplative activity may provide centering before discussion, or writing may precede an activity that draws on narratives. Employing multiple methods for reflection may be more beneficial than utilizing one type of reflection (Hatcher, Bringle, & Muthiah, 2004).

REFLECTION IN LEADERSHIP LEARNING FRAMEWORK

Framed as a tree, the reflection in leadership learning framework (Volpe White et al., 2019) describes three important elements that support reflective practice and leadership learning (Figure 1.1). Grounding ideas provide an anchor in theory and practice. By gaining experience, learning about leadership theory, and being exposed to reflective practice, participants develop a foundation that supports further learning and development. Although educators influence the grounding ideas, they are essential as support structures. The people with whom students reflect play a critical role in drawing out learning from experiences. Educators support learners by providing feedback, encouraging honesty and vulnerability, and prioritizing reflection in curricular and co-curricular settings. The crown highlights transformation and the generative outcomes of reflection. Not all outcomes of reflection in leadership learning are depicted; many outcomes will be driven by context and content. However, the common element of these outcomes is the significance for developing leaders who are engaged in their communities. This framework provides a guiding structure for reflection in leadership learning. It is important not to assume participants understand what it means to reflect. Ashley Curtis and Darren Pierre provided suggestions for framing reflective practice. Their activity, Leadership Development: A Written Reflection Series, is in the written chapter.

EFFECTIVE PRACTICES FOR REFLECTION
Ashley Curtis and Darren Pierre

There are so many options for reflection, it may be challenging for participants to know where to begin with a personal reflective practice. These guidelines can help guide effective reflection.

- **Reflect Daily.** Take a few minutes each day to reflect and make note of impactful events that occurred.
- **Acknowledge Your Emotions.** Ask questions that consider how this experience made you feel and why.
- **Incorporate Multiple Perspectives.** Not only should you consider your own thoughts and emotions around your experiences, but it is important to consider the thoughts and emotions of others.
- **Seek Feedback.** Personal reflection is the first step in understanding what you are thinking and why, but this should be accompanied by processing with others. Share your thoughts with someone to gain an outside perspective, which may create clarity when determining action steps.

REFLECTION MODELS

Utilizing a reflection model, such as the "What? So what? Now what?" model can push the discussion from recapping experiences to applying a critical lens and synthesizing experiences and course materials (Ash & Clayton, 2004). Although this model may seem simple, through an iterative process of asking questions and considering responses, participants can engage in deeper learning.

- **What?** This question is primarily focused on what occurred. The goal is to look at experiences without judgment before ascribing meaning. Some questions may include: What happened? What did you observe? What patterns are taking shape?
- **So what?** This question examines the significance of experience. The process shifts from describing to interpreting and focuses on reactions and evaluation. How did the experience surprise you? What previous experiences may have influenced your reaction? What are the implications of the outcomes?
- **Now what?** This question focuses on implications and application to the future. What did you learn from this experience? How can you apply this to a future experience? What do you need to learn more about to be more effective in your role?

These questions form the basis for many reflection models and provide a grounding for debriefing questions.

Creating a welcoming atmosphere means creating spaces that are inviting for all participants. Amber E. Hampton described considerations for an inclusive space including the layout of the physical space and the mental and emotional preparation for facilitators. Her activity, Dialogue and Leadership Learning, is in the discussion chapter.

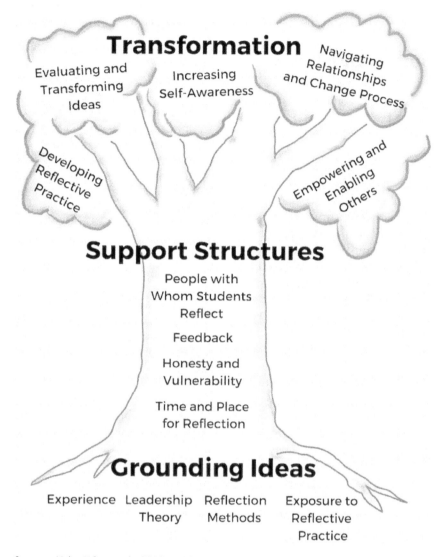

Transformation

Evaluating and Transforming Ideas

Increasing Self-Awareness

Navigating Relationships and Change Process

Developing Reflective Practice

Empowering and Enabling Others

Support Structures

People with Whom Students Reflect

Feedback

Honesty and Vulnerability

Time and Place for Reflection

Grounding Ideas

Experience   Leadership Theory   Reflection Methods   Exposure to Reflective Practice

Source: Volpe White et al., 2019, p. 10). Reprinted with permission.

Figure 1.1.   Reflection in leadership learning framework.

INCLUSIVE REFLECTION
Amber E. Hampton

- **Inclusive Design:** Whenever possible, prepare in advance for participants by leaving spaces open for wheelchair users to use tables or enter a dialogue circle. Similarly, providing materials in alternate languages if any participants do not use English as a first language can help with comprehension and boost participation, reducing the time a person may need to translate while participating.
- **Connect With Triggers or Passion Issues:** Take time to identify your triggers. What are the topics, identities, or themes related to social identity group memberships (gender, race, sexual orientation, socioeconomic status, etc.) that distract you or keep you from being present and engaged? Also take time to confirm your passion issues. On what issues do you have a clear view? What do you believe to be true or right? What aligns with your values? What are you involved in deeply through civic engagement or service to others? These may also be similar to your triggers, and that is okay.
- **Build a Cofacilitator Connection.** If you have a cofacilitator, spend time preparing and reviewing content, as well as building rapport by sharing your trigger and passion issues. This may help to build trust and also support facilitating reflection. Plan time to check in with your cofacilitator following the activity to debrief. Congratulate one another and share feedback for improvement.

ENGAGING GROUPS IN DISCUSSION

In any group discussion, there will be a variety of personalities. Some people may be comfortable sharing while others may be more reserved. These guidelines may help with facilitating conversation.

- **Pose a Question and Wait:** One of the most challenging moments as a facilitator is the silence that follows after you ask a question. Novice facilitators almost always jump in too quickly when no one speaks. Wait. Often participants need a minute to process the question and formulate a response.
- **Ask Open-Ended Questions:** As you develop debriefing questions, focus on open-ended questions, which invite a breadth of responses. For example, rather than asking "Did you learn from your experience?" you might ask "What did you learn from your experience?" or "How did this experience challenge you?"
- **Engage Everyone by Beginning With Writing or Pair-and-Share:** Sometimes it helps to get people talking in smaller groups before sharing with a large group. Ask participants to write responses in notebooks or on a scrap of paper. Alternatively, have participants pair up with the person next to them for a conversation. Once participants have a chance to commit their thoughts to paper, or share with someone else, they may be better prepared, or more likely, to share in a large-group discussion.
- **Invite Sharing:** It can be challenging to balance asking participants to share with honoring their silence, particularly when reflecting on something that is personal or challenging. Resist the temptation to call on people; putting people on the spot is rarely a good idea. To engage people who may not be comfortable talking in front of a group, create opportunities for sharing in pairs or small groups.
- **Managing Different Conversational Tendencies:** If one person dominates the conversation, you can bring other people into the conversation by saying "I would like to hear from some of the people we have not heard from yet." This lets eager participants know to take a break and encourages quieter participants to share.

Reflection is key for developing awareness of self and others. This often includes sharing stories. Julie E. Owen provided guidance for facilitators that may be useful as you prepare to facilitate any reflection activity that invites participants to share about themselves. Her activity, Personal Narratives as Authentic Expression, can be found in the narrative chapter.

HOLDING SPACE FOR SHARING STORIES
Julie E. Owen

Facilitators should note that what seems like a relatively simple activity can be anxiety-producing for participants. This anxiety can have multiple sources—fear of speaking in public; fear of exhibiting vulnerability among peers; worries about how stories may be received or misconstrued; and occasionally, fears about what happens after the story is shared. With such an open-ended invitation to reflection and narration, facilitators need to be ready for any kind of sharing. In the author's past experiences with narrative exercises, participants have shared stories of violence, sexual assault and harassment, eating disorders, migration and undocumented statuses, legal issues, racism, disabilities, ageism, and much more. There are often tears or laughter (occasionally both) accompanying these stories. How facilitators set the tone and parameters of the activity and establish trust in the learning space are vitally important. Facilitators should also be prepared to refer participants (both speakers and listeners) to campus resources if topics are triggering.

Facilitators may also consider the power of sharing their own story. I suggest the facilitator not go first. Although it seems like there would be value in modeling the way, my experience suggests participants tend to conform their stories to the facilitator's which can limit the utility of the activity. Sometimes I offer my story midway through a class or program. Often, I wait for participants to invite me to share. As educators, our values, philosophies, disciplines, and identities shape the curriculum and culture of our classes and programs. In order to create inclusive spaces, we must continue to interrogate our own lenses and positions, and to the extent possible share that learning process with participants. Why would participants risk vulnerability, reflection, and challenge if we are unable to model it ourselves? I also invite participants to explore their personal and social identities and how these shape their learning. Educators should situate learning in participants' experiences (especially vital for participants from underrepresented backgrounds), validate participants as self-authored knowers, and help participants understand the socially constructed nature of knowledge and its application.

FACILITATION

When engaging a group in reflection, effective facilitation goes beyond having a plan or selecting activities. Through developing skills, you can become more comfortable with and adept at facilitating groups in different circumstances. Although many people have experience facilitating, even the most seasoned facilitators can benefit from considering how to support learning and group development as well as practicing skills for facilitation.

- **Provide a Framework for Reflection:** Although some people may be familiar with reflection, other people may not have as much experience reflecting. Framing reflection as a learning process distinguishes it from a one-time activity (White & Guthrie, 2016). Describe reflection and explain the purpose of reflection. You may want to share the learning goals for the activities. This is not telling participants what or how to think, but framing the purpose and takeaways.
- **Create a Space That Is Safe for Sharing:** Educators play an important role in creating and holding space for reflection (Burchell & Dyson, 2005; Guthrie & Jenkins, 2018; Owen-Smith, 2018). Emphasize the importance of listening to others without judgment. Consider developing community guidelines so people can voice expectations.
- **Model Your Expectations:** If the group is doing an activity, everyone should be engaged. People may be more likely to participate if they see the facilitator taking part in the activity. Similarly, people should not observe (i.e., stand around the group and watch activities), but should be engaged as part of the group.
- **Consider Arranging the Group in a Circle:** A circle is a useful shape for groups because everyone can see everyone else, and everyone is equal in the space, though Brookfield (2017) cautioned sometimes circles can make participants feel watched or pressured to engage.
- **Develop an Appropriate Sequence for Your Goals:** You do not have to stick to the plan, but being prepared with a sequence of activities or questions to pose to the group can provide a launchpad from which to begin a dynamic experience.
- **Read the Room:** Do not feel like you have to include an activity just because it was part of the plan. Scanning the room and checking in can help you determine if an activity is appropriate for a group at a particular time. For example, if an activity is emotional or requires focus and a group is struggling to engage, consider another activity or changing the sequence of activities. Having multiple options prepared can be helpful if you need to adapt.

Critical reflection in leadership learning may include reflection that draws on critical thinking skills, encourages students to question assumptions, incorporates critical social theory, or engages participants in action for social justice (Volpe White et al., 2019). Although support from coaches and mentors is important for all reflection, it is particularly important for reflection that challenges assumptions and prepares participants to create positive change (Eyler & Giles, 1999; Mitchell,

Donahue, & Young-Law, 2012; Pigza, 2015). Break Away (n.d.) is a national nonprofit organization "that promotes the development of quality alternative break programs through training, assisting, and connecting campuses and communities" (para. 1). Break Away encourages experiences that engage students in critical reflection in order to become active citizens.

FACILITATING CRITICAL REFLECTION
Break Away

Break Away's vision is to build *a society of active citizens.* An active citizen is an inhabitant of a space who prioritizes community in their values and life choices. This kind of person knows there is no such thing as "not my issue"; they are committed to lifelong learning and self-evaluation. Often, a few catalyzing moments foster a shift in someone's worldview bringing them into a new relationship with community. Reflection is a crucial step in this process and it is essential in service or community-based learning: reflection provides a unique opportunity to process new information *and* plan for future action. The method we suggest mirrors that of *critical reflection*—encouraging a process that goes beyond unpacking your experience. This approach to reflection necessitates the ongoing (and difficult!) work of contextualizing experiences through our individual frames of reference *while also* considering larger systems in our world that perpetuate, alleviate, or maintain social inequity. We believe quality reflection is predicated upon three foundational pieces: a well-built team; a strong curricular framework; and a critical understanding of privilege, oppression, and social justice.

- **Start Before Reflection Begins:** As Audre Lorde (2007) described, the true focus of revolutionary change is to seek the piece of the oppressor that is planted inside of us. Critical self-evaluation broadens our perspectives and initiates the ongoing work of unlearning what we have been previously socialized to believe. Relearning how to navigate the world as stewards of our communities is a difficult process and unlikely to happen among people unfamiliar to one other. In its best iteration, groups of individuals with well-built relationships reflect together creating an environment where participants are able to be vulnerable *and* uncomfortable to ultimately experience growth. Leaders must prioritize relationship building and team development well before formal reflection begins.
- **Keep Reflection Focused and Substantive:** Although any intense and immersive experience requires time to debrief personal highs and lows, ongoing critical reflection expands participants' understanding *of* and individual connections *to* the social issue. Relation-

ships among group members can certainly be strengthened as a result of reflection, but the *substance* comes from examining the root causes of social injustice and collectively brainstorming opportunities for forward-thinking action and organizing.

- **Know Where You Want to Go:** Quality reflection plans are built from established learning outcomes. Learning outcomes, or *what one hopes a participant is able to know and do by the end of the experience,* are developed by leaders before an experience begins. Outcomes tied to education, orientation, and training (Break Away, n.d.) set parameters for what participants will learn in relation to the social justice issue(s); partner organization, host community, service project; and skill development. Each day participants engage in service work, reflection goals will bring the group closer to overall outcomes. Although there is a high likelihood you will deviate from the original agenda, planning with an intended end in mind ensures each component fits within the larger vision.

- **Elevate Unheard Perspectives:** There are many aspects of an immersive community-based learning experience that require careful orchestration, but what often causes the most worry is facilitation. A strong facilitator guides group members through a process while encouraging *all* to participate. Although a leader's inclination may be to serve as an *impartial* facilitator, the reality of our own identities, experiences, and worldview make this impossible. Working within an unjust world requires us to examine the power dynamics at play within our groups. A strong facilitator seeks, instead, to be *multipartial* (Program on Intergroup Relations, 2019)— rejecting dominant norms (i.e., people will get what they deserve if they work hard enough) and elevating underrepresented voices to balance social power.

Reflection can often be seen as an afterthought: to digest what we have done and what has been learned. We see it as the first step: another day of service or a life of prioritizing community, reflection is preparing us for what lies ahead.

FACILITATION AS EXPERIENTIAL LEARNING

Becoming a reflective facilitator is an experiential process, which makes facilitators of reflective leadership learning both students and educators simultaneously. Reflection is a powerful pedagogical tool, learning outcome, philosophy, and strategy for learning assessment. Leadership and reflection are both relational processes: through collective reflection, there is greater potential for sustained action and positive change. By engaging leadership learners in reflection, we enhance their capacity to question assumptions, evaluate beliefs, learn from experiences, and create change.

REFERENCES

Ash, S. L., & Clayton, P. H. (2009). Generating, deepening, and documenting learning: The power of critical reflection in applied learning. *Journal of Applied Learning in Higher Education, 1*(1), 25–48.

Break Away. (n.d.). Eight Components of a Quality Alternative Break. Retrieved from http://alternativebreaks.org/wp-content/uploads/2014/06/8_Components2017.pdf

Brookfield, S. D. (2017). *Becoming a critically reflective teacher* (2nd ed). San Francisco, CA: Jossey-Bass.

Burchell, H., & Dyson, J. (2005). Action research in higher education: Exploring ways of creating and holding the space for reflection. *Educational Action Research, 13*(2), 291–300.

Eyler, J. (2001). Creating your reflection map. In M. Canada & B. W. Speck (Eds.), *New directions for higher education: No. 114. Developing and implementing service-learning programs* (pp. 35-43). San Francisco, CA: Jossey-Bass.

Eyler, J., & Giles, D. E. (1999). *Where's the learning in service-learning?* San Francisco, CA: Jossey-Bass.

Guthrie, K. L., & Jenkins, D. M. (2018). *The role of leadership educators: Transforming learning.* Charlotte, NC: Information Age.

Hatcher, J. A., Bringle, R. G., & Muthiah, R. (2004). Designing effective reflection: What matters to service-learning? *Michigan Journal of Community Service Learning,* 38–46.

Lorde, A. (2007). *Sister outsider: Essays and speeches.* Berkeley, CA: Crossing Press.

Mitchell, T. D., Donahue, D. M., & Young-Law, C. (2012). Service learning as a pedagogy of Whiteness. *Equity & Excellence in Education, 45*(4), 612–629.

Owen-Smith, P. (2018). *The contemplative mind in the scholarship of teaching and learning.* Bloomington, IN: Indiana University Press.

Pigza, J. M. (2015). Navigating leadership complexity through critical, creative, and practical thinking. In S. R. Komives & K. L. Guthrie (Eds.), *New directions for student leadership: No. 145. Innovative learning for leadership development* (pp. 35–48). San Francisco, CA: Jossey-Bass.

Program on Intergroup Relations: University of Michigan. (2019). Retrieved from https://igr.umich.edu/about

Suskie, L. (2018). *Assessing student learning: A common sense guide* (3rd ed.). San Francisco, CA: Wiley.

Volpe White, J. M., Guthrie, K. L., & Torres, M. (2019). *Thinking to transform: Reflection in leadership learning.* Charlotte, NC: Information Age.

White, J. V., & Guthrie, K. L. (2016). Creating a meaningful learning environment: Reflection in leadership education. *Journal of Leadership Education, 15*(1), 60–75.

TABLE OF ACTIVITIES

Section	Activity	Page	Contemplative	Creative	Digital	Discussion	Narrative	Written	Group Size
Contemplative	Finding Your Mission Blueprint	13	X			X			1–20
	Forest Bathing Promotes Contemplation and Reflection	15	X			X			10–20
	I Am, Because: A Journey of Contemplative Reflection on Values (Part 1)	17	X						10–15
	I Am, Because: A Journey of Contemplative Reflection on Values (Part 2)	19	X						10–15
	Labyrinth Contemplation: A Focus on Leader, Identity, Values, and Beliefs	20	X						Any
	Listening to Understand	21	X						10–30
	Oracle Cards as Tools for Intuitive Leader Reflection	22	X						Any
	Stretch and Reflect: Explore Your Inner Self Using Active Relaxation	23	X						Any
	Talk, Walk, and Listen: Partner Contemplative Walk	25	X			X			Any
	Zooming in on Leadership Moments	26	X						Any
Creative	Collaborative Art as a Means for Understanding Team Leadership	31		X					Minimum 4
	Framing Leadership in Your Communities	32		X					Any
	The Music Within You: Leadership Reflection Through Musical Messages	33		X					5–20
	A Playwright's Reflections	34		X				X	2–24
	Pop-Up Concerts	35		X					6–10
	Theater Is a Team Sport	36		X				X	5–10
	Tree of Alignment	38	X	X					Any
	Whole Self as Leader	39		X					Any
	Zoom: A Visual Reflection Tool	40		X					1–30
Digital	7-Day Online Leadership Challenge	44			X				Any
	Better Together Blogging	46			X			X	6–10
	Building an Integrative Learning Portfolio	47			X			X	1–25

Category	Activity	Page							Size
Digital (continued)	Collaborative Reflection Video on VoiceThread	48			X				4–30
	Digital Leadership Is Going to Go Viral	49			X	X			Any
	Leadership Snapshot: Meaning-Making Through Digital Artifacts	51			X	X			5–25
	A MEMEingful Reflection	52			X				Any
	Video Values Clarification	53				X			Any
Discussion	Communities as Assets	56				X			15–50
	Community Dialogue	57				X		X	8–30
	Connecting Leadership Action With the Pillars of Sustainability	58				X			5–20
	Dialogue and Leadership Learning	59				X			15–30
	Highlights, Lowlights, Insights, and Be-Mights	62				X			3–15
	Invitation to Intentionality: An Exploration of Our Purpose and Authentic Selves	63	X			X			Any
	Jeffersonian Conversation/Dinner	65				X			5–100
	Mind Mapping and Exploring the "Leader Box"	66				X			Any
	Structured Dialogue Across Difference	67				X			2–Any
	Toxic Management/Potential Leadership?	69				X			2–15
Narrative	Belief Statements	73				X	X		Any
	Concept Mapping	74				X	X		Any
	Daring to Be Vulnerable: A Leadership Testimonio	74					X		15–20
	An Improvised Tale: The Story Spine Structure	75					X		Any
	Our Stories, Our Voices	76	X				X		8–25
	Personal Narratives as Authentic Expression	78	X				X		Any
	Telling my Leadership Story	79	X				X		Any
	Testimonio: Leader Profile	80					X		5–18
	Using Poetry to Promote Reflection on Experiential Learning	81	X	X			X		5–12
Written	The Big Picture	84				X		X	Any
	Career Ready: Identifying Transferable Skills	85						X	Any
	Crafting a Leadership Philosophy Statement	86						X	Any

Written (continued(	Leadership Development: A Written Reflection Series	87						X	Any
	1-Minute Reflection Paper	89				X		X	Any
	T.I.P.S. for Leadership Learning	90						X	Any
	What's in My Leader House?	92	X					X	Any
	Written Leadership Portfolios: A Longitudinal Tool for Reflective Learning	93			X			X	Any

CHAPTER 2

Contemplative

Contemplation and introspection play a significant role in developing awareness of self and others by promoting "the exploration of meaning, purpose, and values" (Barbezat & Bush, 2014, p. xv). Contemplative knowing is rooted in spiritual traditions (Owen-Smith, 2018), but can be used in secular settings (Barbezat & Bush, 2014). Although not an exhaustive list, the Center for Contemplative Mind in Society outlined many contemplative practices (Figure 2.1). Both silence and listening are important elements of using contemplative practices for reflection. Owen-Smith (2018) observed, "We are a culture that fears silence and one that is far more comfortable with noise" (p. 29). However, it is in silence that we are able to connect to ourselves and allow insights to emerge (Owen-Smith, 2018). Similarly, we often do not prioritize listening as it is perceived as a passive act (Owen-Smith, 2018), but deep listening requires full engagement. The Center for Contemplative Mind in Society (n.d.) described deep listening in the classroom:

> Deep listening requires that students witness their thoughts and emotions while maintaining focused attention on what they are hearing. It trains them to pay full attention to the sound of the words, while abandoning such habits as planning their next statement or interrupting the speaker. It is attentive rather than reactive listening. Such listening not only increases retention of material but encourages insight and the making of meaning. (para. 3)

Through contemplative practices, participants can develop self-knowledge and also appreciate a deep connection to others that develops community (Barbezat & Bush, 2014).

Meditation and Mindfulness. Meditation is one frame for contemplative practice. Drawn from several traditions, two common elements of meditation are "a deep focus and the intention of developing insight" (Barbezat & Bush, 2014, p. 22). Mindfulness is both a process and an outcome; mindfulness involves awareness of and focus on the present moment without judgment (Barbezat & Bush, 2014). The Center for Contemplative Mind in Society (2018) recommended mindfulness resources including tools, readings, and webinars in order to promote social justice and engage in conversations about race. Healthcare professionals who participated in a mindfulness class and journaled about a mindful practice said mindfulness brought discomfort and uncertainty while also facilitating reflection and supporting professional practice (Nugent, Moss, Barnes, & Wilks, 2011). Webster-Wright (2013) proposed a synergistic relationship between mindfulness, as a practice of stillness and openness, and inquiry, as an analytical critique. The interplay of mindfulness and analysis fosters creative possibilities; mindful inquiry can be "a reflective journey from the chatter of the world, through the heart of stillness, to sit with paradoxes and uncertainties, emerging refreshed and revived at the very least, and on occasions with a new spark of an idea" (Webster-Wright, 2013, pp. 564–565). Engaging students in mindfulness requires educators to engage in and become familiar with contemplative practices (Barbezat & Bush, 2014; Davis, 2014; Lucas, 2015). Beginning an experience with a mindfulness activity may help students focus and prepare for discussions and activities (Barbezat & Bush, 2014). Barbezat and Bush (2014) cautioned "We can encourage students to strengthen their attention, sustain their commitment, cultivate equanimity and openness, realize insights, and appreciate interconnection only if we are on that path of awakening ourselves" (Barbezat & Bush, 2014, p. 91).

Labyrinth. An example of contemplative reflection is experiencing a labyrinth. Often confused with a maze, which is a puzzle to be solved, a labyrinth is a winding path that moves in turns toward a center point for meditation or reflection. Early research indicates the value of the labyrinth may be in the connection between physical responses that facilitate mental processes conducive to reflection (Bigard, 2009). The documented uses and benefits of walking a labyrinth may include: pondering a question or problem, thinking critically about a topic or academic area, examining commitments, inspiring creativity, connecting with other people, meditating, experiencing gratitude, reducing stress, or connecting to the physical self (Artress, 2006; Ferre, 2007; West, 2000). It is difficult to

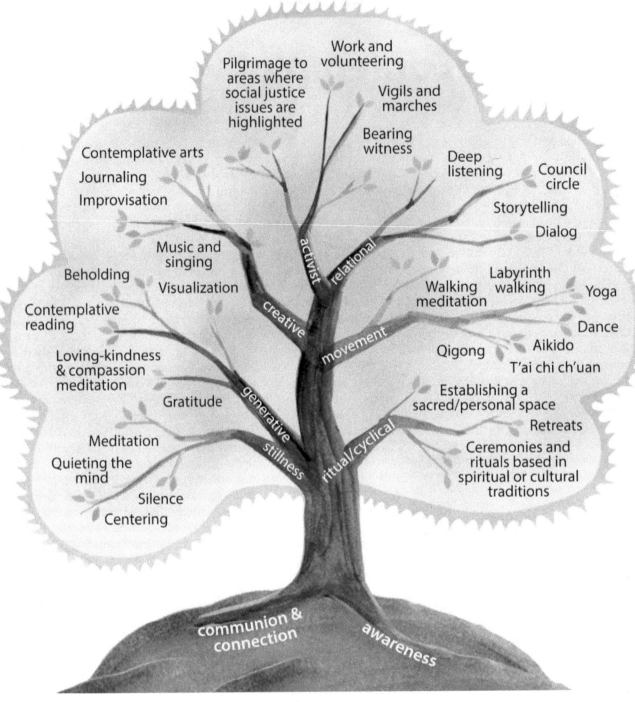

FIGURE 7.1.   Tree of contemplative practices. Reprinted with permission from http://www.contemplativemind.org/practices/ tree. Copyright 2014 by The Center for Contemplative Mind in Society.

know how many institutions of higher education have labyrinths because the labyrinth may not be well advertised or the structure may be temporary (Sellers, 2016). In August 2018, there were more than 130 laby- rinths at colleges, universities, community colleges, and seminaries in 36 states (World-Wide Labyrinth Locater, 2018). There are many possibilities for using labyrinths to facilitate reflection in educational settings. Bigard

(2009) proposed workshops for higher education focused on faculty teaching and learning centers, human resources wellness programs, multicultural programming, academic transitions such as first year experience courses, and student organizations, among others. Students at the University of Central Oklahoma engaged in walking a labyrinth as part of a curriculum aimed at teaching tenants of transformative learning;

one component included developing leadership by walking the labyrinth while reflecting on leaders who impacted their lives and using the labyrinth walk as a metaphor for developing organizational culture (Rudebock, 2016). A labyrinth can provide a space for students to reflect on leadership learning experiences or develop their capacity to engage in leadership.

REFERENCES

Artress, L. (2006). *A sacred path: The labyrinth as a spiritual practice.* New York, NY: Penguin Group.

Barbezat, D. P., & Bush, M. (2014). *Contemplative practices in higher education: Powerful methods to transform teaching and learning.* San Francisco, CA: Jossey-Bass.

Bigard, M. F. (2009). Walking the labyrinth: An innovative approach to counseling center outreach. *Journal of College Counseling, 12*(2), 137–148.

Center for Contemplative Mind in Society. (2018). *Contemplative community in higher education: A toolkit.* Retrieved from http://www.contemplativemind.org/files/ Toolkit021618web.pdf

Center for Contemplative Mind in Society. (n.d.). Deep listening. Retrieved from http://www.contemplativemind.org/ practices/tree/deep-listening

Davis, D. J. (2014). Mindfulness in higher education: Teaching, learning, and leadership. *The International Journal of Religion and Spirituality in Society, 4,* 1–6.

Ferre, R. (2007). *12 reasons to have a labyrinth at your university.* Retrieved from http://www.labyrinthproject.com/ 12university.pdf

Lucas, N. (2015). When leading with integrity goes well: Integrating the mind, body, and heart. In A.J. Schwartz (Ed.), *New Directions for Student Leadership: 146, Developing ethical leaders* (pp. 61–69). San Francisco, CA: Jossey-Bass.

Nugent, P., Moss, D., Barnes, R., & Wilks, J. (2011). Clear(ing) space: Mindfulness-based reflective practice. *Reflective Practice, 12*(1), 1–13.

Owen-Smith, P. (2018). *The contemplative mind in the scholarship of teaching and learning.* Bloomington, IN: Indiana University Press.

Rudebock, D. (2016). Transformative learning: Introducing the labyrinth across academic disciplines. In J. Seller & B. Moss (Eds.), *Learning with the labyrinth: Creating reflective space in higher education* (pp. 56–68). London, England: Palgrave.

Sellers, J. (2016). Introduction: The heart of learning. In J. Sellers & B. Moss (Eds.), *Learning the labyrinth: Creating reflective space in higher education* (pp. 1–14). London, England: Palgrave.

Webster-Wright, A. (2013). The eye of the storm: A mindful inquiry into reflective practices in higher education. *Reflective Practice, 14*(4), 556–567.

West, M. G. (2000). *Exploring the labyrinth: A guide for healing and spiritual growth.* New York, NY: Broadway Books.

World-Wide Labyrinth Locator. (2018). Home. Retrieved from https://labyrinthlocator.com/home

FINDING YOUR MISSION BLUEPRINT
Rolando Torres

- 10–60 minutes
- 1–20 participants

This activity is a self-guided, reflective worksheet where participants develop a rudimentary mission statement/vision. The worksheet is divided into different questions that ask participants to identify their values, how they want to accomplish their values, the impact of living their values, and who the impact would have an effect on.

Learning Goals: Participants will have opportunities to:

- identify the most salient values that guide their decisions, ways of living, and ways of being.
- reflect on how they would like to accomplish living out their values, the impact of living their values, and whom the impact would have an effect on.
- develop a basic, working mission statement they can use to guide them through college, their involvement, their major, and decisions.

Materials: "Personal Mission" worksheet, list of reflective debrief questions (some included, feel free to develop your own), writing utensil

Process:
This activity can be a useful stepping stone to begin priming participants for a larger classroom assignment such as: personal statement papers, personal leadership papers, "why" papers, and larger organizational mission statement creation assignments. This activity can also be used as the first step in a series of activities to help participants develop a vision for their life. Other considerations include using this activity as a primer for helping participants learn the process of sharing their mission/vision statements.

1. Participants will work independently on the worksheets and answer: What are their top values? How would they like to live out their values? What is the result of living out their values? Who or what would they like to impact?

   - *Facilitator Tip:* You can prime the participants to be in a reflective mental space by facilitating a values clarification exercise before this activity.

2. Participants will follow the directions on the worksheet. The facilitator should pause between each section of the worksheet and ask questions such as: How did you choose your top values? What experi-

ences in your life influenced the impact you want to have on the world?

3. Participants will fill in the blank spaces provided at the end of each question with their answers.

   • *Facilitator Tip:* The facilitator should encourage participants to use their own values, populations, actions, etc. in their answers. They are not required to select from the list provided to them by the worksheet. Those are mere examples.

4. A mission statement with blank spaces is at the end of the activity. Using the answers that participants identified in the questions on the worksheet, participants will fill in the blank spaces on the example mission statement.

5. Have participants read their mission statement at the end of the worksheet to the group.

6. Break the participants into small debrief clusters (4–5 participants) or pairs.

Follow up activities that can be done are: a focused discussion on digging deeper into the values, motivations, and impact that the participant wants to have or an activity where the participant can create a vision board for what the world would look like if they accomplished their visions.

Debriefing Questions: Debrief questions could be tailored to many different topics such as leadership, your "why," major selection, and career advancement.

• What are some of the implications of your mission statement?
• What made you decide on the values, populations, impacts, etc. of your mission statement?
• What inspires you most about your mission statement?
• What do you think would be the biggest challenge in enacting your mission statement?
• What experience in your life could you tie into this mission statement?
• How does your mission statement relate to your big picture goals currently? If it does not, what are some adjustments you could make to begin incorporating it into your big picture goals?
• Who are some key allies you could identify to support you in this mission statement?
• What is one small step you could take to live your mission statement? Who is someone that can hold you accountable to that?

PERSONAL MISSION STATEMENT WORKSHEET

1. Review the list below for inspiration to help identify the values that best describe *why* you do what you do. Feel free to use your own words that are not listed. When you are ready, write your top three values in the boxes below.

Achievement	Growth	Peace
Adventure	Harmony	Pleasure
Balance	Honesty	Respect
Beauty	Hope	Security
Creativity	Integrity	Service
Curiosity	Justice	Strength
Faith	Knowledge	Trust
Freedom	Love	Usefulness
Fun	Optimism	Wealth

Top three values:
(1) _____   (2) _____
(3) _____

2. Review the list below for inspiration to help identify the words that best describe *how* you want to live out your values (i.e., by or through). Feel free to use your own words that are not listed. When you are ready, write your top 2 words in the boxes below.

Administering	Empowering	Operating
Advocating	Facilitating	Organizing
Analyzing	Giving	Planning
Building	Helping	Providing
Collaborating	Inventing	Representing
Creating	Leading	Researching
Developing	Managing	Restoring
Educating	Motivating	Solving
Entertaining	Observing	Strategizing

Top two ways to live out your values:
(1) _____   (2) _____

3. Review the list below for inspiration to help identify the word that best describes the desired *result* of implementing your values. Feel free to use your own word. When you are ready, write your top word in the box below.

Awareness	Health	Positivity
Creativity	Human Rights	Reflection
Connection	Hope	Safety
Education	Inclusion	Security
Empowerment	Independence	Social Justice
Equity	Inspiration	Sustainability
Excellence	Leadership	Unity
Freedom	Mindfulness	Wellness
Happiness	Motivation	Wisdom

Top result of implementing your values:

_____

4. Review the list below for inspiration to help identify the word that best describes *who* or *what* you want to impact by implementing your values. Feel free to use your own word. When you are ready, write your top word in the box below.

• Animals	• Immigrants	• People who are illiterate
• Athletes	• Legal systems	• Political systems
• Businesses	• LGBTQ communities	• Social services
• Children & youth	• Low-income communities	• Spiritual communities
• College students	• Medical systems	• Survivors
• Communities	• People experiencing homelessness	• Underrepresented groups
• Education systems	• People in prison	• Veterans
• Environment	• People with disabilities	• Women
• Families		
• Formerly incarcerated		

Who or what you want to impact:

_____

MY MISSION STATEMENT

I am driven by a passionate belief in _____,
_____, and _____.
(Insert answers from Question #1)

I plan on living these values by/through
_____ and _____ …
(Insert answers from Question #2)

… to achieve _____ …
(Insert answer from Question #3)

… that impacts_____.
(Insert answer from Question #4)

Example:

I am driven by a passionate belief in <u>freedom</u>, <u>reconciliation</u>, and <u>justice</u>.

I plan on living these values through <u>education</u> and <u>rehabilitation</u> …

… to achieve <u>equity</u>…

… that impacts <u>children and youth</u>.

FOREST BATHING PROMOTES CONTEMPLATION AND REFLECTION
Jane McPherson

• 60 minutes–1 hour 15 minutes
• 10–20 participants with 2 facilitators

Forest Bathing—also known as *Shinrin Yoku*—is a strategy for reconnecting people to the natural world. Although research on Forest Bathing is young, a recent systematic review found that forest therapy may lower blood pressure, improve heart and lung function, boost the immune system, reduce inflammation, decrease perceived stress and stress hormone levels, reduce anxiety and depression, and increase cognitive function (Oh et al., 2017). In this contemplative practice, forest bathing will be experienced as a group, but with opportunity for participants to tune into their own physical, emotional, and spiritual experience. Individual reflection and group participation will both be promoted.

Learning Goals: Participants will have opportunities to:

• experience nature, and be able to report on what they saw, heard, smelled, felt, and tasted.
• experience a deliberate slowing down of their pace. They will be able to reflect on how the slow and attentive experience of focusing on their senses differs from usual pace and experience.
• learn about the physical and psychological value of time in nature.
• critically reflect on the ease or complexity of accessing nature, and consider the role of nature in learning, mental health, and physical wellness.

Materials: Sturdy footwear for walking and appropriate clothing to protect from weather, any necessary insect repellent and sunscreen, drinking water, safe place for participants to leave belongings, paper and writing utensil, bell for facilitators

Process:
The ideal forest bathing experience brings participants into a forest or natural setting that is away from busy streets and urban noises. Facilitators should prepare participants in advance for the experience by recommending appropriate clothing, footwear, insect repellent, sunscreen, et cetera. Facilitators should also learn about any fears or concerns that participants may have, since all participants may not feel comfortable in a natural setting. Accessibility should be assured for any participants in wheelchairs or with varying physical abilities. Participants should know that facilitators want them to be safe and comfortable during the experience.

PRIOR TO FOREST BATHING (if possible): Provide participants with a reading, podcast, or video link with which they can familiarize themselves (see References listed below).

1. **EXERCISE 1:** Walk as a group on a path in the woods. (~30 minutes)

   - **PREPARATION:** Prepare participants for the walk by describing the trail. (The ideal trail is not too narrow). Explain where the trail is heading and warn them about roots, poison ivy, etc. Explain that in 10–15 minutes, you will come to a clearing where you will form a circle and share your experiences. Plan for one facilitator to lead the group and set the slow pace, and for one facilitator to follow behind the last participant. Safety and preparation are key.

   - *DIRECTIONS FOR THE WALK: We will now take a walk as a group in silence. We will walk slowly and deliberately, breathing deeply, and becoming very aware of our surroundings and of our bodies within them. Though we are walking together, we will seek to create some distance between us, so that each of us is surrounded by a thick layer of forest air. We will walk slowly taking in our surroundings. What do we see? Smell? Hear? Taste? Feel? Can we feel the forest without touching it? On our faces? On our skin? Is there breeze? Can you feel energy or heat from your colleagues? Or from the trees? The river? The birds? What is happening inside your body? Does it feel good? Strange? Familiar? Can you feel your breath or heart slowing down?*

   - **DEBRIEF THE WALK:** Silently indicate for all participants to form a circle. The facilitator should collect a natural object, perhaps a stick or stone, that will indicate whose turn it is to talk. The facilitator will break the silence by welcoming everyone to the clearing, explaining about the "talking stick (or stone)," and then ask who would like to share their experience. The stick/stone will then be passed person to person as group members share their observations and reflections. No specific debriefing questions are necessary.

2. **EXERCISE 2:** Solitary reflection in the woods. (~30 minutes)
   - **DIRECTIONS:** Participants will be asked to spread out now in pairs or small groups to find a place to lean or sit or lie down. This is time for reflective individual thinking and writing. Participants might be asked to really tune in to their feelings at this moment and in this place. They might be asked to reflect on how comfortable they feel in nature and why they think that is. Did they grow up visiting nature? Do they believe that all people have access to nature? Do they feel that being in nature is valuable and should be made available to others? Participants should be told that the facilitator will ring the bell once when it is time for them to bring closure to their reflections. ~30 minutes later, the facilitator should ring the bell heartily inviting everyone back to the circle for group sharing.

Debriefing Questions:

As with the first exercise, sharing can begin by asking participants if they have anything they would like to share. This opening can be followed by more specific questions:

1. What did you notice when you were paying attention to your senses? To your feelings?
2. What did you notice about your heart and lungs? About your legs and arms? How does your body feel?
3. We have been out here in the woods for ____ minutes. How does the passage of time feel to you? Long or short? Why?
4. How easy or difficult was this experience to organize and prepare for? What does it mean that nature is accessible or inaccessible? In our society, who has access to green space? What does this mean for our health?

References:

Oh, B., Lee, K. J., Zaslawski, C., Yeung, A., Rosenthal, D., Larkey, L., & Back, M. (2017). Health and well-being benefits of spending time in forests: Systematic review. *Environmental Health and Preventive Medicine, 22,* 71–82. doi:10.1186/s12199-017-0677-9

Resources:

Barton, J., & Pretty, J. (2010). What is the best dose of nature and green exercise for improving mental health? A multistudy analysis. *Environmental Science and Technology, 44,* 3947–3955. doi:10.1021/es903183r

Haile, R. (2017, June 30). 'Forest Bathing': How microdosing on nature can help with stress. *The Atlantic.* Retrieved from https://www.theatlantic.com/health/archive/2017/06/forest-bathing/532068/

Natural Capital Project. (n.d.). Retrieved from https://natural-capitalproject.stanford.edu/

I AM, BECAUSE: A JOURNEY OF CONTEMPLATIVE REFLECTION ON VALUES (PART 1)
Gabrielle Garrard

- 35–40 minutes
- 10–15 participants

The "I am, because: A Journey of Contemplative Reflection on Values" (Part 1) activity encourages participants to reflect on their core values as a leader. We affirm that each participant brings unique perspectives and lived experiences to their leadership style. As values-driven leaders, we are better equipped to articulate our "why" and purpose to others. The activity is best paired with a second part found in the following pages that engages participants in a meditation on the people and places that have influenced these values.

Learning Goals: Participants will have opportunities to:

- discern which values they hold most saliently.
- reveal connections between their values and their role as a leader.

Materials: "Values Discernment" worksheet, writing utensils

Process:
1. Pass out the Values Discernment Worksheet and make sure each participant has a writing utensil. (2 minutes)
2. Ask the participants to complete Part 1 of the worksheet. (8 minutes)

   - Read out the first statement: *I have the capacity to be a leader. I bring unique talents and values.* Instruct participants to rewrite the phrase 4 times on their worksheet. The practice of reaffirming our own capacity to be leaders through our unique values and talents is important because often times we are socialized to believe otherwise. We recognize that leadership is for everyone. (2 minutes)
   - Give the participants 2–3 minutes to rewrite the phrases on their worksheet. (2–3 minutes)

- Move on to Part 2 of the worksheet. Explain to the participants that they will now have time to reflect on and grapple with what they feel are the values most central to their lives. The table they see on their worksheet can be used as a starting place for their thoughts. Emphasize that the table of values they see is by no means exhaustive, and is meant to be used as a means to get their thoughts centered on potential values. (3 minutes)

3. Tell the participants they have 5 minutes to read over the listed values and write in values of their own choosing. (5 minutes)
4. After the 5 minutes is up, check in with participants to see if they need more time. When everyone is ready to move on, then instruct the participants to read the "Questions to Consider" on their worksheet. It may be helpful to read each question aloud once as well. (3 minutes)
5. Instruct the participants to narrow down the values they see most present in their lives to no more than 10. Give the participants 6–7 minutes to reflect on this. Once everyone has finished, ask the participants to pair and share about what the process felt like to them. (10 minutes)
6. After participants have finished pairing and sharing, ask the participants to narrow down their list to the top three values they feel guide them most strongly in their lives. Give them 5 more minutes to process and reflect. (5 minutes)
7. If the activity is pressed for time, I would encourage the facilitator to instruct the participants to select only one top value, instead of three.

Debriefing Questions:
- Was it difficult to narrow down your values to your top three? Why or why not?
- What was your process for narrowing down your values?
- How do you grapple with the difference between values that others expect of you and the values you expect of yourself?

Resource:
Martin, J. (2016, September 21). *An introduction to Ignatian contemplation.* Retrieved from https://www.americamagazine.org/content/all-things/easing-contemplation

"I Am, Because" Values Worksheet
Leadership Affirmations

Today I affirm the following (rewrite the phrases 4 times):

- I have the capacity to be a leader. I bring unique talents and values.

- _____

- _____

- _____

- _____

Discerning my Central Values

Below is a table filled with values that can be used as a starting place for this activity. By no means is this list exhaustive—there are hundreds of potential values that can be used which are not listed here. It is merely meant to be used as a means to get you reflecting on potential values.

Example Values:

Authenticity	Adventure	Autonomy	Balance	Boldness	Compassion
Community	Creativity	Empathy	Faith	Growth	Happiness
Honesty	Justice	Kindness	Knowledge	Learning	Love
Loyalty	Optimism	Peace	Respect	Service	Spirituality
Stability	Success	Transparency	Wealth	Wisdom	Wonder

Other Values Not Listed:

Use the following spaces to write-in other values that you find missing from the above examples that you would like to consider for your own top values.

Questions to consider as you focus on the values most central to how you live your life:

1. Have I thought about this value today? In the past week? Month?
2. Is this value congruent with my actions? Or is this an aspirational value?
3. Am I inexplicably drawn to some of these values over others?
4. How do family and friends describe me? Which values do I associate with this description?
5. What is the first thing I want a stranger to notice about me?

My Top 10 Values (in no particular order)

_____   _____   _____   _____   _____

_____   _____   _____   _____   _____

After further directions from your facilitator, take the time to discern your top three values.

1. _____

2. _____

3. _____

I AM, BECAUSE: A JOURNEY OF CONTEMPLATIVE REFLECTION ON VALUES (PART 2)
Gabrielle Garrard

- 35-45 minutes
- 10-15 participants

The "I Am, Because: A Journey of Contemplative Reflection on Values" (Part 2) activity encourages participants to reflect on where they derive their top values from. It draws from contemplative prayer in the Jesuit Catholic tradition, which is used to center thoughts and encourage awe and awareness of the individual's sources of motivation and grounding (Martin, 2016). In this activity, although secular, encourages participants to reflect on the meaning and purpose of their own lives through a guided meditation of their central values in silence. Silence is an important part of this activity because it allows the individual to interrogate their thoughts and find their unique grounding in a chaotic world where there are often outside expectations. The process of discerning and reflecting on our values should be from inside ourselves to the outside world rather than vice versa, and this is often best accomplished in silence.

Learning Goals: Participants will have opportunities to:

- contemplate where in their lives they derive their values from.
- reaffirm the meaning and purpose of their lives.

Materials: "Values Discernment" worksheet from Part 1

Process:
1. If at all possible, this activity should be facilitated outside in an open space because of the Jesuit Catholic belief that we can derive more thought in the wonder and awe of nature and creation.
2. Start with framing the importance of contemplation. Emphasize how contemplative activities allow us to gain insight into our most personal thoughts and allow us to lead from a more whole-hearted space.
3. Now that participants have their top three values (from Part 1), it is time to begin their contemplative reflection. Guide them through this reflection by asking them to close their eyes and repeat the first value on their list silently in their head. The tone of your voice should be soft and your words should be concise. (2 minutes)
4. Ask them to relax their bodies and feel the value in various parts of their being. Tell them to start with their fingers and toes, pause, then to their chest and heart, pause, and then their head. Give enough time to focus on each part and when the time feels right, ask them to move on to the next part of their body. (7 minutes)
5. Ask them to visualize where they see the value in the world around them as they silently repeat this word to themselves. (3 minutes)
6. After a few minutes, ask them to reflect on where and from whom they learned this value. Tell them to think of the people who have modeled it for them (3 minutes).
7. Repeat the reflection for the second value. (12 minutes)
8. Repeat the reflection again for the third value. (10 minutes)

Debriefing Questions:
- Was it easy or difficult to be present in the contemplative reflection?
- Where did you feel the values in your body? In our surroundings?
- What emotions did you feel during the contemplative reflection?
- Did specific people come to mind when asked to reflect on where you learned these values from?
- How did this activity help refocus your leader identities?

Reference:
Martin, J. (2016, September 21). *An introduction to Ignatian contemplation.* Retrieved from https://www.americamagazine .org/content/all-things/easing-contemplation

LABYRINTH CONTEMPLATION: A FOCUS ON LEADER IDENTITY, VALUES, AND BELIEFS
Erica Wiborg

- 30-60 minutes
- Any size group

This activity is designed to facilitate contemplation on a core value that connects to one's leader identity through experiencing a labyrinth. Often times it is not feasible, depending on time and location, to walk a labyrinth; however, this activity utilizes a printable finger labyrinth that can be facilitated at any time or place.

Learning Goals: Participants will have opportunities to:

- name a core value that connects to their leader identity, as evidenced by the illustration of their value.
- demonstrate contemplative reflection in regards to their leadership experiences, as evidenced by an intentional labyrinth experience.

Materials: Meditative or reflective music, colorful writing utensils, copy of labyrinth for each participant. You might consider searching Google images or websites for a printable finger labyrinth. We recommend a classical 7 circuit labyrinth (i.e., Cretan design).

Process:
1. Labyrinth Introduction (2 minutes)
   - Describe how for the next 20–60 minutes (depending on planned time), the group will be spending time in contemplation on their leader identity through a specific reflection experience utilizing a labyrinth. Pass out the printed labyrinths.
   - Share a brief description of a labyrinth (see Resources), citing that they are often confused with a maze; however, they are actually a winding path that moves in turns toward a center point. There is one-way in and one-way out, and labyrinths symbolically represent a journey toward understanding or enlightenment.
2. Core Value Reflection Set-Up (8 minutes)
   - Explain the purpose of this reflection will be to understand a core value that connects to their leader identity. Ask participants to take a minute to silently think about who they are as a leader and what they care about in this world.
   - Request that they keep this reflection in mind as they select one core value they hope to contemplate today in regards to their leadership experiences. Have them, with the color pencils, write or draw the core value at the center of their labyrinth.

3. Facilitating the Labyrinth Experience (10 minutes)
   - Explain that there is no right way or wrong way to experience a labyrinth, but for the purposes of this time, you will describe the possible steps for contemplation.
   - Request that participants plant their feet on the ground, square themselves to the paper, and move away any additional distractions from their table.
   - State that once the music starts, they will start at the opening and slowly follow the path with their finger until they get to the center. They can pause here for reflection, and then they will follow the path back out until the reach the same place they entered.
   - Describe that as they journey into the center, they should focus on following the path. When they get to the center, they can stay as long as they need or want to reflect on what experiences connect to their core value. As they journey out, have them reflect on what this core value empowers them to do.
   - Clarify questions, and start the music. Bring the group back together once everyone has completed their labyrinth experience.
4. Connecting Across Experiences (10 minutes)
   - Debrief the experience focused on the process/experience with the labyrinth and the content/learning in regards to leader identity.
   - Close with gratitude and encouragement to carry this experience into their life.
5. If your campus or city has access to a physical, public labyrinth, this activity can be adapted for walking a labyrinth. To find out if your campus or city has one visit the World-Wide Labyrinth Locator at https://labyrinthlocator.com. Depending on your group size, walking a labyrinth could take longer than utilizing a finger labyrinth for reflection.

Debriefing Questions:
- What was that process like for you? Did anything surprise you? Comfort you? Challenge you?
- What was the value you reflected on? What leadership experiences were connected to that value?
- What have you learned about yourself and your beliefs through this process?

Resources:
FSU Labyrinth. (n.d.). Retrieved from http://labyrinth.fsu.edu/walking-the-labyrinth
The Labyrinth Society. (n.d.). https://labyrinthsociety.org/
Veriditas. (n.d.). Retrieved from https://veriditas.org/

LISTENING TO UNDERSTAND
Julie LeBlanc

* 40–45 minutes
* 10–30 participants (ideally even to discuss in pairs)

This reflection activity emerges from the idea that we should more often listen to seek understanding, rather than to agree, disagree or rebut another's statements. Listening involves not just hearing another's words but comprehending their meaning by being truly present. The hope is this activity allows participants to deeply connect with other's shared meaning—or differed meaning—of an experience through paired discussion. Listening is especially important for leadership learning as we seek to acknowledge, illuminate, and understand diverse perspectives in both classroom and cocurricular settings.

Learning Goals: Participants will have opportunities to:

* practice introspection to facilitate understanding of their perceptions, meaning making, and attitudes.
* practice listening to hear and understand another's perspective, rather than listening to respond.
* learn from others to foster empathy and relational leadership.
* broaden their perspectives in a shared space with peers.

Materials: copies of the prompting questions, open space for participants to spread out for discussion

Process:

The facilitator should introduce the reflection activity as a time and space for participants to practice deep listening with a partner. Participants are put into pairs by numbering off and have about 30 minutes to answer prompting questions about their learning experience.

Within the 30-minute time frame, the facilitator will prompt participants to utilize the time accordingly:

* 5 minutes of prep time for participants to think about their responses to the prompting questions (individually; they can jot notes or think in silence). The prep time allows participants to ground themselves and center their thoughts before engaging in the activity.
* 5 minutes for person A to talk
* 5 minutes for person B to summarize their understanding of person A's contributions
* 5 minutes for person B to talk
* 5 minutes for person A to summarize their understanding of person B's contributions
* 5 minutes for the pair to discuss their feelings about the reflective process (How did this exercise feel? What was challenging about it? What was affirmed for you? What is still unclear?)

Debriefing Questions:
* What did you learn about yourself by participating in this experience?
* What did you observe during the experience?
* How did you feel heard during the experience?
* If you did not feel heard, why do you think this was so?
* What alternate viewpoints did you observe or experience today?
* What type of leadership did you embody during this experience?
* What type of leadership did you see others enact during this experience?
* If you could describe your current emotion/feeling about the experience in one word, what would it be? Why?
* Why does it matter that you gained this experience today?

The facilitator may choose to debrief with participants regarding the process of reflection (in order to solidify understanding of deep listening and contemplative reflection) or they may choose to have selected participants share their contributions in the large group space.

Resources:

Brown, V. (2016, June 21). *What happens when you really listen: Practicing empathy for leaders.* Retrieved from http://www.couragerenewal.org/empathetic-listening-for-leaders/

Stamwitz, A. V. (2012, November). *If only we would listen: Parker J. Palmer on what we could learn about politics, faith, and each other.* Retrieved from https://www.thesunmagazine.org/issues/443/if-only-we-would-listen

ORACLE CARDS AS TOOLS FOR INTUITIVE LEADER REFLECTION
Juan Cruz Mendizabal

- Readings should take 10–15 minutes per participant
- Any size group

Oracle cards are symbols of intuitive epistemology that challenge Western, postmodern ways of knowing, ripe with potential to assist the leader in trusting their intuition when navigating dilemmas. As individuals, groups, and communities *practice* leadership while simultaneously *making meaning* of their leadership, oracle cards are tools that can provide a framework to leaders who might struggle to understand the significance of metacognition in the leadership process.

Learning Goals: Participants will have opportunities to:

- appreciate the value of *intuition* as a distinct—yet complimentary—way of knowing in tandem with other "knowing" sources such as self-assessments, feedback, and scholarly literature.
- utilize an oracle card reading as a tool for affirming a leader's role in a leadership process, challenging a leader's conscious and unconscious approaches to a specific situation/goal/dilemma, and providing specific words and phrases of focus to serve as a springboard for a leader's continued reflection.
- sustain their collective reflection efforts after participating in a group oracle card reading, holding peers accountable for remembering the revelations, insights, and calls to action from the cards' messages and implementing those findings into daily leadership practice.

Materials: The only requirement is an oracle card deck with which the group feels comfortable. These are available online, at spiritual stores, and popular bookstores and may be categorized as angel cards, oracle cards, or reflection cards. There are hundreds of decks available based on themes ranging from chakra work to life purpose to the environment. When selecting a deck, a group should let the cards "choose them" by noticing which decks fill them with positive energy at first sight or touch.

Process:

Most people are nervous when participating in an oracle card reading for the first time, especially when in a group with others. The role of the facilitator is to lead each participant through their reading following the steps outlined. To diffuse any nervousness among participants, the facilitator should emphasize the utility of oracle cards as a tool to provide structure and language to the reflective process. They should also describe how an oracle card reading is best experienced in community with others who are aware of a common situation, goal, or dilemma. Therefore, it is best to utilize oracle card reflections later in a group's life cycle when the group has meaningful knowledge of one another beyond a surface level. Finally, the facilitator should be clear that oracle cards are not fortune telling cards, but rather affirmation cards that will reveal what the participant is consciously or unconsciously thinking and feeling about a specific situation. Therefore, oracle cards are just a "beginner" to deep reflection, as participants begin with information from an oracle reading and then continue reflection individually and communally with those in their group.

A suggested experience includes one facilitator with 3–4 participants who will all participate in individual card readings. Suggested placement is all participants and the facilitator sitting in a circle, each participant waiting their turn for their individual reading while the others observe and offer feedback when appropriate. Ideally, when participants are observing, they will add complexity to the reading based on individual interpretation, questioning, and their own intuition, provided they have context of the situation the participant asked about. (The group can adjust for time by simply adding or subtracting the number of participants, though each individual's reading should take approximately 15 to 20 minutes.)

When an individual participates in the reading, the facilitator will lead them through the following steps:

1. Setting a clear intention (1 minute): The facilitator should ask the participant to set an intention by answering the following questions rhetorically, perhaps with their eyes closed and in a meditative state: *Is your reading meant to clarify a point of confusion? Should it affirm a decision? Should it provide information you might not otherwise be aware of? What knowledge or feeling do you seek from this process?*

2. Clearing energy from oracle cards (1 minute): This ensures the reading will use only the energy and intuition of the card's current handler. An imaginative participant might clear the energy by meditatively holding the deck facedown and visualizing cleansing light surrounding the deck. A physically inclined participant might hold the deck facedown with their nondominant hand and make a fist with their dominant hand to lightly pound the energy from the top of the deck. A gentler physical approach could involve holding the deck facedown and gently blowing on the cards to release the old energy. Regardless of the method, the participant should be sure that only their own energy remains after this step. Only the participant—

never the facilitator—should hold the cards during a reading.

3. Asking the right question (1 minute): The participant should fan the cards, facedown, across their chest, making physical contact with as many cards as possible. As the cards are in place, the participant should silently ask a specific question that supports the intention they stated earlier. The participant should avoid asking yes or no questions, but instead ask, "What is the purpose of ...," "Should I ...," or "What will ..."?

4. *Locating energy, spirit, person, or other source of intuitive assistance* (1 minute): Still silently, the participant should activate whatever energy is supporting their intuition in this reading. Is it a spirit guide, deity, nature, ascended master, or a loved one who has passed? The participant should intentionally communicate in partnership with this energy and ask for guidance.

5. Process of card selection (1 minute): There is no right or wrong way to select the cards provided that the cards are facedown and anonymous until they are chosen. Typically, a three-card spread of past, present, and future most effectively helps the participant focus on the question and answer.

6. Revelation of answers (10–15 minutes): Each card is revealed individually. The reader explains the official guidebook explanation while the participant takes note of any card imagery or descriptive words of particular interest or resonance. Additional observers can also note trends, connections, or narratives presented explicitly or implicitly in the card layout.

7. Personal reflection, motivation, and application of lessons learned (takes as long as needed): See debrief questions.

Debriefing Questions:

The debrief should be organic and reflect the main takeaways and tone of the group. A debrief is appropriate after each participant's reading as well as after the entire group has participated. Some sample questions are: What did the participant learn? In addition to the process of information acquisition, what did the process of intuitive knowing feel like? How many of the "answers" did the participant already know, but simply needed the oracle cards to affirm? Note: Because the cards likely affirm participants' perspectives while challenging them to be more honest and active in their current situation, participants might have immediate vulnerable reactions to the cards. The reader and observers should help the participant make sense of what lies before them.

References:

Like many mystical practices and traditions, oracle card readings are primarily passed down and communicated orally. However, every deck includes instructions and a background in its accompanying guidebook.

STRETCH AND REFLECT:
EXPLORE YOUR INNER SELF USING ACTIVE RELAXATION
Daniel Marshall

* 20–30 minutes
* Any size group, depending on space availability (at least 1 foot beyond the edge of mat is sufficient)

This activity is designed to create an active space where participants can calm their mind, body, and senses to focus on and listen to their physical self. This is practice toward becoming more self-aware. Facilitators will guide participants through a series of stretching techniques and breathing exercises to relax the body and reflect on how they feel.

Learning Goals: Participants will have opportunities to:

* focus on breathing to center the mind and body.
* explore their inner self to reflect on their personal well-being.
* relax and become more aware of their physical self.

Materials: yoga mat or towel to sit on, blanket or jacket for the final relaxation, chairs (if participants need accommodations)

Process:

1. Below is a table outlining the stretch sequence with position descriptions and safety cues to share with participants. If you are using a theme, such as a wrap-up where participants reflect about the semester, a question can be asked during each stretch or pair of stretches. Hold each position for 2 to 3 minutes and inform participants that each stretch should be taken to a point of slight discomfort.

   * When instructing the stretch sequence, be aware of the volume and clarity of your voice to ensure you do not overpower the space.
   * When encouraging participants to breathe, instruct them to take deep breaths by inhaling and exhaling through the nose.

Body Position Transitions	Cues
Comfortable seated position	• Sit comfortably and close your eyes • Let your arms relax and start to take deep breaths in and out • Begin to deepen the breath by fully inhaling, allowing your chest to expand, and then slowly exhale • Begin to relax the mind and clear your thoughts in order to be here in the moment with yourself
Comfortable seated position to forward fold	• Take a deep breath in, lifting your arms up and extending through your finger tips to the ceiling • As you exhale, slowly fold forward, walking your fingertips out to the front • Continue to remain seated and allow your chest to fall toward the floor, keeping your sitting bones grounded • Hold this position and continue to breathe
Forward fold to corner fold (both corners)	• Walk your arms to a front corner of the room • Reach as far as you can and hold • Repeat on the other side
Corner fold to chest opener	• Walk your arms back to the center, then slowly roll back up to the starting position • Release your arms, pulling them back toward the floor behind you, slightly past your hips with your palms down • Pull your shoulders back and lift your chest toward the ceiling, feeling a stretch across your chest • Extend your legs in front of you and flex your feet so your toes point to the ceiling
Chest opener to spinal twist	• Walk your hands back to your hips, relaxing your shoulders • Lift and lengthen the spine through the crown of the head • Gently twist to the right, bringing the left hand to the outside of the right thigh • Place the right hand behind you to lift and open the chest • Repeat on the other side
Spinal twist to extended leg forward fold	• Release back to the starting seated position • Taking a big deep breath, sweep your arms up over your head, reaching your fingertips toward the ceiling • As you exhale, hinge at your hips, reaching your hands out toward your toes • Relax your lower back and hamstrings as you settle into the stretch • Repeat on other side
Extended forward fold to neck relaxation	• Release the stretch by lifting your chest up • Relax your shoulders back to starting position, palm on the floor by your hips • Let your right ear fall toward your right shoulder • Switch toward the left side • Return your head to the starting position
Neck relaxation to final relaxation	• While seated, place your hands on the floor by your hips • Lower your body to the floor, lying flat with your hands at your side • You may place a blanket behind your head for support or use it as a cover if the temperature in the room is cooler • Draw attention to your breathing by taking big deep breaths in and out • As you lie there, relax your body and let your muscles melt into the floor • Listen to your body and take the chance to reflect on your experience today

• It is important to note that you may have people that need accommodations to participate. This includes not being able to get on the floor, lie down, or sit in a stretched position. Emphasize that the participant should be comfortable, so any adjustments they need to make are okay.
• This sequence can also be performed in a chair. The primary difference is the start position, where participants will sit with their lower back against the back of the chair by sliding as far back into the chair as possible with feet flat on the floor.

Debriefing Questions:
• How do your mind and body feel now compared to when you first started?
• How has today's activity impacted your overall feeling of well-being?
• What feelings did you experience throughout this activity?
• What did you learn about yourself throughout this activity?
• How do you believe you can use this method of stretching and reflecting in the future?

Resources:
Carlson, C. R., Collins, F. L., Nitz, A. J., Sturgis, E. T., & Rogers, J. L. (1990). Muscle stretching as an alternative relaxation procedure. *Journal of Behavior Therapy and Experimental Psychiatry, 21*(1), 29–38.
Rama, S., Ballentine, R., & Hymes, A. (2007). *Science of breath: A practical guide.* Honesdale, PA: Himalayan Institute.
Wilkinson, A. (1992). Stretching the truth: A review of literature on muscle stretching. *The Australian Journal of Physiotherapy, 38*(4), 283–287.

TALK, WALK, AND LISTEN:
PARTNER CONTEMPLATIVE WALK
Erica Wiborg

- 40 minutes–60 minutes
- Any size group

This activity merges three contemplative practices: walking meditation, deep listening, and dialogue. Partner contemplative walks can be a powerful tool to connect with each other through storytelling, listening, and shared meaning-making, particularly on the topic of identity.

Learning Goals: Participants will have opportunities to:

- practice deep listening skills, as evidenced by their participation in the contemplative walk with a partner.
- describe their personal reflections on identity, as evidenced by their ability to reconcile and respond to the prompts.

Materials: have a printed instructional card that lists out the contemplative listening tips and the prompts for every participant. Below is an example of the card we recommend printing.

Contemplative Listening Tips:	Questions to Respond to:
To the speaker: This time is yours, if you run out of things to say, feel free to simply be silent. When you are ready, speak.	Respond to the following sentence prompt: "I am …"
To the listener: Your job is to listen in silence. You may feel an urge to coach, identify, or chime in—this is normal, but simply notice when this occurs and refocus your attention to your partner.	What life experiences, identities, or relationships are you recalling in response to this prompt? How do they relate in meaningful ways?
To both partners: Make sure to share the time and ensure both people get the opportunity to speak and listen. End by thanking each other.	As a result of this contemplation, what have you learned about yourself as a leader?

Process:
1. It is best to limit the partners to one on one, rather than groups of three or more.
2. You may decide to shorten or lengthen the walk, depending on what your group needs. In addition, consider if you would like the group members to select their partner or if you would like to facilitate a random count-off prior to facilitating the walk.
3. This activity is recommended for outside, weather permitting. When I facilitate, I have everyone leave their bags in the room, besides one phone to look at the time or in case of emergency, and I stay with their items. Have an alternative weather plan if need be.

4. Contemplative listening tips and activity introduction (10 minutes)
   - To begin, divide the group into pairs, and share that they will be participating in a contemplative activity that will challenge them to reflect and actively listen.
   - Open with a general discussion on what active listening means. Seek clarification and consideration for the differences between listening and active listening, listening to respond and listening to understand, and what it means to be heard. If they are having trouble brainstorming, it might be useful to prompt the participants to think back to a situation where they felt heard and recall what was present in that situation.
   - Describe how they will be participating in a partner contemplative walk and pass out the activity cards. Remind the group of what they just brainstormed and refer them to the contemplative listening tips, specifically highlighting the sharing of time. State that they can leave everything in the room and that they will have until a specific time to return to the space. They can walk wherever they would like, but they must return back at the time given and follow the prompts.
   - Instruct them to quietly read the prompts and when their partner pair is ready, they can transition to their contemplative walk.
5. Partner contemplative walk (20 minutes)
   - As they return by the time you stated, welcome them back and thank them for engaging in the walk.
6. Connecting Across Experiences (10 minutes)
   - Debrief focusing on the process of engaging in a contemplative walk, active listening, and the prompts on identity.
   - Close with gratitude and encouragement to carry this experience into their life.

Debriefing Questions:
- What was that process like for you? What was it like when you were the speaker versus when you were the listener?
- Was it difficult to practice the tips of contemplative listening? If so, why?
- What connections were revealed between you and your partner in relation to your experiences, identities, and relationships?
- How does learning with and from others enhance the leadership process? How might you integrate

these reflections and skills into your everyday life on campus and in the communities you care about?

Resources:

Knefelkamp, L. (2006). Listening to understand. *Liberal Education.* Retrieved from https://files.eric.ed.gov/fulltext/ EJ744028 .pdf

The *Contemplative Listening Tips* card was inspired from the LeaderShape Institute curriculum.

ZOOMING IN ON LEADERSHIP MOMENTS
Courtney Holder

- 1 hour 10 minutes
- Any size group

Practicing individual contemplation and meditation can help participants wade through mind chatter, center themselves in the midst of distractions and challenges, and enhance awareness of emotions and environment. This activity asks participants to reflect on a recent leadership moment and engage in mindfulness that can be applied to future leadership moments.

Learning Goals: Participants will have opportunities to:

- enhance awareness of one's feelings and behaviors.
- develop focus and attention within a leadership experience.

Process:

When planning for this activity, the physical space is the most important consideration. While the space can be indoors or outdoors, consider finding a place free from interruptions and with comfortable seating (carpet, soft ground, soft chairs). Ensure the space is free from loud noises and other people will not be walking into the area. The facilitator should allow for ample time by pausing when providing each prompt or direction. Avoid rushing through to allow participants ample opportunity for contemplation.

Introduction (5 minutes)
- Explain to participants that mindfulness is the practice of shifting our attention inward. Through mindfulness, they may become aware of thoughts, feelings, and actions without interpretation or judgment.

Activity (1 hour 5 minutes)
1. Begin the activity by asking participants to spread out and find a comfortable place to sit or recline.

Participants should be at least a few feet from each other and find a position that allows them to remain still and comfortable for several minutes. (5 minutes)
2. Have participants close their eyes. Instruct participants to take three deep breaths, inhaling and exhaling slowly. The facilitator may want to state "inhale" and "exhale" to guide participants. (5 minutes)
3. Ask participants to recall a recent leadership moment. If this activity is part of a larger experience (class session, retreat, training), direct participants to the activity or simulation that was just completed. Pause for a moment to allow participants to recall their moment. Encourage participants to focus on and envision a specific situation. (5 minutes)

- Prompt variation: Direct participants to think of the last time they were engaging with a group and things did not go well or as planned. This could be in a student organization meeting, study group, presentation, work setting, helping a friend or family member, et cetera.

4. Ask participants to imagine they are on a balcony overlooking the scene as that leadership moment was taking place. As they are on the balcony, they have a camera with a zoom lens. (45 minutes)

- First, participants start with the widest view of the scene—examining the broad context and environment: (10–12 minutes)
  - What was the purpose of the group, meeting, or activity?
  - Why were people there?
  - What time of day was it? What did the space look like?
- Ask them to zoom in slightly to the movement and behaviors around them: (10–12 minutes)
  - Who was in the room? Who was far away from you? Who was nearby?
  - Who was talking? What was their tone? What was their message?
  - What did you notice about others' body language? Were they engaged, excited, detached, or distracted?
  - Who was included? Who was not included?
  - Where was people's attention?
- Then, ask them to adjust their lens—zoom in a bit more to their own movements and behaviors: (10–12 minutes)
  - What did you say? How was it received?
  - Notice your breathing: Was it slow and steady? Short?
  - Notice your body: Was it tense, relaxed, tired, energized?

- How was your body language? Were you engaged, excited, detached, distracted?
  - Where was your attention?
  - What did you do? How did your actions align with your values?
- Lastly, ask participants to zoom in as close as possible on themselves—internally to their feelings and thoughts: (10–12 minutes)
  - What were you feeling in that moment?
  - What were you thinking but refrained from saying? Why?
  - How connected did you feel to those you were interacting with? Did you feel supported and valued?
  - How connected did you feel to the group's purpose or goals?
  - How did you feel about the outcome?

5. Direct participants to slowly start to zoom back out from themselves to the people and movement nearest them, then those farthest from them, and finally the entire balcony view of the scene. When they are ready, ask them to open their eyes. (5 minutes)

Debriefing Questions:
- What did you feel or notice during the activity?

- What felt most natural for you during the exercise? What was more difficult?
- How much detail could you recall about your leadership moment?
- What aspects of your experience were easy to recall? What was more difficult to recall?
- Thinking back, what do you wish you would have noticed about the context, others, or yourself in the moment?
- How can mindfulness—increased awareness and presence—enhance your leadership?
- Think about your week ahead. What event (meeting, exam, project) is on your calendar that might evoke feelings of stress, anxiety, worry, or nervousness? What could you do to practice mindfulness before or during that event?

Resources

Goleman, D. (2013). *Focus: The hidden driver of excellence*. New York, NY: Harper.

Mindful. (n.d.). Retrieved from https://www.mindful.org/

Rock, D. (2009). *Your brain at work: Strategies for overcoming distraction, regaining focus, and working smarter all day long*. New York, NY: HarperBusiness.

Thakrar, M. (2017, June 28). How to create mindful leadership. Retrieved from https://www.forbes.com/sites/forbescoachescouncil/2017/06/28/how-to-create-mindful-leadership/#6b364234342a

CHAPTER 3

Creative

Creative reflection methods provide a breadth of opportunities for leadership learning. Guthrie and Jenkins (2018) highlighted the role of art in supporting creativity and innovation in leadership education. Through their creations, artists both reflect the world as they see it and envision possibilities. Broadly speaking, "the vocation of the artist is whatever medium is to reveal the truth of the human condition and to enlarge our imagination of life, through the exploration of the beautiful and the sublime, the ordinary and the degraded" (Daloz Parks, Keen, Keen, & Daloz Parks, 1996, p. 229). Similarly, leaders work in groups and communities to create a vision for how the world can be (Guthrie & Jenkins, 2018). Creative reflection encompasses a broad range of activities that may include music, role-play, theater, and visual arts, among others.

Music. Music can be used as a powerful pedagogy in leadership education, especially in connection with reflection. Often when structured reflection time is given, music is played to provide an environment conducive to reflection. However, music provides more opportunity for leadership learning than playing it in the background. Hall (2010) stated, "Music affords students a 'personal experience,' one that educators can use to stimulate thought and reflection. Reflection then leads to action—action that ultimately leads to student learning" (p. 109). Scholars have discussed how participating in a musical chorus increases awareness of listening habits and helps participants realize the importance of emotional relationships in a group (Purg & Walravens, 2015). Choral participation also results in "memories with momentum" that can result in retaining leadership skills and concepts (Sutherland, 2013, p. 38). Parush and Koivunen (2014) argued practicing skills of directing a choir presented leaders with a variety of competing demands. Navigating these contradictions helped develop the capacity to tolerate paradoxes and to make meaning of the essential virtues of the creative self. Music is a powerful pedagogical tool for framing leadership learning.

Role-Play. McKeachie (1986) defined role-play as an active learning strategy where learners act out assigned roles in either case scenarios or unstructured situations.

Role-play, a common pedagogy in education, has been utilized in a broad range of disciplines to address learning across cognitive, psychomotor, and affective domains (Rao & Stupans, 2012). Role-play activities provide opportunities for learners to engage in a variety of leadership situations and to take on roles students are unlikely to encounter elsewhere. Perhaps one of the most effective applications for this strategy is providing students opportunities to practice varying leadership styles, skills, behaviors, situations, dispositions, and attitudes while exerting some control of the practical consequences. For example, students may play roles of positional authority such as a chief executive officer, boss, president, or principal—statuses that are often far beyond the reach of a traditional undergraduate—or perhaps more supportive, followership roles (Sogurno, 2003; Tabak & Lebron, 2017). Role-play can also be used to demonstrate leadership styles such as autocratic, democratic, and laissez-faire (Sogurno, 2003); various points of view around a particular problem, concern, or issue (e.g., interest groups, law makers, citizens); and potentially how racial, religious, or socio-economic backgrounds can shape one's lived and leadership experiences (Frederick, 2000; Kornfeld, 1990). In doing so, learners relate new and potentially unfamiliar roles and behaviors to practical situations, prompting reflection, stronger retention of information, and more ingrained learning.

Theater. Theater-based curricula is frequently used in leadership education (e.g., Meisiek, 2004; Mirvis, 2005); however, more innovative use of theater for reflection needs to be explored in the context of leadership education. Currently, various methods from improvisational (improv) theater (Gagnon, Vough, & Nickerson, 2012) to classical acting and role-play (Guthrie & Jenkins, 2018) are used in leadership education. McCarthy and Carr (2015) used live stage plays in a management course to teach lessons in conflict, power, and leadership. Another example is Soumerai and Mazer (2006) who required students to participate in productions of theatrical tributes to inspirational historical figures. Most of the research in theater as a pedagogy in leadership education relates to improv.

Scholars found improv skits improve creative thinking and problem solving (Pruetipibultham & Mclean, 2010), strengthen individual and collective empathy (Katz-Buonincontro, 2015), and foster difficult discussions (Meisiek, 2004). Additionally, Huffaker and West (2005) introduced tenants of improv that translate well to learning collaborative leadership in the classroom including being present, being fit and well, listening, willingness to be adaptable, and accepting offers (which means working with what you have).

Visual Arts. Visual arts, whether interpreting or creating, can be a powerful leadership pedagogy (Guthrie & Jenkins, 2018). Adler (2015) referred to the interpretation of visual arts as aesthetic reflection. In a study focused on leadership development, participants used images from the Leadership Insight journal (Adler, 2010) that included "paintings and wisdom from many of the world's most insightful leaders" (Adler, 2015, p. 49). According to Adler (2015), "Reflecting on the visual imagery of the paintings quickly takes managers beyond the dehydrated language and minimal aspirations of economics, accounting, and finance and allows them to go beyond day-to-day reality and return to possibility" (p. 49). Similarly, Purg and Walravens (2015) found students became better observers when they analyzed leadership through the metaphor of visual arts. Students also realized the power of metaphors; they were not only aware of their own leadership style through understanding different styles of art, but they could also talk more about their leadership style.

REFERENCES

Adler, N. J. (2015). Finding beauty in a fractured world: Art inspires leaders-leaders change the world. *Academy of Management Review, 40*(3), 480–494.

Daloz Parks, L. A., Keen, C. H., Keen, J. P., & Daloz Parks, S. (1996). *Common fire: Leading lives of commitment in a complex world.* Boston, MA: Beacon Press.

Fredrick, P. J. (2000). Motivating students by activating learning in the history classroom. In A. Booth & P. Hyland (Eds.), *The practice of university history teaching* (pp. 101–111). Manchester, England: Manchester University Press.

Gagnon, S., Vough, H. C., & Nickerson, R. (2012). Learning to lead, unscripted: Developing affiliative leadership through improvisational theatre. *Human Resource Development Review, 11*(3), 299–325.

Guthrie, K. L., & Jenkins, D. M. (2018). *The role of leadership educators: Transforming learning.* Charlotte, NC: Information Age.

Hall, J. L. (2010). Teaching with music: An alternative pedagogy for leadership educators. *Journal of Leadership Studies, 3*(4), 108–110.

Huffaker, J. S., & West, E. (2005). Enhancing learning in the business classroom: An adventure with improv theater techniques. *Journal of Management Education, 29*(6), 852–869.

Katz-Buonincontro, J. (2015). Decorative integration or relevant learning? A literature review of studio arts-based management education with recommendations for teaching and research. *Journal of Management Education, 39*(1), 81–115.

Kornfeld, E. (1990, September). Representations of history: Role-playing debates in college history courses. *Perspectives on History.* Retrieved from https://www.historians.org/perspectives/issues/1990/9009/9009

McCarthy, J. F., & Carr, S. D. (2015). Igniting passion and possibilities through the arts: Conflict, collaboration and leadership through live stage performances. *Journal of Leadership Studies, 9*(1), 30–32

McKeachie, W. J. (1986). *Teaching tips: A guidebook for the beginning college teacher.* Lexington, MA: DC Heath & Co.

Meisiek, S. (2004). Which catharsis do they mean? Aristotle, Moreno, Boal and organization theatre. *Organization Studies, 25,* 797–816.

Mirvis, P. H. (2005). Large group interventions: Change as theater. *Journal of Applied Behavioral Science, 41,* 122–138.

Parush, T., & Koivunen, N. (2014). Paradoxes, double binds, and the construction of 'creative' managerial selves in art-based leadership development. *Scandinavian Journal of Management, 30*(1), 104–113

Pruetipibultham, O., & Mclean, G. N. (2010). The role of the arts in organizational settings. *Human Resource Development Review, 9*(1), 3–25.

Purg, D., & Walravens, A. (2015). Arts and leadership: Vision and practice at the IEDC-Bled School of Management. *Journal of Leadership Studies, 9*(1), 42–47.

Rao, D., & Stupans, I. (2012). Exploring the potential of role play in higher education: Development of a typology and teacher guidelines. *Innovations in Education and Teaching International, 49*(4), 427–436.

Sogurno, O. A. (2003). Efficacy of role-playing pedagogy in training leaders: Some reflections. *Journal of Management Development, 23*(4), 355–371.

Soumerai, E. N., & Mazer, R. (2006). Arts-based leadership: Theatrical tributes. In M. Klau, S. Boyd, & L. Luckow (Eds.), *New Directions for Youth Development, No: 109. Youth leadership* (pp. 117–124). San Francisco, CA: John Wiley & Sons.

Sutherland, I. (2013). Arts-based methods in leadership development: Affording aesthetic workspaces, reflexivity and memories with momentum. *Management Learning, 44*(1), 25–43.

Tabak, F., & Lebron, M. (2017). Learning by doing in leadership education: Experiencing followership and effective leadership communication through role-play. *Journal of Leadership Education, 16*(2), 199–212.

COLLABORATIVE ART AS A MEANS FOR UNDERSTANDING TEAM LEADERSHIP
Jessica Chung

- 20–30 minutes
- Minimum 4 participants

In the 1950s, Roger Sperry discovered the two halves of the human brain, and came to find the left-brain preferred logic, language, and sequence, whereas the right brain preferred visual, artistic, and abstract ideas (Pink, 2005). In general, U.S. education teaches students through a very left-brain style, focusing on presenting information in a sequential and logical manner; however, we know the right-brain style is also a valuable way of learning and processing (Farmer, 2004). This activity can serve as a validation of right-brained learners and leaders as well as a metaphor for leadership practice.

Learning Goals: Participants will have opportunities to:

- draw parallels between their artistic journey/process and leadership journey/process.
- become more aware of their preferences for reflection.

Materials: large table for all participants, watercolor paint palettes, paint brush for each participant, cups of water to clean paint brushes, paper towels for excess paint, 2 sheets of watercolor paper for each participant

Process:
There is a high level of flexibility in this activity. Please adapt it to suit your audience, budget, time, or specific leadership lesson. For example:

- If you focus on team building, note particular group dynamics such as comfort, trust, encouragement, or hesitation
- If you focus on revealing or accessing personal expression styles, note individual signs of confidence, hesitation, frustration, or concentration
- If you focus on encouragement of risk taking, innovation, or experimentation, debrief the feelings of the process

Watercolor is the original format of this activity; however, it can be cost intensive, so you can also adjust by offering a wide variety of art supplies. Participants may express discomfort with engaging with art. Since the U.S. education system has highly rewarded students who perform well in prescribed ways, art becomes a risky area that connects artistic ability with

achievement. Participants may seek clarity or a "right answer" for how you want them to perform the art. Avoid giving direction; rather, encourage participants to trust themselves to experiment.

1. Briefly anchor the group in the benefits of practicing with right-brain focused activities; often we default to left-brain activities that are verbal and logic based, rather than spending time with creativity and play. This can also be a helpful tool in processing and activating other ways of learning. (2 minutes)
2. If you have time and want to encourage more artistic play, allow for 10 minutes of individual experimentation with the art supplies. Practice using the brushes and paints in various ways:

   - Wet on wet watercolor technique: Wet the brush, gather paint. Apply paint to the paper. Add other colors into the shape while paint is still wet to blend colors together.
   - Wet-on-dry watercolor technique: Wet the brush, gather paint. Apply to the paper. After drying, layer other shapes and colors on top.
   - Blend two colors together by using water.

3. Transition to the group activity. *"For the next part of the activity, begin with a fresh, blank sheet of paper. We will be going in rounds. Each round, I'll read a prompt and you can interpret it however you choose. Go with whatever comes to mind; avoid overthinking, because there is no right way to do it."*
4. First round: Use paintbrush (or other tool) and draw two shapes. Color them in. (60–90 seconds)
5. Instruct participants to pass their paper to the left. Pass the paper left between every round; repeat for as many rounds as you wish for 60–90 seconds each round. Here are some ideas for rounds; feel free to invent your own prompts.

   - Add a set of parallel lines
   - Add a second layer of detail or color to a shape
   - Balance it out with another shape somewhere
   - Overlay 3 circles somewhere
   - Draw two rectangular outlines
   - Add another color outline to a shape
   - Add something you think it needs

6. Repeat until the participants seem to have enough time to get in the rhythm of the activity and there is enough experience for the debrief reflection.
7. Debrief (5–10 minutes).

Points that may emerge from the debrief include: fear regarding their artistic ability and therefore their willingness to take risks for fear of being wrong or looking dumb.

Some may find this activity liberating because of its abstract nature and freedom to express themselves. Some, who prefer using their right-brain skills, may find this activity validating of their own preferences and modes of expression in less-structured or free-form ways.

Debriefing Questions:

- What was this like for you? Is art something you enjoy? How did that impact how you engaged with the activity? What happens when we engage from a place of perceived strength or deficiency?
- How do you feel about your original painting?
- What does this teach us about ourselves? Need for control? Trusting others? Trusting self to add what is needed? Trying new things? My own preference for process?
- What does this teach us about how we work with one another?

References:

Farmer, L. S. J. (2004). Left brain. Right brain. Whole brain. *School Library Media Activities Monthly, 21*(2), 27–28.

Pink, D. (2005). *A whole new mind: Moving from the information age to the conceptual age.* New York, NY: Riverhead Books.

FRAMING LEADERSHIP IN YOUR COMMUNITIES
Sally R. Watkins

- 60 minutes–2 weeks
- Any size group

Photography can be an intentional lens used to facilitate observation and capture moments demonstrating leadership. Undoubtedly artists embrace the role observation and reflection play in identifying, capturing, and framing the concepts and themes they explore in their artwork. This activity is an opportunity for participants to be the artist, identifying, reflecting on, and capturing the leadership moments in their daily life. In the process of developing a leadership gallery, and artist statements, participants rely on reflection for making meaning and translating the images of leadership they experience in their communities.

Learning Goals: Participants will have opportunities to:

- reflect on their personal identities and the communities they align with.
- reflect on how the leadership process shows up in their chosen communities.

- share images of leadership (or concepts related to leadership) in their communities via photo gallery.

Materials: either disposable camera, digital camera, or phone with camera, paper, access to a printer or print-shop, painters tape, tacks, method of hanging the images for the gallery, and a method for journaling—notebook, digital tool

Process:

Also note, the final gallery show might be one picture for each participant that they identify as the strongest representation of leadership in their communities and their artist statement thus can be determined based on the number of people participating and the method used to display the images and statements.

1. Reserve a gallery space. If this is not available, use the hall of an office space. You can also use the walls of a room for a temporary display.

   - It is possible to shift the means of display to participant presentations depending on the context of the curricular or cocurricular leadership learning setting.

2. Have participants identify 2–3 communities they engage with on campus and charge them to observe the communities to identify leadership concepts in action. This can be a structured process by delineating the number of hours or specific situations, such as a group meeting, or ask participants to observe their communities over a period of time such as 2–3 weeks.

3. Ask participants to capture instances of leadership they observe in the communities—acknowledge these should not be staged photos, but candid moments that arise when they are present. One benefit of digital photography is the ability to take numerous photos and curate the final selection for the gallery. Once participants pick the image(s) they plan to display, if their photographs include identifiable images, the artist should obtain permission from the subjects to use their likeness in the photo gallery.

4. In the process of narrowing their images for display, the participants should spend time reflecting and developing a narrative that translates why they perceived the image(s) to be representative of leadership. Additionally, participants should note the concepts and ideas they explored in the process of documenting leadership in their communities and any other unique aspects of the process they hope to translate to people interacting with their images. The process is significant and informs their artist statement, which accompanies the image in

the gallery. It may be helpful to introduce concepts related to observation, reflection, and making artist notes (journaling) related to the technique(s) the individual used to capture the image(s) as well as decisions related to subject matter and thoughts or ideas that emerge across the creative process.

5. Assign participants a gallery day to present their image(s) to the larger group and share their artist statement and other outcomes of the process. This may be in a group meeting or during a class session. In either setting, the larger group should be able to interact with the artist and the images following the presentation and complete a reflection on the experience.

Debriefing Questions:
For presenters in the classroom or a gallery space:

- How did observing and reflecting on leadership shape your interactions with the community?
- How did reflecting on your personal identities and communities strengthen your connection to them?
- Why did you choose the images you displayed?

For gallery visitors: As an exit activity, individuals that engage with the images in the gallery can be asked to engage in personal reflection and take a moment to respond to the following questions:

- How did spending time with these images shape your comprehension of leadership?
- How do the leadership concepts and themes the artist captured in these images mirror leadership in your own communities? Differ?
- Which image stood out to you? Why?

Resources:
5 tips for writing a memorable artist statement. (n.d.). Retrieved from https://www.artworkarchive.com/blog/5-tips-for-writing-a-memorable-artist-statement

Barrett, T. (2018). CRITS: A Student Manual. Bloomsbury Publishing. A text on the value of the critic in the artistic process.

International Center of Photography. (n.d.). Retrieved from https://www.icp.org/

PhotoVoice. (n.d.). Retrieved from https://photovoice.org/

Segars, G. (2007). A participatory photography toolkit for practitioners and educators. Compiled for the Cultural Agents Initiative. Retrieved from http://wendylut-trell.ws.gc.cuny.edu/files/2010/08/visible_toolkit.pdf

THE MUSIC WITHIN YOU: LEADERSHIP REFLECTION THROUGH MUSICAL MESSAGES
Jesse Ford

- 50 minutes–1 hour 40 minutes
- 5–20 participants

Music has been used throughout history as a mechanism to trigger reactions, memories and reflection (Scherer, 2004). Although these triggers often have both positive and negative responses from listeners, music has the ability to inform our reflection within leadership development. This activity will provide participants with a better understanding of how reflection through music can expand their views on leadership.

Learning Goals: Participants will have opportunities to:

- define personal thoughts, opinions, and ideas of leadership and leader identity through music.
- examine the connections between personal leadership definitions and the diversity of thought within theory formation.
- synthesize knowledge and use creativity to explore on how leadership as a multilayered and a diverse pedagogy is needed to lead our ever-changing global society.

Materials: a computer with music editing software

Process:
Part 1

1. Ask participants to choose a song that reminds them of a memory, reaction, or moment when they had to engage in the process of leadership or establish a leader identity.
2. Next, have participants use a mobile device, computer, or another method to select the 20–25 seconds of the song that most resonates with their memory.
3. In a group setting, invite participants to explain their song selection and why it reminds them of a time they engaged in the process of leadership or established their leadership identity (if it is a large group, small group clusters can also be effective).

Part 2

4. The facilitator should combine the song clips to create a compilation of all material selected by the participants. I recommend using music editing software to create one file, but is not necessary. The facilitator can explore other methods for completing this process.

The compilation should be played for the larger group to start a dialogue around reflection and leadership. The overall goal is to discuss how leadership is displayed in music culture.

Debriefing Questions:
Part 1

- What do you think the purpose of this activity was?
- How does music impact your reflection of leadership and leader identity?

Part 2

- Is there anything about the song compilation you heard that surprised you?
- What are some common messages from participants' song selections?
- How are you feeling right now?

References:
Scherer, K. R. (2004). Which emotions can be induced by music? What are the underlying mechanisms? And how can we measure them? *Journal of New Music Research, 33,* 239–251.

A Playwright's Reflections
Jennifer Batchelder

- About 60 minutes (pending the length of your script)
- 2–24 participants

In this activity, participants become playwrights as they reflect. The ideas, experiences, and concepts explored by characters during scenes are likely a product of the writer's own interests, experience, or ideas. This activity uses the concept of narrative learning (Clark & Rossiter, 2008) to engage participants in reflection through story telling.

Learning Goals: Participants will have opportunities to:

- reflect on a selected topic or issue and reflect their own identities.
- identify ways their identities intersect and impact the way they respond to the topic.

Materials: one writing utensil and two pieces of lined paper per participant

Process:
Throughout the activity, it is helpful to be comfortable with silence in the room, but also be open to ques-

tions your participants may have about the topic, characters, scene, or conversation. Rather than giving answers, ask participants probing questions about their perspective and how their characters might see the situation. If they have experienced something similar to the topic addressed by the play, it can be a reflection of what they remember or how they wish it happened. As noted, these scenes incorporate identity and may contain personal information participants may not be comfortable sharing with the group. Keep this in mind for the discussion and any modifications of the activity.

1. Think about a concept or experience to reflect on (this can be assigned by the leadership educator). Some ideas may include a small or large personal change, describing a specific feeling, defining #Adulting, and any other topic of conversation.
2. *For this activity, you will become a playwright and focus on two characters for your scene. One of the characters should be someone who is a reflection of yourself and the other character can be anyone you could see yourself having a conversation with about this topic (friend, family member, mentor, etc.). This person can be fictional or based on someone you know.*
3. *To start, describe the two characters. What demographics do they possess? What do they believe? What experiences have brought them to where they are? Do they have an original opinion on the topic? Are they open to hearing the other person's perspective? Are they the type of person who will change their mind? (about 10–15 minutes)*
4. *Provide your audience (the facilitator and group) with the scene and a backstory. Where are you? What day/time/year is this scene happening? Why are they reflecting on this topic or experience? Where are they and why are they at this location? Who else is around? Is there someone or something that is creating a barrier to your conversation (i.e. noise, taboo, another person). (5–10 minutes)*
5. *Write two pages of dialogue between the two characters discussing the topic (the page length varies based on time allotted). Remember that dialogue goes back and forth. Have the characters ask questions and try to break down the concept or experience to each other and incorporate their identities as a way to explain the way they are responding. (15–30 minutes)*

- Remember, there is not a correct way for how stories are told—they can be happy, sad, successful, or defeating. As the playwright, they have the control over the ending (or nonending).

Variations:

- The facilitator may choose the length of the script. Longer scripts will call for more time, but also allow for a deeper dive into participants' understanding of the topic, their identity, and how they intersect.

- This activity is written for a single cocurricular workshop, but it could be incorporated into the classroom by stretching it over a few sessions through the stages of understanding the topic, reflecting on the characters, setting the scene, and writing out the dialogue.
- You may ask participants to share the dialogue, but be aware of time and the potentially private nature of the content the participants may write.

Debriefing Questions:
- How did this playwriting experience help you to reflect on the topic?
- What was it like to write a character that you related to? Did you make any changes to this character (name, background, beliefs)? If so, why?
- Who did the second character represent and why did you choose to have the conversation with them?
- Why did you pick the location of the conversation?
- How do you relate to this scene?
- Have you tried to have this conversation before? Did it follow the story you wrote, or did you write an alternative ending?
- What new insight do you have about yourself or the topic as a result of this playwriting process?

References:
Clark, M. C., & Rossiter, M. (2008). Narrative learning in adulthood. *New Directions for Adult and Continuing Education, 119,* 61.

POP-UP CONCERTS
Grady K. Enlow

- 60 minutes–2 hours
- 6–10 participants per group (may have multiple groups)

This learning activity intended for a music-related course consists of the planning and implementation of a series of three or four pop-up concerts throughout the semester by the entire class, or subgroups of the class, depending on its size.

Learning Goals: Participants will have opportunities to:

- improve their skills in observation and reflection.
- improve their capacity for audience and group member empathy.
- recognize elements of concert planning, promotion and assessment that could improve audience members' experience.
- recognize relational leadership dynamics.
- advance in their leadership identity development.

Materials: generated by the participants, such as press kits, press releases, programs, handbills, posters, and social media posts

Process:

1. Facilitator describes activity and assigns groups. For the first pop-up concert, the participants should identify a group member who is willing to perform a pop-up concert at a determined location on campus or in the community (likely within walking distance for the class). The performance should only last 10 minutes, and the remainder of the group or class members should observe the concert and people who are present or pass by during the concert. No other instructions are provided for the first concert.
2. Following the concert, the participants are asked to reflect on what took place in the planning and execution of the concert, including group members' participation and audience reaction, and write a brief (approximately 100–250 word) summary of their reflection.
3. Facilitator leads discussion bringing participants to consensus of two to three elements of planning, promotion, articulation, or assessment that could improve the next concert.
4. Next pop-up concert is held, after which participants again reflect on experience and summarize their reflection with potential improvements.

5. Facilitator leads discussion bringing participants to consensus of two to three elements of planning, promotion, articulation, or assessment that could improve the next concert (repeat steps four and five once, if needed).

6. Final pop-up concert is held, after which participants reflect and summarize their overall learning experience through the activity and submit the final project packet of materials created to promote and support the final concert; these materials may include handbills, posters, social media posts, programs, press kits, press releases (preconcert and postconcert), audience interaction and response tracking, et cetera.

7. Facilitator leads discussion encouraging all participants to share their reflections to enhance group learning and individual leadership identity development.

Potential variations for this activity include the number of group members, the overall number of pop-up concerts in succession for the course, and the number of new elements added to each successive pop-up concert, including the total number included for the final concert.

Participants' observations and reflection on those observations after each concert are a vital part of this learning activity.

Debriefing Questions:

After the first concert, participants should be asked questions only from the first two bullets:

• What did you observe about the audience members' experience of and/or response to the concert? What might have improved audience members' experience or response?

• What did you learn about leadership from your experience working with the group to plan and execute the concert? What might have improved group effectiveness?

After subsequent concerts, the following questions should be asked, as well:

• How did each added element improve audience members' experience or response?

• How were you able to apply relational leadership components to this next phase of group planning and execution?

Resources:
Beeching, A. M. (2010). *Beyond talent: Creating a successful career in music* (2nd ed.). New York, NY: Oxford University Press.

Cutler, D. (2010). *The savvy musician: Building a career, earning a living, and making a difference.* Pittsburgh, PA: Helius Press.
Komives, S. R., Lucas, N., & McMahon, T. R. (2013). *Exploring leadership: For college students who want to make a difference* (3rd ed.). San Francisco, CA: Jossey-Bass.
Wallace, D. (2008). *Reaching out: A musician's guide to interactive performance.* New York, NY: McGraw Hill.

THEATER IS A TEAM SPORT
June Dollar

• 45–60 minutes
• 5–10 participants

This activity uses the process of creating and producing a theatrical work to better understand how leaders need to evolve complex processes and sometimes adapt to the wildly creative personalities involved. By participating in theater, we are able to weave multiple theories of leadership into the creation of a play.

Learning Goals: Participants will have opportunities to:

• learn about themselves as leaders through self-examination.
• practice adaptation and team work.
• analyze the process of determining what role each team member will play.

Materials: computer, props, set pieces, costumes, a room of sufficient size to accommodate the play and an audience

Process:
It is helpful for the facilitator to have a familiarity with the participants, whether any of them have participated in a play or theatrical production previously. This activity works best when creation from start to finish happens over a predetermined number of meetings.

1. **Have participants do research.** Participants should bring copies of scripts to first meeting (these can be found online at no cost). A good recommendation is to have participants read the play out loud for 10 minutes. Reading some scripts online can help participants decide the structure of the play they wish to create.

   • Encourage participants to decide what story they want to tell and how far the story should go. They should also discuss details like how space will influence characters and what props they could use.

2. **Who will be the director?** Participants will decide who the director will be. In this role, the director tends to be both a transactional and situational leader. The group might decide to have several directors who will choose the cast.

3. **Writing the script.** Spending time on the script is crucial as it describes the setting and any type of stage direction. This can take up to 2 hours of collective work.

- Here is an example from Shakespeare's Romeo and Juliet:

  Scene II, The Capulet's orchard (THE SETTING)

  Juliet appears at her window (STAGE DIRECTION)

  ROMEO: (standing below Juliet's window) [STAGE DIRECTION]

  But, soft! What light through yonder window breaks? It is the east and Juliet is the sun! Arise, fair sun, and kill the envious moon ..."

  JULIET: O Romeo, Romeo! Wherefore art thou Romeo? Deny they father and refuse thy name! Or, if thou wilt not, be but sworn my love and I'll no longer be a Capulet!

  ROMEO: (as an aside to himself) [STAGE DIREC-TION]

  Shall I hear more, or shall I speak at this?

  JULIET: (Looking down at Romeo) 'Tis but thy name that is my enemy. Thour art thyself, though not a Montague.

  (There is clearly more to the scene but this should give you a good illustration of how script formatting, stage direction and scene-setting should work.)

4. **Staging.** Once the director or directors are chosen, the group should write the script, decide on the props, and gather the costume pieces. The director should provide the staging. When a director provides stage direction (for example from what direction the actors enter the stage, how the actors move

about during the scene if at all for example), each actor will write down their stage direction in the script, paying close attention to how fellow actors enter the stage prior. This process of perfecting the play through rehearsal is the practice of leadership.

- Keeping a journal of this process and how it connects to leadership can assist in the overall reflection and meaning making of this activity.

5. **The performance.** After the play is performed, group debriefing should occur playing close attention to the connection to leadership learning.

Debriefing Questions:
- How did you choose the subject of the play?
- How did you select the roles including the director and the person casting the show?
- What about the activity was stimulating or fun? What was challenging?
- How were you able to apply leadership theories during the activity?
- Did the team find the activity intimidating? If no, why not? If yes, why and how did they overcome the initial intimidation?
- How did you balance group members who had strong opinions about how the activity should play out?
- Aside from being a theater professional, what do you need to better perform your role? For example, how could you work on speaking in front of a group or thinking on your feet if something goes wrong?

Resources:
Carter, P. (1994). *The backstage handbook: An illustrated almanac of technical information* (3rd ed.). New York, NY: Broadway Press.
Crook, P. B. (2016). *The art and practice of directing for theatre.* New York, NY: Routledge.
Hatcher, J. (2000). *The art and craft of playwriting.* New York, NY: Story Press.

References:
Writing a Play. (2019). Retrieved from https://www.theatre-ontario.org/resources/training-resources/school-tools-for-high-school/writing-a-play.aspx

TREE OF ALIGNMENT
Laura Osteen

- 1 hour 10 minutes
- Any size group

This activity is an opportunity to reflect upon core values, daily choices, visions for change, and the resulting alignment or misalignment of our core, choices, and change.

Learning Goals: Participants will have opportunities to:

- clarify and claim their own values, choices, and visions.
- identify specific choices to align self and bring about positive sustainable change they wish to see in their community.

Materials: blank paper, colorful writing utensils

Process:

1. Provide a quick review of the Social Change Model (SCM) of Leadership Development (Higher Education Research Institute, 1996). (5 minutes)

   - *Consider how the Social Change Model (SCM) would be significantly different without one of the three circles. Without Individual? Nothing would actually get done. Without Group? Individuals would burn out/crash before change became sustainable. Without Community? Change would be irrelevant to the intended. Does power exist with the alignment of these circles? How do the arrows in the model represent power created or lost? (5 minutes)*

2. Draw Tree of Alignment (30 minutes)

   - Hand out paper and coloring pencils. Describe task to reconsider the SCM as a tree imagining each of the three sections as our roots, our trunk, and our crown (branches) of our own tree.

3. Roots: Choice to Act—Individual Context

   - Describe and Prompt: *What motivates you to act? Why are you driven to be where you are right now? Who and what guides your choices? Motivation to act often comes from within—we act on something we care about or believe is important. The lifelong learning process of understanding and knowing self is central to our capacity as a leader and follower.*
   - Draw: *Reflect on these prompts to draw the roots of your tree, using symbols, words, and images to*

reimagine the Individual context of the SCM. As a compass for our behavior, our values often define what we believe is important and guide our decisions. Reflect upon what and who you value. In addition, these values are grounded in our sense of identity. Reflect upon and draw your roots as an expression of who you are—how do you define yourself?

4. Trunk: How we Act—Group Context

   - Describe and Prompt: *While our values may ground and guide us, do they always? What else influences our ways of being? The trunks of our tree represent our choices with others to do what you say you will do. Integrity in leadership is examining the choices we are making daily with our time, resources, and relationships.*
   - Draw: *Reflect on these prompts to draw the trunk of your tree, using symbols, words, and images to reimagine the Group context—as the day to day choices you are living right now. How do you spend your time, attention, money? What people, groups, communities do you give your personal resources to? What choices are you making right now? What do you prioritize in your day? Week?*

5. Crown: Vision—Community Context

   - Describe and Prompt: *Visions allow us to dream beyond what we think is possible, to imagine a better tomorrow for our communities. What better tomorrow are you leading or following to? What is your desired impact for that tomorrow?*
   - Draw: *Reflect on these prompts to draw the branches of your tree, using symbols, words, and images to reimagine the Community context as the crown of your tree. What is your why? Why are you committed to creating change? What compels you? What could happen if you focused all your energy on a single passion that you hold? What does your community need for a better tomorrow? What would evolve? Change?*

6. Give participants time to ensure they finish all three sections.

Debriefing Questions:

1. Invite participants to practice a deliberate sharing experience by gathering in groups of 3 to share their trees. (15 minutes) Each person has 4 minutes to share, the other two are listeners. If the speaker stops talking in their 4 minutes, listeners stay silent. The speaker owns their time to share and reflect. After 4 minutes switch roles. Prompt participants with these questions:

   - What surprises you? What are you most proud of? What do you most wonder about?

- Where are your roots, trunk, and branches in alignment? Where are they not?

2. Invite groups of 3 to engage in open conversations to react to each other's sharing and identify action steps to increase the alignment of their core, choices, and change. (5 minutes)

3. Large Group Sharing: (10 minutes)

- Open up to reactions on the deliberative sharing model of speaking and listening. After responses, remark on how infrequently we get 5 minutes to explore what is in our heads or hearts before being interrupted for someone else's train of thought.
- Then focus specifically on their trees. What emerged in your conversations?
- Finally, why is alignment of your tree important? Alignment creates power through:
  ○ Developing Trust—people follow/are drawn to individuals who walk their talk
  ○ Building Commitment—we are motivated and sustained by the cause not external factors
  ○ Creating Energy—propels us forward because we are motivated when values, passion, and behavior grow together

4. Closure: (5 minutes)

- Connect back to tree metaphor: a tree grows in direct relation to its roots (i.e., the crown and branches of a tree will be the same size as the root structure). Sustainability of a tree is in its congruence with itself.
- Everyday there are moments to act, when you have the opportunity to lead and/or follow through the choices you make. How are you aligning these choices? Look around you. You are not alone, this is not a single tree, this is a forest of possibilities—how will you support the growth of your colleague/peer standing tall next to you?

References:

Higher Education Research Institute. (1996). *A social change model of leadership development* (Version III). Los Angeles, CA: University of California Higher Education Research Institute.

WHOLE SELF AS LEADER
Kathy L. Guthrie

- 30 minutes
- Any size group

In this activity, participants reflect on their whole selves as leaders through drawing a picture of themselves. Participants will reflect on their identify, capacity, and efficacy as both a leader and follower. Art is a valuable pedagogy for leadership learning (Guthrie & Jenkins, 2018), and can provide space for reflection.

Learning Goals: Participants will have opportunities to:

- identify how they demonstrate leadership knowledge, skills, and abilities.
- reflect on personal aspects that either benefit or negatively influence their engagement in the leadership process.
- discuss personal aspects that make up their whole self and how these show up both as a leader and a follower.

Materials: flip chart paper (1 piece per participant), markers or colorful writing utensils

Process:

1. Make sure each participant has a piece of flip chart paper and a few markers or colorful writing utensils.
2. Ask each participant to draw an outline of self on paper. This could physically be an outline of themselves (they will need to have a friend help) or a stick figure. (5 minutes) It is good to provide various examples of pictures of self so participants understand it can be simple.

3. Next, instruct participants to add parts of self that relate to the leadership process, both as a leader and a follower. For example, when they think of self as a leader, what parts of their body is being used and for what specifically? Parts of self to pay attention to may include, but are not limited to: head, eyes, mouth, ears, heart, hands, feet and so on. (15 minutes) Examples may include:

4. Once each participant has finished their picture, have them get into pairs to discuss their drawings. (10 minutes)

Debriefing Questions:
- Each participant should discuss what parts of self they chose to highlight in relation to the leadership process, both as a leader and follower.
- What part of yourself do you feel is the most important as a leader? As a follower?
- How was this process of identifying specific aspects of self in relation to the process of leadership?
- Are there aspects of self, either regarding leader or follower, you wish were represented on your picture?

References:
Guthrie, K. L., & Jenkins, D. M. (2018). *The role of leadership educators: Transforming learning*. Charlotte, NC: Information Age.

ZOOM: A VISUAL REFLECTION TOOL
Kerry L. Priest

- 30–60 minutes
- Up to 30 participants (per set of pictures)

Zoom is a graphic children's book by Istvan Banyai (1995) that can be used as a visual reflection activity. It is a series of images that progressively "zoom" out and can be used to reflect on learning/changed perspectives, others' perspectives, and systems. An Internet search of "zoom activity" turns up multiple training websites that illustrate variations of this activity (e.g., http://www.wilderdom.com/games/descriptions/Zoom.html). This version has been adapted specifically as a reflection for leadership learning.

Learning Goals: Participants will have opportunities to:

- describe the role of perspective taking in leadership learning and development.
- reflect on course learning (content and experience) through multiple perspectives (self, others, system).

Materials: *Zoom* book (paperback) that has been disassembled into a deck of 30 images (pages with image on one side, blank on other). You may wish to laminate cards, however, they will hold up with careful use.

Process:
Zoom can be used to help draw connections to concepts of socially responsible leadership (Komives & Wagner, 2016), adaptive leadership (Heifetz, Grashow, & Linsky, 2009), and vertical leadership development (Petrie, 2014). The activity could be used to talk about observations and interpretations within systems, perspective, communication, or group process.

Introduce the activity by stating to the group: *"The goal of this game is to put the cards in the proper order, the order reveals a story."*

1. Distribute cards, face down, 1 per person (or modified based on number in group). If using less than 30, some people may have multiple pictures, or you may need to divide the "deck" into a smaller set of images. If there are more than 30 participants, consider adding a second set of images (i.e., *Re-Zoom*, Bayani, 1998).
2. *Without showing others your card, take a look at your cards for 30 seconds. Make silent observations.*
3. *Turn card face down. Each person in the group now has 30 seconds (to 1 minute, depending on size of group) to describe your picture(s) to the rest of the group. There are no questions or comments across participants at this step.*

4. *Pick up cards and look again at your image for 45 seconds in light of learning what others' pictures are.*

5. *Cards down. You have 30 more seconds each to describe your picture with any additional detail to the group. Again, no cross talk as people are sharing.*

6. *With cards still down, in this step your whole group may now discuss for 3 minutes what you think the order/story might be. Remember, no peeking at others' cards!*

7. *Take 30 more seconds to view your cards.*

8. *Cards down. Now, as a team you have 4 minutes to lay out the cards in order with blank sides up.*

9. *Finally, turn cards over and lay them out and see how well you did!*

10. Make any adjustments necessary and proceed to debrief.

Some insights may include:

- We each come to class with our own "pictures" of leadership; now we have added to our story of what leadership is and what we can do as leaders. We can continue our story through involvement as participants and eventually in life, careers, families, or communities.

- There is an intentional pattern of development of our leadership identity and capacity that mirrors our guiding framework of leadership for the common good (self, others, society). Through our learning, we have sought to move from focus on individual achievement only towards group performance and impacting community systems.

Variations:

- At Step 9, you could ask groups to put cards in order without speaking.
- If one deck is divided between smaller groups, once the stories are revealed you can do a gallery walk to see how the images between groups are connected.

Debriefing Questions:
General Debrief:

- What is special about these images and their order? What is a key factor in ordering this story?
- What were some obstacles you faced in accomplishing the task?
- How did you overcome those obstacles? What skills were necessary?
- The name of this activity is Zoom. It's about perspective. As we approach a new year in this course/program, how has your perspective changed compared to when you started? What do you see now that you didn't see then? How does it help you?
- What does it mean that your group only had part of the story?

Advanced Debrief:

- How might this exercise also be a metaphor for our learning process this semester?
- As you think about your (our) work this semester, what is the bigger story we are a part of? How will our work support continued progress?

References:

Banyai, I. (1995). *Zoom.* New York, NY: Puffin Books.

Banyai, I. (1998). *Re-zoom.* New York, NY: Puffin Books.

Heifetz, R., Grashow, A., & Linsky, M. (2009). *The practice of adaptive leadership.* Boston, MA: Harvard Business School.

Komives, S. R., Wagner, W. E., & Associates. (2016). *Leadership for a better world: Understanding the social change model of leadership development* (2nd ed.). San Francisco, CA: Jossey-Bass.

Petrie, N. (2014). Vertical leadership development—Part 1: Developing leader for a complex world (White Paper). Center for Creative Leadership. Retrieved from https://www.ccl.org/wp-content/uploads/2015/04/VerticalLeadersPart1.pdf

Zoom & Re-Zoom. (2009). Retrieved from http://www.wilderdom.com/games/descriptions/Zoom.html

CHAPTER 4

Digital

Beyond social media, technology encompasses "digital learning tools and platforms in which students, faculty, and administrators can share and critically examine leadership theories and identities" (Ahlquist & Endersby, 2017, p. 5). As the role of technology in learning continues to expand, it is important for educators to embrace technology in their work and consider digital identity development (Ahlquist, 2016). Digital identity development adds a layer as both students and educators negotiate how they show up in online environments (Ahlquist, 2016; Gordon Brown, 2016). Active learning extends to digital spaces. Guthrie and Meriwether (2018) proposed a digital leadership engagement strategy to support mentoring, coaching, and advising students. Through clear and consistent engagement, using tools to manage content, and capturing measurable outcomes, educators can engage students in online spaces to support a sense of belonging (Guthrie & Meriwether, 2018). As technology expands, leadership educators should consider how to engage students in the digital sphere in making meaning of their leadership experiences, as well as supporting all students in developing technology competencies.

Social Media. Since the introduction of Facebook in 2004, and with the proliferation of social media platforms, the role of social media in education has been an ongoing dialogue (Stoller, 2013). The prevalence of social media challenges educators to consider what, if any, role these platforms should play in learning and reflection. While social media may not allow for in-depth dialogue, there is some expectation that "an interaction on Twitter, a comment on Facebook, or a response to a blog post can be the start of multiple conversations" and social media exchanges may prompt deeper in-person interactions (Stoller, 2013, p. 6). In a study of students perceptions of social media in a leadership classroom, students cited benefits including enhanced communication, ease of connection, and having a tool for networking (Odom, Jarvis, Sandlin, & Peek, 2013). Disadvantages included social media as a distraction, discomfort with technology, loss of face-to-face interaction, and lack of access to consistent Internet (Odom et al., 2013). Although there were benefits,

given the drawbacks, researchers recommended social media be an add-on or optional component of courses in order to enhance connections (Odom et al., 2013). As a tool for creating change, the Pew Research Center (2018) found around half of Americans surveyed used social media for some form of political or social-minded activity in the previous year. In examining case studies of recent social media activism through a leadership lens, Gismondi and Osteen (2017) outlined five "Rs" for practice:

> A *reminder* to welcome dissent, to *respect* the transformational impact of technology, a *reality check* that you have to be there, the *relationship* potential in your reach, and the *recognition* that online narratives reflect offline pain, joy, and the possibility for transformative social change. (p. 70, emphasis in original)

The transformative power of social media invites leadership educators to embrace technology broadly and engage in learning with students regarding how to use technology for positive change.

Digital Storytelling. Storytelling is a powerful tool for learning and reflection; digital stories are "short vignettes that combine the art of telling stories with multimedia objects including images, audio, and video" (Rossiter & Garcia, 2010, p. 37). Digital stories contribute to learning and reflection by giving voice, encouraging creativity, and requiring self-direction or self-authorship (Rossiter & Garcia, 2010). The Center for Digital Storytelling provided seven steps for building digital stories, and the process begins with owning insights and emotions (Lambert, 2013). Developing a digital story is a reflective process. Building upon digital stories, Baldwin and Ching (2017) highlighted the features of interactive storytelling that enhance its potential: dynamic presentation, data visualization, multisensory, interactivity, and narrative. By including these elements, which are often used in journalism, learners can engage with stories in a non-linear way and become more active in the learning process (Baldwin & Ching, 2017). This type of active learning may support telling complex stories of leadership learning.

Blog. A blog, abbreviated from web log, is a type of technology that allows users to post content displayed in reverse chronological order. Blogging is similar to journaling in that blogging entails "writing regularly about ideas that are personally meaningful, as they emerge" (Freeman & Brett, 2012, p. 1040). Unlike journals, many blogs published online are public forums that are designed to promote interaction among readers and writers through the comment feature (Freeman & Brett, 2012). In a review of literature, Duarte (2015) found the benefits of blogging in education clustered in three areas: students' engagement or sharing knowledge, learning, and relationships. In studies examining blog content between groups of students who received different guidelines, leadership educators found providing more structure for blog posts, including a framework for reflection (Gifford, 2010) or structured blogging guidelines (Cain, Giraud, Stedman, & Adams, 2012) resulted in posts that demonstrated deeper critical thinking as opposed to open-ended blogging. Blogs can be a significant tool for student learning, but they require input and structure from educators in order to scaffold reflection and provide timely, substantive feedback.

REFERENCES

Ahlquist, J. (2016). The digital identity of student affairs professionals. In E. T. Cabellon & J. Ahlquist (Eds.), *New Directions for Student Services*: No. 155. *Engaging the digital generation* (pp. 29–46). San Francisco, CA: Jossey-Bass.

Ahlquist, J., & Endersby, L. (2017). Editors notes. In J. Ahlquist & L. Endersby (Eds.), *New Directions for Student Leadership*: No. 153. *Going digital in student leadership* (pp.5–8). San Francisco, CA: Jossey-Bass.

Baldwin, S., & Ching, Y. H. (2017). Interactive storytelling: Opportunities for online course design. *TechTrends, 61*(2), 179–186.

Cain, H. R., Giraud, V., Stedman, N. L. P., & Adams, B. L. (2012). Critical thinking skills evidenced in graduate students blogs. *Journal of Leadership Education, 11*(2), 72–87.

Duarte, P. (2015). The use of group blog to actively support learning activities. *Active Learning in Higher Education, 16*(2), 103–117.

Freeman, W., & Brett, C. (2012). Prompting authentic blogging practice in an online graduate course. *Computers & Education, 59*, 1032–1041.

Gifford, G. T. (2010). A modern technology in the leadership classroom: Using B logs for critical thinking development. *Journal of Leadership Education, 9*(1), 165–172.

Gismondi, A., & Osteen, L. (2017). Student activism in the technology age. In J. Ahlquist & L. Endersby (Eds.), *New Directions for Student Leadership: No. 153. Going digital in student leadership* (pp. 63–74). San Francisco, CA: Jossey-Bass.

Gordon Brown, P. (2016). College student development in digital spaces. In E. T. Cabellon & J. Ahlquist (Eds.), *New Directions in Student Services: No. 155. Engaging the digital generation* (pp. 59–73).

Guthrie, K. L., & Meriwether, J. L. (2018). Leadership development in digital spaces through mentoring, coaching, and advising. In L. J. Hastings & C. Kane (Eds.)., *New Directions for Student Leadership: No. 158. Role of mentoring, coaching, and advising in developing leadership* (pp. 99–110). San Francisco, CA: Jossey-Bass.

Lambert, J. (2013). *Full circle*. Retrieved from https://www.storycenter.org/storycenter-blog/blog/2013/2/26/full-circle.html

Odom, S. F., Jarvis, H. D., Sandlin, M. R.,& Peek, C. (2013). Social media tools in the leadership classroom: Students' perceptions of use. *Journal of Leadership Education, 12*(1), 34–53.

Pew Research Center. (2018). *Activism in the social media age*. Retrieved from http://www.pewinternet.org/2018/03/01/social-media-use-in-2018/

Rossiter, M., & Garcia, P. A. (2010). Digital storytelling: A new player on the narrative field. In M. Rossiter & M. C. Clark (Eds.), *New Directions for Adult & Continuing Education: No. 126. Digital storytelling: A new player on the narrative field* (pp. 37–48). Hoboken, NJ: Wiley.

Stoller, E. (2013). Our shared future: Social media, leadership, vulnerability, and digital identity. *Journal of College and Character, 14*(1), 5–10.

7-DAY ONLINE LEADERSHIP CHALLENGE
Virginia L. Byrne

- 15 minutes a day for 7 days
- Any size group

The 7-Day Leadership Challenge is an example of an online cocurricular program that can help participants reflect on the intersection of academics, work experiences, and campus involvement. Hosted via social media, participants can post their responses to each day's question to earn points. Other participants will benefit just by reading the reflections of their peers.

Learning Goals: Participants will have opportunities to:

- reflect on their experiences with leadership by responding to online challenges.
- connect leadership ideas to participant experiences by reading others' responses.

Materials: an institutional, public social media account on Twitter, Facebook, or Instagram, participants will need a public account as well.

Process:
Explain the "7-Day Online Leadership Challenge" to participants:

- **Rules:** Every morning the facilitator will post a new challenge on the social media account. Participants then have 24 hours to earn up to 4 points before the next challenge is posted. After each day, the facilitator will moderate the posts and determine who earned points.
- **Engagement:** Facilitators may respond to students' posts with a "Thank you!" message. If desired, host a Challenge Completers Party with coffee or pizza for the top 10 participants.
- **Points:** Earn points each day by responding to the challenge. Earn 1 point for each of the following: (A) relevant response to the challenge, (B) relevant photo with your post, (C) relevant video with your post, and (D) supporting comment on another person's post.

Example Posts:

- **Example #1:** We believe leadership is a process of knowing yourself, what you contribute, and how you can best work with others to make a change in your community. The leadership learning process is about inner work and self-development just as much as it is about learning how to work with others. Watch this TED talk on passion. Who makes your eyes "shiny"? How do you define your own success? http://www.ted.com/talks/benjamin_zander_on_music_and_passion
- **Example #2:** Leadership exists through powerful relationships. No one can be a leader alone. Often the greatest leaders have a partner who can see their true selves and can challenge the leader's thinking. Watch this short TED video on How to Start a Movement. What do you think about the way the speaker discusses the importance of followers? https://www.ted.com/talks/derek_sivers_how_to_start_a_movement
- **Example #3:** Follow the link to an instrument called *The Moral Foundations Questionnaire* (http://www.yourmorals.org/explore.php). This instrument will give you some data regarding your own moral foundations. After taking the questionnaire, you will get your results and the graph, which shows how your responses line up with the thousands of others who have taken it so far. Post your reaction. How does this change your perception of terms like *liberal* and *conservative*?

- **Example #4:** Today we focus on how we empathize and understand others. Conflict can often come from decisions that were made without considering multiple perspectives. Watch this TED talk called "Danger of a Single Story." What is your reaction to this video? How can you avoid only hearing a single story? http://www.ted.com/talks/chimamanda_adichie_the_danger_of_a_single_story.html
- **Example #5:** Leadership is in response to the needs of our community. What are your reactions to the below quote? How have you identified a need in your community? How do you know your work is relevant? *"To my mind, you cannot speak about the need for leadership within our communities without being prepared to take on responsibility yourself. It's not enough to point the finger at those who have let us down and to expect others to come forward and fix our problems. Nor can anyone afford to call themselves a leader unless they truly have the interests of our community at heart. Too many people like to think they are leaders and too many are identified by the media as leaders who are not really leaders at all." Jackie Huggins,* Author and Activist
- **Example #6:** Today we focus on how you and everyone else in your community creates change. Watch this TED video called "The Antidote to Apathy." What is your reaction? Since citizenship extends beyond voting, how do you stay informed about needs and issues relevant to your community? How do you foster a community where everyone has a voice and access to power? http://www.ted.com/talks/lang/en/dave_meslin_the_antidote_to_apathy.html

References:

Adichie, C. N. (2009). *The danger of a single story* [Video file]. Retrieved from https://www.ted.com/talks/chimamanda_adichie_the_danger_of_a_single_story

Meslin, D. (2010). *The antidote to apathy* [Video file]. Retrieved from https://www.ted.com/talks/dave_meslin_the_antidote_to_apathy?language=en

Moral Foundations Questionnaire. (n.d.). Retrieved from http://www.yourmorals.org/explore.php

Sivers. D. (2010). *How to start a movement* [Video file]. Retrieved from https://www.ted.com/talks/derek_sivers_how_to_start_a_movement

Zander, B. (2008). *The transformative power of classical music* [Video file]. Retrieved from https://www.ted.com/talks/benjamin_zander_on_music_and_passion

BETTER TOGETHER BLOGGING
Jillian M. Volpe White

- 30 minutes–1 hour 30 minutes for several works (this works best over the course of several weeks)
- 6–10 participants

In this activity, participants post to a collective blog, which allows them to share responsibility for content. This encourages a variety of perspectives, creates opportunities for interaction, and allows participants to not feel singularly responsible for blog content. Through collaborative blogging on experiential learning, participants can share a variety of perspectives and engage in discussions with each other and blog readers about leadership learning.

Learning Goals: Participants will have opportunities to:

- process experiences through a collaborative blog by posting in response to prompts.
- engage in discussion with peers and facilitators about experiential learning.
- receive and respond to feedback through comments on their reflective posts.

Materials: access to a smartphone, tablet, or computer as well as Internet, use of a site such as Wordpress.com to create a blog.

Process:

Blogs are most effective when posts are consistent, meaning they may not be an effective reflection tool for temporal projects. One way to ensure regular contributions by a group of participants is to have people select a day of the week when they will post content; consider developing a calendar for the group to see who is posting on which days. Finally, blogs are most effective when they become dialogic. The facilitator should plan to comment on posts and encourage others to read and comment on the blog.

1. At the beginning of the experience, introduce blogs and blogging. Consider sharing a few examples of blogs you read.
2. Let the group know they will be responsible for posting regularly to a shared blog. Have the participants sign up for dates to post.
3. Provide the better blogging handout. Additionally, you could provide a list of scaffolded prompts for participants in case they need ideas.
4. Let the group know they should plan to read and comment on other posts.
5. At the end of the experience, facilitate a large group debrief.

Debriefing Questions:

- How did you go about developing the content for your posts?
- What was challenging about this process?
- How did comments from other people further prompt reflection?
- What insights did you gain about your experience through blogging and reading posts?

HANDOUT: BETTER BLOGGING

Ideas for Blog Posts

A blog that recounts what someone does daily (like a journal or a diary) is okay, but a blog with creative and compelling posts is more engaging. Use these ideas to jump-start your blogging. Keep a list of potential posts in a notebook or planner.

- Interview someone (get their permission before posting about the interview).
- Make a list. Some examples: three memorable experiences, 10 skills I've developed, five websites that inspire me, etc.
- Write about social issues. Compare social issues at a national or global level to observations in your local community.
- Tell a story.
- Describe your schedule for the typical day/week.
- Create a post with just pictures.
- Create themed days: Mind Dump Monday, Weekly Friday Recap, or Ten Questions Thursday.
- Post about a book, movie, or song that inspired or challenged you.
- Share links to your favorite websites.
- Write about goals you have for the future and plans for achieving those goals.
- How-to _____: anything you know or learned.
- Take questions from readers in the comments and answer them in the next post.

Suggestions for Blogging

- Write about what you know best.
- Infuse posts with your interest in the topic.
- Post frequent updates and keep posts short (500 words or less; 250 words is usually enough).
- If you feel like your post is getting too long, create a cliffhanger or develop a series.
- Give posts catchy titles that generate interest.
- Make posts easy to scan by using bullet points or subheadings and breaking long sections of text into paragraphs.
- When possible, include pictures.
- Include timely content by commenting on current events or including links to relevant news.

- Check facts and cite sources.
- Pose questions to readers at the end of the post to generate discussion in the comments.
- Set alerts in your calendar so you remember to post.
- Check spelling and grammar before publishing posts.

BUILDING AN INTEGRATIVE LEARNING PORTFOLIO (EPORTFOLIO)
Patrick M. Green and Brody C. Tate

- 2–4months
- 1-25 participants

Learning portfolios allow participants to build a digital collection of their learning—to make learning visible—throughout their curricular and cocurricular experiences. An integrative learning portfolio encourages participants to connect, or integrate, their learning within and across programs and learning experiences. This activity will instruct educators on how best to guide participants to building an integrative learning portfolio, in which participants reflect upon and connect their learning holistically.

Learning Goals: Participants will have opportunities to:

- curate and narrate the learning artifacts presented.
- organize the portfolio with named tabs that provide cohesive structure.
- design the portfolio with multi-media representations that support the artifacts.
- reflect on their learning by connecting multiple artifacts.

Materials: ePortfolio Platform (Watermark, Weebly, Wix, etc.) and a system to send and/or store portfolio links (Google Form, email, Learning Management System assignment tab, Excel spreadsheet)

Process:
Using the Social Change Model of Leadership as a framework (Higher Education Research Institute, 1996) reflections aim to elicit four domains of self, community, society, and change. Participants deepening their understandings of their social capital, leadership and values compound their connections to their realms of social influence, leading to a broader purpose of connection to society, citizenship or the world (Komives & Wagner, 2016). Change, or action, is the last domain in which we ask participants "what now?" and where they should take this knowledge and use it for the benefit of social good, personal leadership, and development.

1. Introduce the learning portfolio at the beginning of the program as a way for participants to:

   - collect evidence of their learning, often referred to as "artifacts,"
   - reflect upon the artifacts and learning that occurred, and
   - connect learning by linking artifacts together and synthesizing learning experiences.

2. Develop milestones and checkpoints for participants by creating assignments for submission into their portfolio throughout the program. Encourage creativity by including opportunities for participants to engage in written work, as well as oral presentations (e.g., PowerPoint or Prezi), research projects or posters, artwork, picture slideshows, videos, word clouds, or other creative representations.

3. Near the end, have the participants develop a final reflection in which they review their progress throughout the course or program and discuss their learning.

The key to a portfolio is not necessarily the medium but rather the message. The goal is for participants to critically think about experiences while curating a visible representation of their own learning in words. By empowering participants to reflect and demonstrate their learning, we offer the agency to articulate what they have learned in connection to their backgrounds, identities, and in- and out- of class experiences as participants come to understand the complexities of leadership capacity.

Debriefing Questions:
- How did the experiences in this course affect your personal, intellectual, civic, and/or professional development?
- How did you connect your in-class and out-of-class experiences to the course topics thus far?
- What is your action plan to live out the goals you have set forth in this course and beyond?
- Review an artifact that is one of the best quality examples of your work and write a narrative about it. What were some of the most interesting discoveries about your own knowledge, skills, and values while working on this artifact?
- Describe an experience this semester where you were challenged in this course. How did you navigate this experience and what did you do to address the challenge?

Resources:
Sample portfolios are helpful to spark participants' imaginations. Visit the Learning Portfolio Program at

Loyola University Chicago, and review the gallery of sample participant portfolios: www.luc.edu/eportfolio.

References:

Higher Education Research Institute. (1996). *A social change model of leadership development* (Version III). Los Angeles, CA: University of California Higher Education Research Institute.

Komives, S. R., & Wagner, W. E. (2016). *Leadership for a better world: Understanding the social change model of leadership development*. Hoboken, NJ: John Wiley & Sons.

COLLABORATIVE REFLECTION VIDEO ON VOICETHREAD
Virginia L. Byrne

- 5–6 weeks
- Groups of 4–6 people

Using VoiceThread, participants can create, share, and collaborate on reflections through testimonial videos and video clips, as well as text and slides. After posting the VoiceThread, their peers and the facilitator can view, comment, and offer a video response – all within the video itself. This interview assignment asks participants to work in groups to interview a person they see as a leader in their community and share their findings with the class in the form of a VoiceThread.

Learning Goals: Participants will have opportunities to:

- conduct an interview with a person who they identify as a leader.
- synthesize and compare their interview results with the class content.
- create a VoiceThread video that demonstrates their interview reflections using any relevant video clips or photos, text-based facts or data, and personal narrative.

Materials: a VoiceThread subscription (may be included within Learning Management System)

Process:

1. In assigned small groups, participants need to select and interview one person they see as a leader in their community: campus, city, field of study, et cetera. The interview should consist of 10 questions that will examine the leadership learning story lived by the selected person. All members must be present at the interview. Additional directions for participants may include:

- Select a leader who inspires you and/or who you have seen make a difference in the community. Use this opportunity to meet someone fascinating.
- Send a professionally written letter/email to the leader you would like to interview.
- Determine seven questions (in addition to the three below) to ask in your interview.
  - Interview questions: How would you describe leadership? How do you differentiate between leadership and management? (ask for a personal story). We study leadership as a process of making positive community change. Explain a time in your career when you felt like you were making a change.
- Conduct your interview. If approved by the interviewee, video record the interview. Ask them questions about their leadership learning story. Do not assume that your language and assumptions about leadership are shared with the person you are interviewing.

2. Next, ask participants to analyze the content of the interview. They should consider how the beliefs, assumptions, and practices of the person interviewed relate to what was discussed in class. Ask participants to reflect on their interviews and compare findings to what has been covered in class.

3. In part 3, instruct participants to create a 3–5-minute long VoiceThread capturing their analysis.

- Encourage participants to use the different features of VoiceThread to share their reflections and the lessons they learned.
- Participants should submit the VoiceThread to the class page on the Learning Management System.

4. Participants should individually watch each group's VoiceThread, and add comments or questions to the VoiceThread using text or video comment features as necessary. Each person in the class should comment on two group's VoiceThreads.

5. As a class, participant groups will discuss the VoiceThread project and their design choices. Groups will synthesize comments from peers while discussing their project.

Debriefing Questions:

- What media did you consider including in your VoiceThread?
- How did the different media formats help you convey your findings to your audience?
- Looking across all the group VoiceThreads, what themes about leadership emerge?

Resources:

Brunvand, S., & Byrd, S. (2011). Using VoiceThread to promote learning engagement and success for all students. *Teaching Exceptional Children, 43*(4), 28–37.

Ching, Y. H., & Hsu, Y. C. (2013). Collaborative learning using VoiceThread in an online graduate course. *Knowledge Management & E-Learning: An International Journal, 5*(3).

Gillis, A., Luthin, K., Parette, H. P., & Blum, C. (2012). Using VoiceThread to create meaningful receptive and expressive learning activities for young children. *Early Childhood Education Journal, 40*(4), 203–211.

DIGITAL LEADERSHIP IS GOING TO GO VIRAL
Courtney "Pearson" Pearson

- 30-60 minutes
- Any size group

Social media has transformed how leadership occurs and the digital spaces where leaders emerge. Platforms such as Twitter and Instagram have made concepts such as "following" everyday language and allowed digital leadership to develop. This activity allows participants to explore and define digital leadership by reviewing their Twitter account and the account of someone they recently followed. This activity is specifically crafted for Twitter but can be modified for other social media platforms.

Learning Goals: Participants will have opportunities to:

- identify and explore the digital leadership education pillars (Ahlquist, 2017).
- identify their personal digital leadership philosophy.
- review profiles of digital leaders and apply concepts of digital leadership.

Materials: personal device (cell phone, computer, tablet), access to connect to Internet, worksheet

Process:

Social media has created an indention in our society, community, and higher education institutions. Ahlquist (2017) defined digital leadership as "heartware of technology in higher education. Heartware is your internal operating system as a whole person in the digital age—with core values, life mission, and passion.... Heartware is about humanizing tech through human operations and relationships" (p. 55). Ahlquist (2017) also developed the Digital Leadership Education Pillars and Digital Reflection Model tools "that can be used by leadership educators to create intentional curricula built around critical thinking and reflection on social media" (p. 54). This framework is rooted in the following: "holistic digital identity, including prioritizing relationships, strategic communications, leadership philosophy, and embracing change" (Cabellon & Ahlquist, 2016, p. 8).

1. Begin by opening a discussion on what participants think digital leadership includes:

   - Based on your definition of leadership, does leadership exist on social media? Why or why not?
   - How does the way in which you define digital leader challenge or support your definition of leader? Of follower?
   - Consider one relationship developed on or established by Twitter. How has it demonstrated leadership? Why or why not? How?

2. Ask participants to reflect by completing the following handout. Consider also asking participants to complete the handout about themselves as a digital leader. Use the questions to guide them.

   - Who or what (company, organization, institution, or department) have you "followed" on Twitter in the last 90 days? Complete the handout on your selected "digital leader."
   - Why did you "follow" them?
   - Who or what (company or organization) has "followed" you on Twitter in the last 90 days?
   - How have you engaged with this "leader" (someone you follow)?
     - Retweets?
     - Likes?
     - Shares?
     - Messages?
     - Replies?
     - Comments?

Debriefing Questions:
- How has social media influenced leadership?
- What is a follower?
- How is the definition of this term different in leadership than within social media?
- How does digital leadership develop on Twitter?
- Are different social media platforms more suitable for digital leadership? If so, which ones? How?

References:

Ahlquist, J. (2017). Digital student leadership development. In J. Ahlquist & L. Endersby (Eds.), *New Directions for Student Leadership: No. 153. Going digital in student leadership* (pp. 47–62). San Francisco, CA: Wiley.

Cabellon, E. T., & Ahlquist, J. (Eds.). (2016). Editor's notes. In *New Directions for Student Services: No. 155. Engaging the digital generation* (pp. 5–10). San Francisco, CA: Wiley.

Header Content:
- *What image or text appears at the top of the account's profile?*
- *What does their header say about them or their leadership?*

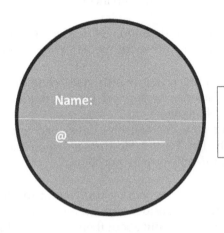

Name:

@_____

Bio Content:
- *What does the account choose to share about themselves in this limited space?*

Location:

Joined _____

Linked Site:

_____ Following   _____ Followers

What, if anything, does the number of followers indicate leadership?

How does this digital leader exemplify individual digital leadership skills (digital identity, digital wellness, digital decision making)?

How does this digital leader exemplify global skills (digital reputation, digital community building, digital leadership)?

How does this digital leader define leadership?

How does this digital leader engage in leadership?

Has this leader "gone viral"? If so, for what?

LEADERSHIP SNAPSHOT:
MEANING-MAKING THROUGH DIGITAL ARTIFACTS
Natasha H. Chapman and Naliyah Kaya

- 1+ weeks to create and upload their digital artifact
- Approximately 60-75 minutes for sharing
- 5–25 participants divided into small groups of 5

Using digital imagery, this activity will allow participants to draw from the verbal and the nonverbal to make meaning of the complex phenomena of leadership. Participants will create a digital artifact about leadership that requires them to make a creative choice and then reflect back on why they made the choice with the intention of stimulating deeper learning and understanding (Chapman & McShay, 2017). The process of sharing and examining artifacts with others promotes social learning, perspective-taking, and the development of a collective definition of leadership as a baseline for future leadership learning (Kaya & Chapman, in press; Maxwell & Greenhalgh, 2011).

Learning Goals: Participants will have opportunities to:

- explore personal assumptions, beliefs, and ideas about leadership.
- use digital imagery to examine leadership from diverse perspectives.
- engage in the process of reflection with peers.

Materials: personal device(s) with Internet connection and sound (one per small group), poster paper, and colorful writing utensils

Process:
When introducing the activity, facilitators should go over photography and filming laws specifically defining public spaces versus private spaces (Klosowski, 2012).

1. Explain to participants they will be creating a digital artifact that reflects leadership from their point of view. This artifact can be a photo or a 1–2-minute video that captures leadership in action, serves as a metaphor or example of leadership, or portrays a personal belief, value, feeling or expression of leadership.
2. Give participants one or more weeks to complete the activity and provide a shared space, such as a social media platform, in which they can upload their digital artifacts. Consider creating a class account and share the login credentials with participants who can then individually upload their examples. An alternative is to designate a hashtag for the activity, as long as participants have a public account associated with the social media platform. If you are using a learning management system, you could choose from several sharing tools that are available.
3. Once participants have uploaded their digital artifacts, build in time for sharing and discussion. Break participants into small groups of 4–5 and have them share their digital artifact, describe its significance, and explain the reasoning behind their choices. Since some artifacts may include audio, consider using a large room where small groups can intimately share their digital artifacts and hear one another. During this exchange, group members should thoughtfully and carefully interrogate and listen for common themes in response to the prompt, "Leadership is …". Providing 30–40 minutes should be sufficient.
4. Participants can use the following prompts to facilitate small group discussions:

- Walk through your decision to capture or create this image or video. What was significant about the event, symbol, image or situation you captured or created?
- How does the photo or video reflect leadership? What does your digital artifact say about your assumptions, beliefs, value, or understanding of leadership?
- What role did your personal, social, and leader identities play in what you created or captured?
- How do the following themes present themselves in your digital artifact (if at all): power, relationships, influence, change, identity, process, traits, environment, or context?
- What do others see in this photo or image that was not described by the creator?
- What connections can you make to the leadership concepts, models, and theories we have previously discussed (if relevant)?

5. Provide poster-paper and markers for small groups to organize and document themes, ideas, and questions from their discussion in a visible way.

Debriefing Questions:
After sharing in small groups, bring the participants together for 30 minutes as a large group to discuss themes, highlights, and takeaways related to the prompt, "Leadership is…". Large group debrief questions can include:

- What common themes emerged from your small group discussion? What meaning do you give to this? What was missing from your digital artifacts or your conversation? Why do you think that is?

- What role did identity, culture or difference play in your small group discussions? What emerged from the conversation that you had not considered?
- Consider our artifacts as a whole. What narrative have we produced about leadership? How would you describe our collective definition of leadership?
- Has this activity given you more or less clarity on your understanding of leadership? Why? What new questions or curiosities do you have about leadership or your role as a leader? In what ways has your perspective about leadership been informed by this activity and how does that make you feel?

References:

Chapman, N., & McShay, J. C. (2017). Digital stories: A critical pedagogical tool in leadership education. In B. T. Kelley & C. A. Kortegast (Eds.), *Engaging images: Utilizing visuals to understand and promote student development research, pedagogy, and practice.* Sterling, VA: Stylus.

Kaya, N., & Chapman, N. (in press). Leadership: Changing the narrative. In K. L. Guthrie & D. M. Jenkins (Eds.), *Transforming learning: Instructional and assessment strategies for leadership education.* Charlotte, NC: Information Age.

Klosowski, T. (2012). *Know your rights: Photography in public.* Retrieved December 2, 2018, from https://lifehacker.com/5912250/know-your-rights-photography-in-public

Maxwell, C. I., & Greenhalgh, A. M. (2011). Images of leadership: A new exercise to teach leadership from a social constructionist perspective. *Organization Management Journal, 8*, 106–110.

A MEMEINGFUL REFLECTION
Ana Maia Wales

- 30–55 minutes
- Any size group

A meme is a popular image, video, or text that has been replicated and passed to others repeatedly, mostly through social media. In popular culture, individuals use memes to express themselves. This digital expression is then imitated, reproduced and slightly altered to covey different meanings. This type of digital reflection can be used by facilitators to evaluate participants' growth after participating in a variety of leadership development experiences.

Learning Goals: Participants will have opportunities to:

- create an image and phrase to describe their attitudes and beliefs *before* engaging in the program or experience.

- create an image and phrase to thoughtfully evaluate their attitudes and beliefs *after* engaging in the program or experience.

Materials: share with participants a link to the Meme Generator: https://imgflip.com/memegenerator

Process:

For the purposes of this activity, participants may use images in pop culture or a photograph they have taken themselves. Note: It is easier for participants to find an image on the Meme Generator (https://imgflip.com/memegenerator) that depicts their thoughts, feelings or emotions and then add text to it through the website than to create their own image from scratch.

Activity Before the Program or Experience

1. Begin by describing the purpose of this digital reflection: to provide participants with a platform to describe their attitudes and beliefs *before* and *after* engaging in the program or experience. Describe the use of a meme in this reflection by illustrating to the participants the memes shown below (see Figures 1 and 2) or memes of your own creation that exemplify an individual's feelings before participating in the activity. These meme example can be shown in-person, in class, through a group chat, or on a learning management system such as Blackboard or Canvas.

2. At the beginning of an experience of leadership development activity, invite participants to create a meme to describe how they feel *before* engaging in the program or experience (see meme for an example). Encourage participants to be creative. It may help for them to find an image first that related to their attitude and/or beliefs and then add the text. Then, have participants supplement the image with a brief 2–4 sentence description about how they feel.

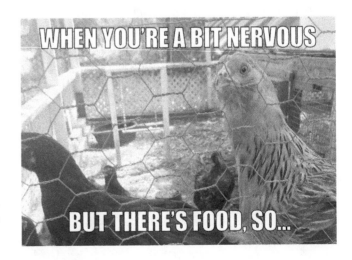

Activity After the Program or Experience

3. After participants engage in the experience or leadership development activity, invite them to create or find a meme to describe how they feel *after* participating in the program or experience. Supplement the image with a brief 2–4 sentence description to further clarify the meme they created.

Debriefing Questions:
*   How did your attitudes and beliefs change throughout this experience?
*   Were you surprised by any other participant's reactions?
*   Did you notice any themes emerge across the group? Which memes were similar?
*   From observing the group's memes, why did most individuals feel *insert suggested theme here* before engaging in this experience?
*   From observing the group's memes, who do you think had the most impactful experience? How come?
*   What skills did you acquire from this activity?
*   How does your experience connect to your development as a leader?
*   How will you approach a similar experience in the future? Would you select a different meme to describe how you would feel before engaging in this activity a second time?

Reference:
Meme Generator. (2019). Retrieved from https://imgflip.com/memegenerator

VIDEO VALUES CLARIFICATION
Kathy L. Guthrie

*   1–2 weeks
*   Any size group

In this activity, participants create a three-minute video to describe their personal values (Guthrie, 2012). Once completed, participants upload their videos to YouTube or a similar platform where others can access and view the values videos.

Learning Goals: Participants will have opportunities to:

*   clarify personal values through critical personal inquiry and reflection.
*   develop and edit a personal video portrait of their values.
*   identify themes of fellow participant's values.

Materials: a list of values, personal device with video capability (i.e., smart phone, tablet, computer), access to YouTube or similar platform for entire group

Process:
Berk (2009) discussed potential outcomes of using video in teaching, which include attracting participants' attention, capitalizing on participants' imagination, generating interest in content, and focusing participant concentration. Although any video platform can be used, YouTube is an incomparable resource for videos, with diverse material from many locations it is created to share content of personal opinion pieces, historical events, and media clips (Guthrie, 2012). Video production is an educational process, especially for those who do not regularly create videos. Remind participants this activity does not require high technical capacity, but encourage them to focus on content and to experiment with the technical aspect if they are new to video creation.

1. Introduce the activity of developing a video portrait of their values. Explain to participants that this is a 3-minute video where they describe their personal values. (2 minutes)
2. Briefly discuss why clarifying personal values is important in learning leadership (2 minutes)
3. Provide participants with a list of 50–75 values. Some commonly identified values include:

    *   Achievement
    *   Adventure
    *   Autonomy
    *   Challenges
    *   Change

- Community
- Competence
- Competition
- Cooperation
- Creativity
- Diversity
- Environment
- Education
- Excellence
- Excitement
- Faith
- Fame
- Family
- Flexibility
- Freedom
- Friendship
- Happiness
- Health
- Honesty
- Integrity
- Loyalty
- Money
- Order
- Play
- Power
- Privacy
- Recognition
- Relationships
- Safety
- Service
- Spirituality
- Status
- Wealth
- Work

4. Ask participants to quietly reflect on which 10 values are of greatest importance to them currently, and have them circle or mark those 10 values. (15 minutes)
5. In groups of 5–8 (depending on group size) have participants gather and discuss what values they chose and why. This is allowing time and space for participants to reflect on what they personally value. In a digital space, this could be in a group video chat or discussion board format. (20 minutes)
6. Now that participants have started reflecting on their values, they have one week (or an appropriate time for the specific context) to create a three-minute values self-portrait. The values self-portrait is framed as a confessional, where the participant is talking directly to the camera and discussing 3–5 personal values in a clear and concise manner. Have participants post values self-portrait to a common platform where group members have access. (1–2 weeks)
7. Once posted, participants are encouraged (or required, depending on context) to view fellow group members' videos and reflect on what they experienced and learned. (45 minutes)
8. Finally, the group will reconvene to reflect on the experience. Some potential questions are below.

Debriefing Questions:
- How did you personally come to narrow what you valued to the ones discussed in your values self-portrait?
- What common themes, if any, did you find across the group?
- Why is it important to know your personal values in relationship to the process of leadership?

References:

Berk, R. A. (2009). Multimedia teaching with video clips: TV, movies, YouTube, and mtvU in the college classroom. *International Journal of Technology in Teaching and Learning, 5*(1), 1–21.

Guthrie, K. L. (2012). YouTube: Beyond lectures and papers in leadership education. In C. Cheal, J. Coughlin, & S. Moore (Eds.), *Transformation in teaching: Social media strategies in higher education* (pp. 93–113). Santa Rosa, CA: Informing Science Press.

CHAPTER 5

Discussion

As the signature pedagogy for leadership education, discussion is an important instructional and assessment strategy for developing leadership knowledge (Guthrie & Jenkins, 2018). For each aspect—leadership development, leadership training, leadership observation, and leadership engagement—Guthrie and Jenkins (2018) identified some form of discussion for instruction and assessment including pair and share; face-to-face and online discussion; one-on-one, small, and large group discussion; and peer critical feedback sessions. Additionally, the Multi-Institutional Study of Leadership (Dugan, Kodama, Correia, & Associates, 2012) demonstrated one of the high-impact practices for student leadership development is sociocultural conversations with peers; in fact, these conversations were the strongest predictor of socially responsible leadership capacity. Sociocultural conversations "consist of formal and informal dialogues with peers *about* differences (i.e., topics which elicit a wide range of perspectives) as well as interactions *across* differences (e.g., with people who have different backgrounds and beliefs than oneself)" (Dugan et al., 2012, p. 9, emphasis in original). A group of leadership educators demonstrated the importance of dialogue by hosting a summit that engaged people from leadership programs around the state in intentional and deliberative dialogue for the purpose of enhancing their collective leadership efficacy (Priest, Kliewer, & Stephens, 2018).

Discussion is a common tool for reflection in curricular and cocurricular settings, whether in a small group (Bringle & Hatcher, 1996; Eyler, 2001; Guthrie & Thompson, 2010; Roberts, 2008) or with faculty (Astin et al., 2000). Discussions can take place face-to-face or through an electronic medium such as email or a discussion board (Hatcher & Bringle, 1997; Roberts, 2008). Exchanging ideas with other students in a classroom setting allows students to compare their experiences to the course content and to learn from exposure to alternative points of view (Hatcher & Bringle, 1997; Roberts, 2008). Faculty impact the efficacy of discussion-based reflection. Astin, Vogelgesang, Ikeda, and Yee (2000) noted faculty engagement and frequency of discus-

sions prompted by faculty impacted students perception of their learning experiences in a service-learning course. Discussions can be unstructured, but using prompts or rubrics can enhance discussion by providing focus and setting expectations (Roberts, 2008).

White and Guthrie (2016) described how discussion based courses were a tool for establishing a reflective culture in a leadership certificate program. Participants highlighted discussion as an opportunity to engage with diverse perspectives, and they also said discussion-based courses "challenged students to have a greater role in the learning process" (White & Guthrie, 2016, p. 69). To remedy the challenge of student leaders engaging only with people who shared their viewpoint, University of Northern Iowa developed a *Civic Discourse and Opposing Views* series (Perreault, 2012). The series was designed to help students become more willing and able to listen to views with which they disagreed, an important skill for leaders (Perreault, 2012). Many colleges and universities host dialogue programs or events to encourage students to engage with others purposefully and with an intent to listen. Pairing discussion with other methods for reflection, such as journaling, can enhance the value because committing thoughts to paper provides time for participants to process before sharing.

REFERENCES

Astin, A. W., Vogelgesang, L. J., Ikeda, E. K., & Yee, J. A. (2000). *How service learning affects students.* Los Angeles, CA: Higher Education Research Institute.

Bringle, R. G., & Hatcher, J. A. (1996). Implementing service learning in higher education. *The Journal of Higher Education, 67*(2), 221–239.

Dugan, J. P., Kodama, C., Correia, B., & Associates. (2013). *Multi-Institutional Study of Leadership insight report: Leadership program delivery.* College Park, MD: National Clearinghouse for Leadership Programs.

Eyler, J. (2001). Creating your reflection map. In M. Canada & B. W. Speck (Eds.), *New Directions for Higher Education: No. 114. Developing and implementing service-learning programs* (pp. 35–43). San Francisco, CA: Jossey-Bass.

Guthrie, K. L., & Jenkins, D. M. (2018). *The role of leadership educators: Transforming learning.* Charlotte, NC: Information Age.

Hatcher J. A., & Bringle, R. G. (1997). Reflection: Bridging the gap between service and learning. *College Teaching, 45*(4), 153–158.

Perreault, G. (2012). Leadership and civil civic dialogue across "enemy" lines: Promoting the will for dialogue. *Journal of Leadership Education, 11*(2), 237–246.

Priest, K. L., Kliewer, B. W., & Stephens, C. M. (2018). Kansas leadership studies summit: Cultivating collaborative capacity for the common good. *Journal of Leadership Education, 17*(13), 195–207.

Roberts, C. (2008). Developing future leaders: The role of reflection in the classroom. *Journal of Leadership Education, 7*(1), 116–130.

White, J. V., & Guthrie, K. L. (2016). Creating a meaningful learning environment: Reflection in leadership education. *Journal of Leadership Education, 15*(1), 60–75.

COMMUNITIES AS ASSETS
Joi N. Phillips

- 30–45 minutes
- 15–50 people

This activity is designed to help participants consider how their leader identity influences how they think about and approach working with communities. This is an opportunity for participants to understand how their assumptions influence their perception of what "help" is needed in a community. The activity also highlights the need for participants to understand the importance of entering communities ready to learn and support existing efforts from those who intimately understand existing needs and past efforts.

Learning Goals: Participants will have opportunities to:

- explore how their leadership identity influences their perception of community needs.
- understand the influence their perception has on identifying community needs.
- understand the importance of building relationships with communities in order to provide the most needed support.

Materials: stereotypical pictures of a high-income community, stereotypical pictures of a low-income community, flip chart paper, colorful writing utensils, discussion questions

Process:

1. Open with a discussion focused on how our identity as leaders impacts how we view communities and community needs (this is where you can discuss deficit framing versus asset-based framing as this will be a good segue into the next discussion point). (5 minutes)
2. Discuss the idea of all communities having assets (feel free to use the framework of Asset Based Community Development [DePaul University, 2019] to help provide language if needed). (5 minutes)
3. Share that you will now engage in an activity that will help us to think about community in a different way.
4. Show pictures of a high-income community along with the question: What can you bring to this community?

   - Try to use pictures that depict varying identities. This can allow for a more nuanced conversation around the intersectionality of race, gender, sexual orientation, et cetera and how perspective may change or be impacted by varying identities.

5. Have each small group discuss/write ideas on flip chart paper. (5–10 minutes)
6. Have large group discussion: Volunteers from each group are able to share (if you are tight on time be sure to ask groups to add something new to the list that is being created to cut down on redundancy). (10–15 minutes)
7. Next, show pictures of the low-income community, along with the question: What can you learn from this community?
8. Have each small group discuss/write ideas on flip chart paper (this one may take the groups a bit longer to discuss so feel free to adjust the time as needed). (5–10 minutes)
9. Have large group discussion: Volunteers from each group are able to share (if you are running short on time be sure to ask groups to add something new to the list that is being created to cut down on redundancy).
10. Show the following TED Talk: The Story We Tell About Poverty Isn't True by Mia Birdsong (or any other appropriate talk).

Debriefing Questions:
- What was it like to do this activity?
- Which question took the most time to discuss? Why?
- If the group says that it took longer to answer the question focused on high income communities, ask: Why was it so difficult to answer this question?

What assumptions were made based on the pictures shown?

- If the group says it took longer to answer the question focused on low-income communities, ask: Why was it so difficult to answer this question? What assumptions were made based on the pictures shown?
- If you provided pictures that included people of varying identities, ask: What role did [insert identity here] play in how we perceived each community presented?
- How do our assumptions show up in our community work?
- What decisions do we make based on our perception of a community?
- How can our assumptions about what is needed, or not needed, in a community impact how volunteers are received into the community?
- What can you do to minimize the assumptions you bring with you into a community?

References:

Birdsong, M. (2015). *The story we tell about poverty isn't true* [Video file]. Retrieved from https://www.ted.com/talks/mia_birdsong_the_story_we_tell_about_poverty_isn_t_true

DePaul: Asset Based Community Development Institute. (2019). Retrieved from https://resources.depaul.edu/abcd-institute/about/Pages/default.aspx

COMMUNITY DIALOGUE
Steven D. Mills

- 1 hour 30 minutes
- 8–30 participants

This is a format for sensitive community discussions that utilizes both formal expertise and the personal experience, beliefs, and agency of community members. After a 30-minute period of expert presentation on a topic of community concern, the expert, moderator, and participants physically move to a circle of chairs in a separate space where the participants are encouraged by the moderator to express their points of view according to their knowledge and experience. The expert, in this space, is asked not to speak until the end, when they are asked to give brief closing remarks on what they have heard.

Learning Goals: Participants will have opportunities to:

- receive a data-driven overview of a specific community issue or phenomenon.

- broaden their perspectives on controversial topics.
- practice respectful dialogue across different perspectives.
- be reminded of their own agency regarding issues of community concern.

Process:

Arrange two separate areas (preferably in the same general room/space). One area is set up in a traditional lecture format, and the other is simply an open space with chairs arranged in a closed circle for group dialogue.

Two keys to the success of this activity are appropriate choice of topic and adequate prework with the expert speaker. Presentations should feature the exploration of an issue rather than a strident declaration of one exclusive perspective. It is perfectly fine (even preferred) for a speaker to offer their position, but every topic should feature an identifiable and normalized tension between viable perspectives. The moderator should meet with the speaker weeks before the event if possible to ensure that the speaker understands the importance of viewpoint diversity to the culture of the gathering.

1. This activity begins in the lecture space where the moderator introduces the format before welcoming and introducing the expert speaker. In describing the format, it is important for the moderator to begin preparing the participants to shift from passive receivers of knowledge to active creators of knowledge. The moderator may share:

   Before I introduce our speaker, I'd like to start with a little information about the Community Dialogue intention and format. This event has two distinct chapters. We begin in our more traditional learning space, where we feature a speaker with an important idea and a passion for sharing it, and we give them around 30 minutes. We listen, and we question, and we experience the speaker's truth.

   Then, at the end of this offering, we will get up and physically move over into the dialogue space, and the focus shifts from our speaker to our collective consideration of their ideas. Our speaker has the opportunity to witness this process, and offer final words at the end, but their work will have already been done in this space. Think of it like poetry interpretation, which rarely includes guidance from the actual poet, or an important article or movie or event that everyone has experienced on their own and finds themselves passionately discussing and digesting with their broader community the next day. We work out our truth together, as this is our community responsibility, and we get to see where that leads us. Now I'd like to introduce our speaker for the day.

2. After the expert speaker has finished and there has been a brief period for questions and answers, the moderator announces the shift over to the dialogue circle. Once everyone, including the expert speaker, is seated in the dialogue circle, the moderator repeats and embellishes the dialogue instructions by saying something like:

> So now it's our turn to consider this message through the lens of our own knowledge and experience, and [name of expert] is simply witness to this group process. She will have the opportunity to share closing words, but until then I'm going to ask that we don't direct questions to her in this circle.
>
> We ask that you share your own truth, make room for the truth of others, and honor everyone's voice in the circle. We want your thoughts, impressions, beliefs, and emotional reactions to what you've heard from [name of expert], or what you hear from others in the circle. What inspires you, confuses you, or eludes you regarding this topic?
>
> The best dialogue circles are the ones where everyone contributes, so if you've spoken twice and you notice others haven't spoken at all, think about stepping back and making some room. My simple prompt to get things started would be the broadest possible: "What have you heard or experienced so far in this meeting that has special significance for you?"

3. Once the dialogue circle begins, the moderator role is minimal. In the event that participants insist on asking the expert direct questions, a reminder of the expert's expected silence is appropriate, as are occasional process observations regarding any imbalances that may be occurring in the conversation (e.g., only men speaking; one participant dominating). With 10 minutes left, the moderator should direct the expert to offer closing remarks, after which the group should be thanked and congratulated for its community insight.

- There may be a clear desire among some participants to have a distinct and substantive prompt to begin the dialogue circle. Some prefer a clear guiding question directly related to the primary tension in the topic and believe this leads to a more focused group. Others appreciate the open nature of the more universal prompt and believe it underscores the *group's* responsibility for the relevance and usefulness of the evolving conversation.

4. This activity is not verbally debriefed, but it is important to provide each participant with a written evaluation form and the time to record their feedback of the event. This feedback should be compiled electronically and e-mailed out to the group within the week.

CONNECTING LEADERSHIP ACTION WITH THE PILLARS OF SUSTAINABILITY
Elizabeth Swiman

- 30–60 minutes
- 5–20 participants

The purpose of this activity is to highlight the connection of the three pillars of sustainability—environmental, social, and economic issues—with leadership action. Understanding the relationship between sustainability and leadership enables groups to explore the intersectionality of ideas.

Learning Goals: Participants will have opportunities to:

- explain the interconnectedness of the three pillars of sustainability.
- apply local, regional, and international examples to sustainability scenarios.
- understand how different leadership actions (or inactions) can impact sustainability issues.

Materials: 4 cube-shaped cardboard boxes of any size, markers

Process:
- In advance of the activity, write on the six (6) faces of each cube using words representing that particular sustainability pillar. Potential words can include the following but please adapt to particular needs:
  - Environmental—climate change; waste; water; 3Rs (reduce, reuse, recycle); food/food systems; ecosystem/ecosystem services; pollution
  - Social—justice/social justice; people; stakeholders; equity/equitable; quality of life; access; rights
  - Economic—jobs; local; economics of …; growth; tradeoffs; profit; prosperity
  - Leadership—educate; engage; empower; change; do; collaborate; build up

- Three (3) of the cubes represent one of the pillars of sustainability: environmental, social, or economic. The fourth cube represents different aspects to foster leadership capacities.

1. Ask participants to stand in a circle. (2 minutes)
2. Hand the three sustainability cubes to different participants and have them toss the cubes into the center of the circle.
3. Read each word that is face-up on the three cubes so that the whole group can hear. Ask participants to describe examples of local, regional, or international sustainability issues related to the three-

word scenario. Countless word combinations (one from each "pillar" cube) can be created as discussion scenarios. For example:

- Food, local, stakeholders
- Ecosystem services, people, profit
- Waste, quality of life, growth

4. Encourage participants to add additional facts and examples to each scenario to facilitate deeper understanding of the connections between the three pillars of sustainability.

5. Discussion questions for each scenario: (5–7 minutes)

- What is the effect of the issue at hand to under-represented groups? Who is affected in this particular scenario? And how?
- Do you see examples of this scenario in your community?
- What are the local, regional, national, international implications of this particular scenario?

6. Introduce the leadership capabilities action cube to the middle of the circle and reframe the conversation to include how a leadership lens can be applied: (5–7 minutes)

- How can change be created in this scenario?
- Where do you see yourself in this scenario?
- What can you/we/us/the community do to lead an effort to create the change?
- What positive examples already exist in your community? *How* are they addressing the intersectionality of the three pillars of sustainability?

7. Repeat. Utilize different dice tossers each round.

Debriefing Questions:
- What common themes emerged from the scenarios?
- Did you learn about a local, regional, or international issue previously unknown to you?
- Where do you see yourself and your impact in these scenarios?

Resources:
Association for the Advancement of Sustainability in Higher Education. (2018). Retrieved from http://www.aashe.org/
Principles of Environmental Justice. (1996). Retrieved from https://www.ejnet.org/ej/principles.html
Report of the World Commission on Environment and Development: Our Common Future. (1987). Brundtlant Report. Retrieved from http://www.un-documents.net/wced-ocf.htm
UN Sustainable Development Goals. (n.d.). Retrieved from https://sustainabledevelopment.un.org/

DIALOGUE AND LEADERSHIP LEARNING
Amber E. Hampton

- 2 hours
- 15–30 participants with 2 facilitators

This activity is designed based on a wealth of information that notes the effectiveness of using dialogue to connect groups and communities, which can be very effective when used in a leadership or work setting. Use of dialogic practice also requires in-person participation and presence, redirecting participants away from technology and toward human connection.

Learning Goals: Participants will have opportunities to:

- connect dialogue skills and leadership practice.
- recognize one or more of the skills of dialogue as evidenced by identifying *when* they practice one or more skills and identifying *when* others practice one or more skills of dialogue.

Materials: white board and dry erase markers, electronics should include a laptop/computer, projector, and wireless Internet

Process:

1. Centering the Group (10 minutes)

- As the group settles in, reiterate the purpose objectives and schedule so participants are aware of timeline.

2. Introductions (20 minutes)

- Have each person find a partner and share their name and one book, movie, or song everyone in the world should read, see or listen to—and why?

3. Preparation (10 minutes)

- Establish a clear understanding between the difference in dialogue, discussion, and debate.
- Processing Questions:
  - What are some examples of when you have participated in *debate*?
  - When have you seen others participate in *discussion*?
  - What is a good example of *dialogue*?

4. Agreements (10 minutes)

    - Together, create a list of agreements that the group will provide and adhere to (ex: vulnerability, sharing space, etc.). Following the building of the list, invite everyone to agree and allow edits throughout the activity if needed.
    - Processing Questions:
      o What do we need to be aware of to fully participate?
      o What do you each need to feel comfortable sharing your experiences?

5. Shift Space (if needed)

    - Arrange the group into a circle of chairs (no tables, etc. in between)
    - Facilitators should arrange themselves at opposite edges of the circle to maintain eye contact and give nonverbal cues to move the group forward.

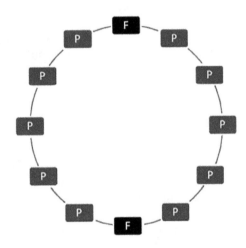

6. Partnering (10 minutes) [handout provided below]

    - Everyone is given a list of the dialogue elements (ex: deep listening, suspending judgments, respect, etc.) and asked to partner with one other person to share which elements will be easy or difficult to practice

7. Shared Experience: Content (10 minutes)

    - The group will engage with a shared reading, video, or speaker. Choose something relevant for the group, a poem or short story works best. Example: Each participant will read one section of the poem (for larger groups, each person reads 1–2 lines around the circle until completed)

8. Group Dialogue: Process (30 minutes)

    - Following this shared content experience, the group will process together where they found connection in their personal lives to the content. Facilitators should appreciate those who share particularly vulnerable stories, but also those who are practicing the dialogic elements. Be sure to also remind participants to:
      o Use the dialogue skills handout to pay attention to your participation and others
      o Maintain eye contact around the circle and use names of participants
      o Speak from personal/individual/lived experiences
      o Draw connections across and identify connections between others

Debriefing Questions:
- Does anyone have an experience they would like to share that came to mind as we read the poem together?
- In learning about each other's stories, we have the potential to be better leaders. Can anyone share an example of when you grew as a leader by learning more about someone's story/lived experience?

HANDOUT: BUILDING BLOCKS OF DIALOGUE
By David Bohm

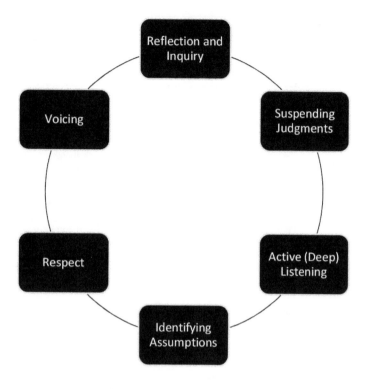

Reflection and inquiry	• Thinking about what you are saying before you say it. • Ask yourself about your reactions to what you want to say and what others say.
Suspending judgments	• Allowing someone to share their experience without using it to judge right/wrong about them or their view
Active (deep) listening	• Listening with mind and heart. • Hearing both the emotion and the content someone shares. • Quieting your own thoughts to fully hear, without the immediate need to respond or question.
Identifying assumptions	• Noticing when you make an assumption about a person (based on appearance or comments). • Noticing and identifying/sharing with the group the assumption you had and where it stems from.
Respect	• Allowing someone to finish their thought before sharing. • Avoiding the use of language that may intimidate or prevent another person from sharing.
Voicing	• Identifying when you have had a turn to speak multiple times, not allowing others space to share. • Sharing in the group as an expert of your own lived experiences.

Discuss with a partner:

Which of the dialogue skills will be the most difficult for you to practice or the easiest to practice *and why*?

Easy Dialogue Skills + Why?	Difficult Dialogue Skills + Why?

In the dialogue:

When you are practicing each element or observe an element being used throughout the dialogue

Dialogue Element	I am Practicing This …	I Notice Someone Practicing This …
Reflection and inquiry	I am …	Someone else …
Suspending judgments	I am …	Someone else …
Active (deep) listening	I am …	Someone else …
Identifying assumptions	I am …	Someone else …
Respect	I am …	Someone else …
Voicing	I am …	Someone else …

HIGHLIGHTS, LOWLIGHTS, INSIGHTS, AND BE-MIGHTS
Shane Whittington

- 3–15 participants
- 10–60 minutes

The purpose of this activity is to "break the ice" with a group that meets regularly at the beginning of every training meeting, typically twice a week, in an intentional and meaningful way. This activity was developed for a group of highly committed participants focused on the process of peer to peer intergroup dialogue (their learning outcomes included engage multiple layers of identity; create an environment that encourages curiosity and awareness; explore social structures and social dynamics; foster a practice for engagement across difference and develop the skills to bring people into and maintain a healthy dialogue space). This activity specifically engages a group in a space of vulnerability and meaning-making through storytelling.

Learning Goals: Participants will have opportunities to:

- grapple with internalized doubt and fear of clear communication.
- practice risk taking (offering words of vulnerability and challenge).
- employ mistake making (via asking questions or sharing an experience of error).
- share healing and joy (heal or be joyous with others in the moment or with self).
- practice authenticity (be kind, be candid, be open) with words.

Materials: paper (or use their electronic device) to have participants collect their thoughts

Process:
Participants should be facing each other in a circle.

1. Describe the activity "Highlights, Lowlights, Insights, and Be-Mights" to participants, which should begin the group's time together.
2. Each participant will have the opportunity to respond to one or all of the prompts: Highlights, Lowlights, Insights, and Be-Mights before proceeding to the next person.

   - During "Highlights", individuals within the leadership group share what is bringing them joy in their personal or professional lives. The participant will begin by saying, "my highlight(s) is (are) …". Typically, a participant will not stop with such a statement, but if they do, as a facilitator please ask: who, what, when, where, how and why.

- "Lowlights" refer to an event, personal situation or thought within the past day, week and/or recent past that elicits sadness, insecurity, error, etc. This is a key moment within the leadership group for members to be vulnerable with their peers. Lowlights are arguably the most important when it comes to creating an open, nonjudgmental space for communication. The participant begins by saying, "my lowlight is…".
- Sharing "Insights," refers to something you noticed that was not immediately obvious or seen, but enlightening. This is a reading-between-the-lines occurrence and moment of clarity. Insights build on the depths of the person and the meaning they create in situations. The participant begins by saying, "my insight is …". Some examples of shared Insights include: A discovery of personal growth; remembering something a family member said that was not significant before, but it is in that moment; an interesting food for thought you learned in one of your classes; a deeper understanding of a sociocultural phenomenon; etc. Note: they may attach an insight to a lowlight, highlight, or be might.
- "Be-Mights," also known as "Might could be possibly," are endeavors that will happen in the future, something being planned or something that the sharer thought about doing, but may or may not act upon. The participant begins by saying, "I might could be possibly be doing …" or "my be-might is …". Be-Mights are important because they give the group a glimpse of the person's possible future acts.

3. This activity shapes the group and also offers the facilitator constant and consistent feedback they may not hear otherwise. Be confidential, but also read between the lines. For example, if participants are constantly sharing how stressed they are about school and/or life, offer the group an opportunity to (as a group) participate in a mental wellness or destressing activity/workshop. This can provide another opportunity to develop the group in a different space.

Debriefing Questions:

When group members are more comfortable, they increase the practice of being more vulnerable and share more personal information about themselves which builds true trust and confidence in the group and the individual. Most often debriefing is not necessary; if it is, a simple check-in or "How do you all feel?" is all that is needed.

INVITATION TO INTENTIONALITY: AN EXPLORATION OF OUR PURPOSE AND AUTHENTIC SELVES
Carlo Morante

- 60 minutes
- Any size group

This activity is designed to ask big questions, which are questions that incite thoughtfulness regarding the topics of life, existence, spirituality, and other philosophical concerns. This activity focuses on three main themes within the context of leadership: identity, authenticity, and purpose. Individual reflection and interpersonal dialogue are at the core of this activity to allow participants to develop self-awareness and engage in sociocultural interactions.

Learning Goals: Participants will have opportunities to:

- examine and explain how authenticity, identity, and purpose intersect with their leader identity and how they engage in leadership.
- listen, observe, and understand the leadership development process of their peers through sociocultural conversations.
- articulate ways in which they could incorporate identity, authenticity, and purpose in their leadership contexts.

Materials: magazines or newspapers, paper, writing utensils, PowerPoint or flip chart paper with instructions and questions

Process:

1. Provide an overview of the activity by briefly introducing identity, authenticity, and purpose in the context of leadership learning. You will also want to create or review community guidelines and let participants know the activity requires three different processes: an individual reflection, a small group dialogue, and a large group debrief. (5 minutes)

   - Facilitators should discuss what "identity" means in this context. The intention is for personal identity and social identity to be explored. The following are some examples you can present to the group:
     - Personal: daughter, student, sibling, athlete, painter, writer, teacher
     - Social: woman, Latinx, young adult, Queer, transgender man, Muslim, middle class, native English speaker, Nigerian

- Participants should not be forced or encouraged to disclose their identities to anyone. Although this activity heavily focuses on identity, the share-out portions invite participants to share their processing rather than share the way they identify.

2. Explain that in individual silent reflection, participants should reflect on how identity, authenticity, and purpose interact with each other, their leader identity, and the leadership process. Provide magazines, newspaper, markers, pencils, and pens and encourage participants to cut images or phrases, draw, write, or simply contemplate identity, authenticity, and purpose. (5 minutes)

   - Participants reflect on the following prompts: (15 minutes)
     - Identity: Who are you? What identities do you think about the most? What identities do you think about the least? Do any of your identities influence your values? If so, in what ways? How do identity and authenticity intersect in your life? Is there a relationship between your identities and your leader identity? Please explain your thoughts.
     - Authenticity: What does authenticity mean to you? What spaces support your authentic self? What aspects of these spaces support authenticity? When is it easier for you to act authentically? When is it the most challenging to be authentic? Do authenticity and your leader identity interact in your life? If so, in what ways? If not, what may be the reason?
     - Purpose: What do you feel is your purpose in life? Is your purpose impacted by your identities? If so, in what ways? Are authenticity and purpose interconnected in your life? Please explain. How are you living out your purpose when you engage in leadership?

3. Encourage participants to find 1–2 other people who they would like to know better or may share a different worldview than them. In a small group (less than 15) or a group with participants who have built strong bonds, pairs may work best. For groups larger than 15 participants, groups of three may work best. (2 minutes)

   - Small groups will explore the following questions: (15 minutes)
     - Did any feelings arise while processing through these questions? If so, what feelings and during which questions? Did you discover anything new about yourself when reflecting on these questions? Describe what you discovered. Which of the three topics was the easiest for you to examine? Which one was the most challenging? Please explain. Are any of these topics currently resonating strongly with you in your personal or professional spheres? Please explain.

4. At the completion of the small group dialogue, invite all groups to come together and form a circle for a large group debrief (see questions below). (15 minutes)
5. Lastly, help tie the learning together for the participants by touching on the concepts of authenticity, identity, purpose, and leadership. Highlight pieces that were shared throughout the activity by participants that may have resonated with the group and demonstrated the essence of the activity's purpose. (3 minutes)

Debriefing Questions:
- What are some themes you heard, observed, or resonated with in today's activity?
- What may be some benefits of developing spaces that invite people to reflect on the intersection of identity, authenticity, and purpose in the context of leadership?
- In what ways can you utilize today's learning to continue your own leader development?
- How can you create an environment within the groups you work with that promotes the exploration and discussion of leadership in relation to identity, authenticity, and purpose?

Resources:
Day, D. V. (2001). Leadership development: A review in context. *Leadership Quarterly, 11,* 581–613.
George, B., & Sims, P. (2007). *True north: Discover your authentic leadership.* San Francisco, CA: Jossey-Bass.
Guthrie, K. L., Bertrand Jones, T., Osteen, L., & Hu, S. (2013). Cultivating leader identity and capacity in students from diverse backgrounds. *ASHE Higher Education Report, 39*(4).
Owen, J. E. (2012). Using student development theories as conceptual frameworks in leadership education. In K. L. Guthrie & L. Osteen (Eds.), *New Directions for Student Services: No. 140. Developing student's leadership capacity* (pp. 17–35). San Francisco, CA: Jossey-Bass.

JEFFERSONIAN CONVERSATION/DINNER
Kimberly Sluis

- 1 hour 30 minutes
- 5–100 participants

It is said that the concept of Jeffersonian Dinners originated in Thomas Jefferson's home in the 1800s. Today, the idea of the Jeffersonian Dinner or Jeffersonian Conversation can be used to facilitate a *single conversation* meant to cultivate reflection, engaged listening, and deep understanding of both self and others. This activity can effectively be used to help participants consider their life experiences and leadership learning and to imagine future applications for what they have learned.

Learning Goals: Participants will have opportunities to:

- reflect orally on their experiences in an uninterrupted setting.
- consider how a single event—or the accumulation of many experiences—might guide their future goals or plans.
- harness the collective wisdom of participants to help each individual more deeply reflect on their own learning.

Materials: tables (circular preferred) to seat no more than 10, chairs, printed question for each table

Process:

Prior to the event, the facilitator will need to come up with a question for the conversation. The question should be provided to participants in advance so they have some opportunity to reflect on what they want to share prior to engaging in the activity. Jeffersonian Conversations work best if each table is considering the same question. A few sample questions include:

- How have the experiences you have had to date shaped the kind of leader you hope to become?
- What have you learned this (weekend/week/year) that changes the way you think about your own future goals or plans?
- What are two or three moments in your life that help define the legacy you want to leave on the world?

1. Invite participants to the event and provide them with the question that will be used to facilitate the conversation.
2. Assign tables/seats to spread out participants who may already know one another and to create diverse table groups.
3. Assign a table facilitator (preferably in advance) who will read the question, ask someone to go first, and remind the group to save any questions/comments until the speaking participant is completely finished sharing. The table facilitator should also be asked to manage time so that each participant has an opportunity to share.

   - The one rule for Jeffersonian Conversations is that only one person speaks (uninterrupted) at a time. They speak until they are finished at which point other participants can ask questions or provide reflections on what the participant has shared.

4. Invite the table hosts to begin the activity.

   - First person shares. (3–5 minutes)
   - Group asks questions and shares reflections on what was shared. (1–2 minutes)
   - Another person is invited to share.
   - Group asks questions and shares reflections on what was shared.
   - Process continues until everyone at the table has shared.

Debriefing Questions:
- What did it feel like to speak uninterrupted?
- What did you learn from speaking your reflections aloud?
- What did you gain from the questions asked by other participants?
- What changed about your understanding of self or others from participating in this activity?

Resources:

Eich, D. (2008). A grounded theory of high-quality leadership programs: Perspectives from student leadership development programs in higher education. *Journal of Leadership & Organizational Studies, 15*(2), 176–187. https://doi.org/10.1177/1548051808324099

Komives, S. R., Lucas, N., & McMahon, T. R. (2009). *Exploring leadership: For college students who want to make a difference.* San Francisco, CA: John Wiley & Sons.

MIND MAPPING AND EXPLORING THE "LEADER BOX"

Cameron C. Beatty, Ashley M. Brown, and Tristen Hall

- 45 minutes
- Any size group

This discussion-based activity focuses on facilitated reflection through mind mapping and exploring the "leader box." A mind map is hierarchical and visually highlights relationships among concepts (Hopper, 2015). The following activity offers a mind mapping reflection activity and a large group discussion "leader box" activity, for participants to consider their preconceived understandings of the definition of leader and what/who informed those understandings.

Learning Goals: Participants will have opportunities to:

- define leader and follower by drawing a mind map.
- develop a leader box and explore their preconceived understandings of who and what a leader is and who/what has informed those understandings.

Materials: any large writing surface such as flip chart paper or whiteboard, markers, two standard-sized sheets of paper for each participant

Process:

Note: plain text sections will indicate notes to guide you through the activity and discussion, not to be directly stated to participants. Italicized sections will indicate sections that you can convey directly to participants, if you so choose.

1. **Mind Mapping:** For this activity, each participant will need two blank sheets of paper (or both sides of one) and a writing utensil.

    - *The mind map is made up of concepts, generally represented by words or phrases and bubbles and branches that are the lines connecting the two. On the branches there will be words or short phrases that explain the connection between the two concepts. (10 minutes)*
    - Have participants create a map for both "follower" and "leader." On one sheet, direct participants to write the word "leader," and on the other sheet, direct participants to write the word "follower," both within a bubble. These words will be the main ideas.
    - From the first bubble, participants will create branches that stem to concepts, feelings, behaviors, and thoughts that are associated with the

main idea. Participants can create more branches off of each new bubble they create.

  - o Example prompting questions to start the mind mapping activity:
    - * How do you define leadership or leader? What messages inform your definition?
    - * How do you define followership or follower? What messages inform your definition?
    - * How do you show up as a leader? What characteristics do you show when enacting leadership?
    - * What qualities are valued/not valued in leadership?
    - * How do you show up as a follower? What characteristics do you show when enacting followership?
    - * What qualities are valued/not valued in followership?

2. **Pair and Share:** When participants have completed the mind map, ask them to share their mind maps with a partner. (5–10 minutes)

3. **Unboxing the "Leader":** This activity is adopted from the "man box" that explores toxic masculinity (Creighton & Kivel, 1992). The activity is intended for participants to explore how they understand who and what a leader is and what has informed those understandings. (25 minutes)

    - *Raise your hand if anyone has ever told you or you've heard someone being told, "You're a leader."*
      - o Write "Be a Leader" on the top of the writing surface.
    - *What does it mean to be a leader? What are the expectations and what is valued? What does a leader look and act like? Share out words and phrases. (3–4 minutes)*
      - o Write responses in the middle of the writing surface (you will eventually draw a box around the responses).
    - *How do we know how a leader is supposed to act or look? Where do these messages come from? (4–5 minutes)*
      - o Here, provide space for participants to discuss and brainstorm. You do not need to record these responses on the writing surface.
      - o Following this discussion, draw a box around the words and phrases already on the writing surface.
    - *Look at the words and phrases we brainstormed together, does this box seem familiar to you? Do you visit this box? When are you in the box, and when aren't you? (2 minutes)*

- *What behaviors and characteristics are not considered leader-like? Who is not considered a leader? Share out words and phrases.* (3–4 minutes)
  - Write the responses outside and around the box.
  - What patterns are you noticing about expectations of leaders? (10 minutes)
    What does this box represent?
  - How do we, as a society, perceive those who do not fit in this box?
  - How do our social identities shape how we are perceived as leaders?
    Based on your experiences, what do you think it means to be a leader?
  - How can we unbox the leader and rewrite what we have up here?

References:

Creighton, A., & Kivel, P. (1992). *Helping teens stop violence.* Alameda, CA: Hunter House.

Hopper, C. H. (2015). *Practicing college learning strategies* (7th ed.). Independence, KY: Cengage Learning.

STRUCTURED DIALOGUE ACROSS DIFFERENCE
Steven D. Mills

- 1 hour 15 minutes
- Any size group

This activity promotes clear guidelines for achieving mutual understanding during the dialogic process. Two-person conversations are structured so that each participant must demonstrate an understanding of the other's point of view on a topic in which there is fundamental disagreement.

Learning Goals: Participants will have opportunities to:

- practice listening skills.
- broaden their perspectives on controversial topics.
- practice empathy by actively reflecting a differing point of view.
- practice building relationship across difference.

Materials: Instruction sheet with topics on one side and process rules on the other

Process:

Staging a brief demonstration before the conversation pairs begin is possible. If this decision is made, the presenters should stage a conversation in which the Listener takes at least three tries to accurately reflect the speaker's position. It should also be emphasized

that the demonstration has been shortened, simplified for time, and is reflective of the demonstrators' personalities. Each conversation will be unique within the structure, and participants should not attempt to replicate the example.

1. **Establishing Positions.** Explain to participants that they will be determining their point of view on a variety of controversial topics and then practicing conversation with someone who holds a different point of view on at least one of the topics. Pass out the *Structured Dialogue Across Difference Topics & Responses* handout (below) to all of the participants and ask them to take 5 minutes to mark their point of view on the continuum associated with each topic statement. Before they begin, briefly go over the instructions on the handout to make sure everyone has the same understanding of how the continuum works. Reiterate that participants should react quickly to the statements, since there will be time to consider the nuances of their position during conversation with their partner. (10 minutes)

2. **Seeking Difference.** Once each person has marked their own topic list, it is time to find a conversational partner. How this is done will be up to the facilitator, but each participant must find another with a significantly different placement on the continuum of responses on at least one of the topics provided. Ideally, partners will find a topic where they are separated from each other in their responses by at least three numerals, with one partner on the Agree side and one partner on the Disagree side. Once conversational partners have been selected, each dyad should find a comfortable space for their conversation. (5 minutes)

3. **Rules of Engagement.** Once partners have been chosen and each dyad is seated together, the rules for the conversation must be clearly communicated. These rules should be printed on the back of the *Topics & Responses* handout (below), so ask each participant to turn their attention to the rules for a quick review. Go over these rules carefully before dialogues begin. (5 minutes)

4. **Dialogue.** Each conversational pairing should last approximately 15 minutes. Ideally, conversational partners can be switched for at least two distinct pairings and still leave time for large group discussion at the end. (30 minutes)

5. **Debrief.** Debrief should allow participants the chance to reflect on the experience and its relevance to their lives moving forward. (20 minutes)

Debriefing Questions:

- What was this process like for you? What did you notice?

- What was the most difficult aspect of this process for you? What was easiest?
- How was your position impacted by this process? What did you learn about your own position?
- How difficult was it to confirm at least one aspect of your partner's position?
- Is there any aspect of this process that may be practical for disagreements going forward?

Resources:
Reflective Listening Overview. (n.d.). Retrieved from https://en.wikipedia.org/wiki/Reflective_listening
RSA Animates. (2013, December 10). *Brené Brown on empathy* [Video file]. Retrieved from https://youtu.be/1Evwgu369Jw

Structured Dialogue Across Difference Topics & Responses

Please <u>circle the number that best represents your feeling for each issue below</u>. We're looking for deep, immediate feelings. If it takes more than a few seconds to decide any one item, skip it.

Strongly Disagree .... **Neutral** .... **Strongly Agree**

1. *Stand Your Ground* laws, which allow lethal force to be applied if someone determines that they are in danger of death or great bodily harm, are good and should be maintained.

2. People who have immigrated *illegally* and have been contributing (employed, law-abiding) members of American society for over 10 years should be given amnesty and granted citizenship.

3. Abortion should be legally prohibited except in extreme cases such as rape, incest, or maternal health issues.

4. Women should be expected to fight in military combat units.

5. A physician should be allowed to assist in the death of a patient suffering with a terminal illness if death is requested by the patient, and the patient is believed to be of sound, unimpaired judgment

6. Electronic communication (texting and e-mailing) in the university classroom should be left to individual student discretion and not restricted by the course professor.

7. Student loans should be restricted in favor of students with majors guaranteeing sufficient income to pay the debt in a reasonable time frame.

Find a dialogue partner that you do not know very well and identify one controversial proposition that the two of you most disagree about. You're looking for an issue on which you are on opposite sides, preferably as far apart as possible. If there is more than one topic on which you substantially disagree, just choose the one you'd most like to understand from a different point of view.

Rules for Practice: Structured Dialogue Across Difference

1. Conversational partners, in turn, will play the roles of *Speaker* and *Listener*. Choose who will play the Speaker role first.
2. The Speaker will then explain their point of view. The Listener will listen with minimum interruptions except for essential clarifications on points of confusion.
3. After the Speaker has finished, and before the Listener can reply, the Listener must repeat 100% of what the Speaker has communicated. This reflection needn't be word for word, but it must reflect 100% of the content to the satisfaction of the Speaker. If the Speaker is not satisfied that the Listener has represented the Speaker's point of view faithfully, the Speaker must provide the necessary corrections and allow the Listener to try again. Only after the Listener has faithfully represented the Speaker's point of view, in full, the Speaker will declare, "Perfect!" The Speaker must maintain a high standard of expectation for the Listener!
4. As a final step before switching roles, the Listener must choose one aspect of the Speaker's argument that appeals to (or at least makes sense to) the Listener, and share that with the Speaker.
5. Roles are switched (Speaker becomes Listener, and Listener becomes Speaker), and Steps 1–4 are repeated.
6. After both conversational partners feel their argument is perfectly understood by the other, you may engage in a broader, unstructured conversation about your topic. If this has not already emerged, it may be interesting for each of you to hear the life experiences that led to your partner's point of view, or how this particular point of view has evolved for each of you over time.

TOXIC MANAGEMENT OR POTENTIAL LEADERSHIP?
Melissa Jarrell

- 25–30 minutes
- 15 participants or less

This activity seeks to examine the differences in leadership and management and allow participants to gain an understanding of both terms. Participants will reflect on their own experiences where they have witnessed both management and leadership.

Learning Goals: Participants will have opportunities to:

- demonstrate a practical understanding of leadership as it compares to management.
- assess the differences in the definitions of leadership and management.

Materials: white board and dry erase markers, writing utensils

Leadership vs. Management

Leadership	Management
Influence Relationship	Authority Relationship
Leaders and Followers	Managers and Subordinates
Intend Real Changes	Produce and Sell Goods and/or Products
Intended Changes Reflect Mutual Purposes	Good/Services Result from Coordinated Activities

Source: Adapted from Rost (1991).

Process:

1. With the information on leadership and management provided, ask participants to reflect about a time they worked with a good manager. Have participants write down a description of what made that an experience of good management. (5 minutes)
2. Next, ask participants to reflect on a time that they experienced or witnessed good leadership. Have participants write down a description of what made that an experience of good leadership. (5 minutes)
3. Once all the participants have completed their descriptions, ask for volunteers to discuss their experience with the larger group. If this is done with a group larger than 15 participants, the facili-

tator can ask participants to get in pairs and discuss with one another. They should note the differences in management and leadership.

- If participants discuss with one another, ask a few participants to share what was discussed and reflect on the conversation.

4. During the discussion: the facilitator will list the characteristics of each term (management and leadership) as participants share. This can be done on a dry erase board or flip chart. (10–15 minutes)
5. As a large group, discuss the differences between management and leadership using the discussion questions below to help facilitate. (5 minutes)

Debriefing Questions:
- How does your definition of leadership differ from your definition of management?
- Did any of the participants struggle with the activity because they thought that management and leadership were the same thing?
- The leadership process often emphasizes relationships. How does this differ (if at all) from a manager/employee/staff relationship?
- Although we have established that leadership and management are different, do you think they can overlap at all? In what ways?

References:
Rost, J. C. (1991). *Leadership for the twenty-first century*. New York, NY: Praeger.

CHAPTER 6

Narrative

The key feature of a narrative is it tells about an event (Abbott, 2008). Each day we create narratives: "As soon as we follow a subject with a verb, there is a good chance we are engaged in narrative discourse" (Abbott, 2008, p. 1). Moon (2010) highlighted some of the ways stories can serve as a tool for learning: encapsulating lived experience from a holistic perspective, engaging emotion and imagination, serving as a tool for reflective learning, and providing engagement in contrast to traditional lecture format. Life narratives can be a pedagogical tool for challenging dominant narratives and developing spaces for learners to engage in critical self-reflection on their identities (Turner Kelly & Bhangal, 2108). In exploring the connections between storytelling, transformative learning, and complexity science, Tyler and Swartz (2012) described the power of students sharing stories, first in pairs, then trios, then larger groups, then altogether. They noted the value of storytelling for reflection: "Key to this process is the ability of listeners and the teller to engage in posttelling conversations that explore the stories in ways that clarify, deepen, enlarge, expose new facets, and experiment with new meaning" (Tyler & Swartz, 2012, p. 465).

Storytelling. Although people may associate storytelling with personal narratives, storytelling can also include stories that are well known or widely shared in a particular setting as well as stories drawn from fiction or fantasy (Moon & Fowler, 2008). McNett (2016) described opportunities for including stories in learning, from sharing brief anecdotes or using stories to link broad concepts to using story as the framework for an entire course. Whether asking learners to create a narrative based on their experience or anchoring experiences in literary narratives, stories in their many forms can be a powerful tool for reflection on leadership learning. At Florida State University, as part of LDR3215 Leadership and Change, students write a personal change experience story where they apply leadership theory to a personal negotiating change. Students consistently reflect that this opportunity to write and share personal stories was a powerful learning experience. As part of a Leadership and Storytelling course at a private university in the northwest, stu-

dents focused on authenticity as they integrated their stories of self with leadership theory (Albert & Vadla, 2009). Narrative can also be a tool for leadership educators. Priest and Seemiller (2018) used narrative approaches to learn how leadership educators developed their professional identities. They combined three approaches: storytelling (past experiences), symbolic interactionism (present beliefs), and anticipatory reflection (future practices) (Priest & Seemiller, 2018). One of their findings was "the use of narratives proved to be a powerful research methodology, yet the process-oriented nature of narratives also offered a self-reflective experience for participants to uncover their thoughts and feelings about their professional identities" (Priest & Seemiller, 2018). At a gathering of leadership educators from 11 programs across the state of Kansas, organizers used story to facilitate an in-depth discussion of collective capacity (Priest, Kliewer, & Stephens, 2018).

Testimonio. A testimonio is a form of reflection where individuals share their experiences with others in the form of writing or dialogue (Reyes & Curry Rodríguez, 2012). Testimonios can be presented as poetry, memoir, lyrics, spoken word, or oral history (Reyes & Rodríguez, 2012). Carmona and Luciano (2014) created a testimonio course in which students read poetry, autobiographies, essays, and stories of Latina women. They explored theories and themes of feminist epistemologies. Students and instructors in this course also wrote and shared testimonios among themselves, which facilitated reflection on their collective experience. Another example of using testimonios in the classroom is having students write a paper reflecting on how their social identities influenced their approach to certain topics (El Ashmawi, Sanchez, & Carmona, 2018).

Poetry. Poetry, like narratives, tells a story that allow people to relate personally to topics or ideas and engage on multiple levels. Poetry can be an effective vehicle for understanding and expressing concepts that may be unfamiliar or difficult to verbalize; in this way, poetry can be an effective tool for engaging students' cognitive and affective dimensions as part of reflection. Mazza (2003) developed a model of poetry therapy practice that includes using preexisting poems or literature (receptive/prescriptive), inviting expressive writing (expressive/creative), and using metaphor or storytelling (symbolic/ceremonial). Only professionals with appropriate credentials should engage in poetry therapy (Mazza, 2003); however, educators can draw on poetic therapeutic techniques to support reflection and build community (Mazza, 2008).

Blake and Cashwell (2004) used poetry in a university setting to facilitate conversations about diversity, and Ingram (2009) wrote about using narrative to engage graduate education students in critically reflective conversations about identity. Furman, Coyne, and Negi (2008) explored the use of poetry to enhance reflection for social work students on a trip to Nicaragua. The instructors hoped through poetry the students would reflect on power and privilege and learn to manage their emotions and feelings in order to become more responsive practitioners. For a group of students in a preservice professional teaching program, reading and discussing poetry in a group invited risk taking as part of reflection (Speare & Henshall, 2014). McPherson and Mazza (2014) used poetry as part of an undergraduate social work course where students engaged in arts-based activism related to human rights. In addition to ongoing spoken and written reflection in class, following the installation of the art, which brought awareness to mass violence and genocide, students were guided to create three poems as a group. Poetry is a creative form of reflection that allows instructors to facilitate conversations with students about difficult topics and can also serve as a catalyst for creating responses in the form of group or individual written expression.

REFERENCES

Abbott, H. P. (2008). *The Cambridge introduction to narrative* (2nd ed.). Oxford, England: Cambridge University Press.

Albert, J. F., & Vadla, K. (2009). Authentic leadership development in the classroom: A narrative approach. *Journal of Leadership Education, 8*(1), 72–92

El Ashamwi, Y. P., Sanchez, M. E. H., & Carmona, J. F. (2018). Testimonialista pedagogues: Testimonio pedagogy in critical multicultural education. *International Journal of Multicultural Education, 20*(1), 67–85.

Blake, M. E., & Cashwell, S. T. (2004). Use of poetry to facilitate communication about diversity. *Journal of Poetry Therapy, 17*(1), 1–12.

Carmona, J. F., & Luciano, A. M. (2014). A student-teacher testimonio: Reflexivity, empathy, and pedagogy. *Counterpoints, 449,* 75–92.

Furman, R., Coyne, A., & Negi, N. J. (2008). An international experience for social work students: Self-reflection through poetry and journal writing exercises. *Journal of Teaching in Social Work, 28*(1/2), 71–85.

Ingram, I. (2009). Creative maladjustment: Engaging personal narrative to teach diversity and social justice. *Journal of Women in Educational Leadership, 7*(1), 7–22.

Mazza, N. (2003). *Poetry and therapy: Theory and practice.* New York, NY: Brunner-Routledge.

Mazza, N. (2008). Twenty years of scholarship in the *Journal of Poetry Therapy*: The collected abstracts. *Journal of Poetry Therapy, 21*(2), 63–133.

McNett, G. (2016). Using stories to facilitate learning. *College Teaching, 64* (4), 184–193.

McPherson, J., & Mazza, N. (2014). Using arts activism and poetry to catalyze human rights engagement and reflection. *Social Work Education, 33*(7), 944–958.

Moon, J. A. (2010). *Using story: In higher education and professional development.* New York, NY: Routledge.

Moon, J., & Fowler, J. (2008). 'There is a story to be told …'; A framework for the conception of story in higher education and professional development. *Nurse Education Today, 28*(2), 232–239.

Priest, K. L., Kliewer, B. W., & Stephens, C. M. (2018). Kansas leadership studies summit: Cultivating collaborative capacity for the common good. *Journal of Leadership Education, 17*(3), 195–207.

Priest, K. L., & Seemiller, C. (2018). Past experiences, present beliefs, future practices: Using narratives to re (present) leadership educator identity. *Journal of Leadership Education, 17*(1), 93–113.

Reyes, K. B., & Curry Rodríguez, J. E. (2012). Testimonio: Origins, terms, and resources. *Equity & Excellence in Education, 45*(3), 525–538.

Speare, J., & Henshall, A. (2014). 'Did anyone think the trees were students?' Using poetry as a tool for critical reflection. *Reflective Practice, 15*(6), 807–820.

Turner Kelly, B., & Bhangal, N. B. (2018). Life narratives as a pedagogy for cultivating critical self-reflection. *New Directors for Student Leadership, 159,* 41–52.

Tyler, J. A., & Swartz, L. (2012). Storytelling and transformative learning. In E. W. Taylor & P. Cranton (Eds.), *The handbook of transformative learning: Theory, research and practice* (pp. 455–470). San Francisco, CA: Jossey-Bass.

BELIEF STATEMENTS
Jillian M. Volpe White

- 60 minutes
- Any size group

In this activity, participants are encouraged to consider a quality or belief. While some people may struggle with the word "belief," this can be framed as the tenants that guide our daily actions and frame how we engage with others and the world around us. In this activity, participants use short essays or videos to prompt reflection.

Learning Goals: Participants will have opportunities to:

- engage affective outcomes through reflecting on their identity and sense of self.
- write their own reflections as they relate to prompts or selected texts.
- share written reflections with a group.

Materials: paper and writing utensil for each participant, books or short essays to prompt reflection (suggestions for books with short readings are included in the resource list)

Process:

1. Introduce the significance of sharing one's story as part of reflection and leadership learning (you might draw from the introduction to the narrative section in this text). (10 minutes)
2. Share some examples from essays, books, or media (see variations below) (10 minutes).

   - Prescreen essays or videos to make sure they fit the type of group you are facilitating, the content meets your objectives, and the timing works for your program.

3. Invite participants to consider a quality or belief and write about it. Let them know this should be done without sharing, and you will set a timer to let them know when to come back together. Consider playing instrumental music during this time. (10 minutes)
4. Bring participants back together. Open up for sharing. Participants could read all or part of what they wrote. If the group is larger, start with smaller groups where participants may have more time for sharing or be more comfortable. When people

share, be sure to say "thank you" as an acknowledgment of their bravery and candor. (20 minutes)

   - When it comes to topics like beliefs or qualities, participants may feel the need to share something deep or profound; consider examples that range from serious to lighthearted. It can be helpful to frame beliefs and qualities as the things that impact our everyday actions and add up to our legacy rather than broad or lofty ideals.

5. Discuss the debrief questions as a large group. (10 minutes)

Variations:

- Qualities: In *The Book of Qualities*, Gendler (1988) personifies qualities using rich description. Reflection may focus on one quality or utilize multiple. Invite participants to consider a quality they have or hope to develop and write an essay personifying that quality.
- Beliefs: Based on an NPR series by the same name, *This I Believe: The Personal Philosophies of Remarkable Men and Women* (Allison & Gediman, 2006) essays are short enough to be read in a few minutes. After reading a few excerpts, facilitators should encourage participants to write their own "This I believe" statement.

Debriefing Questions:
- What quality or belief did you write about? (This can be a good question to begin—even if some people shared, it is unlikely everyone was willing or able to share.)
- How did you choose the quality or belief you wrote about?
- What was challenging about this process?
- What insight did you gain from writing about this quality or belief?
- How might this insight influence your actions as someone engaging in leadership?
- When people were sharing, what did you observe about the qualities or beliefs from people in this group?
- How might knowing this about the group help you work more effectively together?

References:
Gendler, J. R. (1988). *The book of qualities*. New York, NY: Harper & Row.
Allison, J., & Gediman, D. (Eds.). (2007). *This I believe: The personal philosophies of remarkable men and women*. New York, NY: Henry Holt and Company.

CONCEPT MAPPING
Julie LeBlanc

- 55–60 minutes
- Any size group

Generating the connections between concepts and systems can be a powerful reflective experience. The purpose of concept mapping is to provide a space for participants to identify, connect, and analyze their ideas about a certain topic. Concept mapping is a beneficial activity in almost any educational setting and can be tailored to your specific context and needs.

Learning Goals: Participants will have opportunities to:

- identify and articulate their knowledge of concepts and systems.
- understand the interconnected nature of concepts and systems through visual illustration.
- learn from others to foster an expanded perspective.
- analyze the varying perspectives among group members.

Materials: blank paper, chart paper, colorful writing utensils

Process:

1. Prior to facilitating the activity, the facilitator should develop the key theme they wish for participants to explore in the concept map.
2. Introduce the activity as an opportunity for participants to reflect upon their experiences and identify connections between concepts and systems. Write the key theme in a circle in the middle of a piece of paper as the starting point. (5 minutes)
3. Based on the key theme selected for your context (see facilitator notes), write the same key theme at their center of the paper. Encourage them to invite participants to begin to identify and draw branches and circles for subthemes and additional branches and circles for more specific concepts. (15–20 minutes)
4. Once participants have completed their individual concept maps, divide the group into pairs so participants can share their concept maps with a partner. This can be a beneficial technique if participants are unfamiliar with each other or if the key theme is challenging or controversial. (5 minutes)
5. Facilitate the creation of the group's concept map by having partners share their subthemes and specific concepts. In the spirit of shared learning and the process-oriented nature of reflection, allow time for the participants to sit with the newly cre-

ated concept map so that new ideas can emerge on the spot. (10 minutes)
6. Additional branches can be added until the group and facilitator feel the concept map includes all relevant concepts, themes, and systems. (5 minutes)
7. Conclude the activity by asking the group the debriefing questions. (15 minutes)

Debriefing Questions:
- What resonates with you about the group's concept map? What surprises you?
- In what ways is your individual concept map similar to the group's concept map? How are they different?
- What conclusions can we draw based on the concepts and systems we identified and developed?

Resources:
Gray, D. E. (2007). Facilitating management learning: Developing critical reflection through reflective tools. *Management Learning, 38*(5), 495–517. https://doi.org/10.1177/1350507607083204

Novak, J. (2010). *Learning, creating, and using knowledge: Concept maps as facilitative tools in schools and corporations.* New York, NY: Routledge.

DARING TO BE VULNERABLE: A LEADERSHIP TESTIMONIO
María Rivera

- 1 hour 30 minutes–2 hours
- 15–20 participants

When practicing leadership, individuals are inevitably faced with vulnerability; the capacity individuals have to identify, confront, and work through their vulnerability can determine their success in the leadership process. Brené Brown (2015) defines vulnerability as "the emotion that we experience during times of uncertainty, risk, and emotional exposure. It is having the willingness to show up and be seen with no guarantee of outcome." Being able to reflect on incidents where they felt vulnerable when participating in a leadership process may allow participants to grow, strengthen, and develop their leadership identity and capacity as they develop self-awareness and self-knowledge.

Learning Goals: Participants will have opportunities to:

- identify and explain a personal leadership experience in which they felt particularly vulnerable.
- translate their experience into narrative form and dissect the elements of the experience and the vulnerability encountered.

- develop and explain how identifying, confronting, and working through their vulnerability has increased their leadership identity.

Materials: Brené Brown's list of Core Emotions (found online), writing utensils

Process:

1. Discuss with participants of the importance of safe space where what is shared in the group will not leave the group and will be honored and cared for as if it was our own story. (5 minutes)
2. Ask participants to identify a situation that occurred while participating in a leadership process that impacted their lives in a significant way. (5–10 minutes)
3. Provide participants with the list of Core Emotions by Brené Brown (see resources) and ask them to identify one or two emotions they experienced in the situation they previously identified. (5–10 minutes)
4. Ask participants to write their testimonio using the experience and the emotion(s) they felt. Allow participants enough time to write their testimonio. (about 30–45 minutes)

   - If the emotions were positive: how these emotions empowered or affirmed their leadership identity.
   - If the emotions were negative: discover how they overcame (or will overcome) the emotions in order to develop their leadership identity.

5. At the end of the time, ask participants to share voluntarily. The process of reading their testimonio out loud to the group requires an additional level of vulnerability, so be patient and remind participants of the importance of safe space where what is shared in the group will not leave the group, and will be honored and cared for as if it was our own story. (30–45 minutes)
6. Debrief (30 minutes)

Debriefing Questions:
- How did it feel to first identify the leadership situation? What emotions did that bring up?
- How did it feel to identify the emotions experienced during that leadership situation? Was it easy or difficult? How in touch are you with your emotions?
- Do you think it is important to be aware of our emotions? Why?
- How does reflecting on our emotions strengthen our leadership identity and leadership capacity?

- What role does vulnerability play in the leadership process? How can being vulnerable lead to affirmation and feeling empowered?

Resources:
Brené Brown Downloads: List of Core Emotions. (n.d.). Retrieved from https://brenebrown.com/downloads/
Brown, B. (2010, June). *The power of vulnerability* [Video file]. Retrieved from https://www.ted.com/talks/brene_brown_on_vulnerability
Brown, B. (2015). *Rising strong: How the ability to reset transforms the way we live, love, parent, and lead.* New York, NY: Random House.

AN IMPROVISED TALE: THE STORY SPINE STRUCTURE
Christopher Ruiz de Esparza

- 10–30 minutes
- Any size with each group 1–7 participants

Participants, either individually or collaboratively, use a series of sentence stems to create reflection stories. The framework helps create a transformation story, which might include a personal change story or an organizational change story. For example, participants can be divided into smaller groups and asked to cocreate a story that illustrates an important lesson, learning outcome, or takeaway. Similarly, groups can use the story spine as part of vision work—the vision statement filling in as the final sentence ("And ever since then …").

Learning Goals: Participants will have opportunities to:

- review and reflect on their progression and developmental journey.
- work independently or collaboratively as a team.
- utilize a process for stimulating new ideas, problem solving, or needs assessment.
- practice communication, storytelling, and presentation skills.

Materials: flip chart paper, slide, handout, note cards or similar with the story spine template displayed for all participants to see and reference

Process:
Stories allow us to describe, explore, and understand *cause* and *effect*, but they also serve as mechanisms for processing and relating our lived experiences. A good narrative is often built from a good structure. For example, one of the most basic story structures is simply a beginning, something happening, and then an ending.

The following structure is just a little more complex, yet can be adapted to generate endless possibilities. As an exercise or game, the story spine activity invites participants to improvise the development of a well-structured story by spontaneously filling in the blank for each line. With iterative attempts, the stories can flex our creative muscles more and more.

1. Present the story spine frame:

   - Once upon a time …
   - Every day …
   - But, one day …
   - Because of that, … (repeated 2–3x)
   - Until finally …
   - Ever since then …
   - The moral of the story is … (optional)

2. Provide a brief description and example of a story using this frame. The frame can be used as a reflection on something that has already happened, or it can be used as a prospective to something we wish to see happen. For example, if used as a reflection following a service-learning trip, *But one day* could be filled in with the experience of participating in that trip. Alternatively, if used as a visioning exercise, the participant's or organization's vision statement could be filled in under *And, ever since then.*

3. Have participants create and/or complete a story one sentence at a time, using the cue words to begin each sentence. Depending on time, participants can practice creating multiple stories or responding to various prompts using the story spine frame. The story spine frame can also be used to help participants create an outline for a talk or presentation.

   - To increase the interactivity and to experience a cocreative process, invite participants to work with a partner or in a small group. Participants can take turns providing a response to each sentence stem of the spine. Depending on the intended application, participants can write out stories on the same topic or theme and share their stories with each other. The entire group can then attempt to identify common themes or elements in the reflections shared. Additionally, participants can debrief their own stories and discuss their emotional reactions, the key learning points, and any implications for future change or action.

Debriefing Questions:
- Did the structure help you or hinder you? How?
- What value does this structure provide? What are key elements that help hone our learning and growth? How could the structure be applied to leadership learning and development?
- *Because of that* reinforces the connectivity (e.g. cause and effect, intent and impact, etc.) in our stories. What can we do to increase our awareness of connectivity in our lives and in our impact as leaders?
- What role does change play in our lives? How does change impact our leadership development journey? Is change inherently good or bad? Planned or unplanned? Internally generally or externally imposed? Does it matter?

Resources:
Adams, K. (2007). *How to improvise a full-length play: The art of spontaneous theater.* New York, NY: Allworth Press.
Koppett, K. (2013). *Training to imagine: Practical improvisational theatre techniques for trainers and managers to enhance creativity, teamwork, leadership, and learning.* Sterling, VA: Stylus.
Pixar in a Box: The Art of Storytelling. (2019). Retrieved from https://www.khanacademy.org/partner-content/pixar/storytelling

OUR STORIES, OUR VOICES
Trisha Teig

- 2 hours–3 hours 30 minutes
- 8–25 participants

In this activity, participants present a creative narrative of their life stories, including how this has shaped who they are and what legacy they will pursue. After hearing each narrative, the group processes through a shared reflection of learning to engender a collective conarrative and establish a deeper connection across participants.

Learning Goals: Participants will have opportunities to:

- engage in reflection, through creative narrative of their life story.
- envision future possibilities, through creative narrative considering their future legacy.
- create a collective conarrative through noticing differences and similarities in their personal stories.
- build relationships through hearing others' narratives and making connections across difference.

Materials: none

Process:

1. Offer the following information in your syllabus or on a handout. Give the information in advance and

allow for plenty of time (several weeks) for participants to prepare to participate in this activity:

- *You will present a creative narrative of your life story, including how this has shaped who you are and what legacy you will pursue. Historically, participants have approached this project by writing a poem, expressing their experiences through song lyrics and music, showing a painting, or creating a slideshow with photos and video of their lives as they present to the class. This assignment is open to your interpretation and is intended to expand our understanding of each other by hearing and appreciating everyone's individual stories. Each participant will have 5–7 minutes to present.*

Questions you *may* ask yourself to prepare for this presentation include:

- What is your family narrative?
- Where do you come from and how does that influence who you are?
- What are your salient (most important) social identities (i.e. gender, race/ethnicity, religious identity) and how do they show up for you?
- How do your most salient identities influence how you see yourself as a leader?
- If you could only state it in two sentences, what would you want your life legacy to be?
- How does your story so far inform your future legacy?

2. This activity requires honesty, clarity about the expectation of vulnerability, and the need for a supportive space to give participants a platform to speak their truths. The facilitator should present their own Our Stories/Our Voices narrative the week before the participants present to give an example and to also show vulnerability and openness to the power of their own story.

3. It is important to be aware that some participants may have more challenging stories than others, and some participants may choose to be more vulnerable than others. It is a delicate balance between creating an open space for hearing the power of stories in a safe, yet brave space (Arao & Clemens, 2013). Facilitators should use caution to ensure participants from historically marginalized identities are not unduly expected to shoulder the burden of vulnerability.

4. All participants should engage in active listening throughout to give respect, grace, and power to the presenter, and participants should listen with empathy, compassion, and love for the person presenting.

5. Following the presentation of all the narratives, the facilitator should share appreciation and acknowledgment for the power and importance of the stories shared. The facilitator should then employ open time for supportive statements of learning and appreciation for all participants.

6. This language can be added if the activity is used as an assignment for a course:

   "Because of the open and creative nature of this assignment, this project is not graded on a scale, and all participants who attend class during presentations and share their story through any creative means will receive full credit."

Debriefing Questions:
- This is an open time for appreciation and acknowledgment for yourselves and your peers. Please give shout outs and love for what we have heard today.
- Why is it important for us to give voice to or share creatively our own lived experiences?
- Where do we see moments of connection in our stories?
- How do we feel connected because we have listened to one anothers' truths?
- What do we envision a conarrative could be for this group?
- How would we tell a collective story, and why might that voice be powerful?

References:
Arao, B., & Clemens, K. (2013). From safe spaces to brave spaces: A new way to frame dialogue around diversity and social justice. In L. M. Landreman (Ed.), *The art of effective facilitation: Reflections from social justice educators* (pp. 135–150). Sterling, VA: Stylus.

Resources:
Bell, L. A. (2008). *Storytelling for social justice: Connecting narratives and the arts in antiracist teaching*. New York, NY: Routledge.
Delgado Bernal, D. (2002). Critical race theory, Latino critical theory, and critical raced-gendered epistemologies: Recognizing students of color as holders and creators of knowledge. *Qualitative Inquiry, 8*, 105–126.
hooks, b. (1994). *Teaching to transgress*. New York, NY: Routledge.
Turner Kelly, B., & Bhangal, N. K. (2018). Life narratives as pedagogy for cultivating critical self-reflection. In J. Dugan (Ed.), *New Directions for Student Leadership: No. 159. Integrating critical perspectives into leadership development* (pp. 41–52). San Francisco, CA: Jossey-Bass.

PERSONAL NARRATIVES AS AUTHENTIC EXPRESSION
Julie E. Owen

- 60 minutes–1 hour 30 minutes
- Any size group

One way to combat the impersonal and often transactional nature of formal learning is to invite participants to share brief authentic stories about their lives and what they care about. These stories are usually linked to class or workshop themes (e.g., gender, leadership, social change) and serve to showcase diverse perspectives and build an inclusive learning community. These stories invite participants to practice risk-taking and contribute to the development of brave spaces in the learning community.

Learning Goals: Participants will have opportunities to:

- reflect on critical incidents and commitments in their lives.
- practice the art of vulnerability and authentic sharing in a community of learners.
- consider connections between lived experiences and the social construction of knowledge.

Materials: prompt for "Personal Narratives as Authentic Expression," access to TED Talk

Process:

Facilitators should note that what seems like a relatively simple activity can be anxiety producing for participants. This anxiety can have multiple sources—fear of speaking in public; fear of exhibiting vulnerability among peers; worries about how stories may be received or misconstrued; and occasionally, fears about what happens after the story is shared. With such an open-ended invitation to reflection and narration, facilitators need to be ready for any kind of sharing. In the author's past experiences with this exercise, participants have shared stories of violence, sexual assault and harassment, eating disorders, migration and undocumented statuses, legal issues, racism, disabilities, ageism, and much more. There are often tears or laughter (occasionally both) accompanying these stories. How facilitators set the tone and parameters of the assignment and establish trust in the learning space are vitally important. Facilitators should also be prepared to refer participants (both speakers and listeners) to campus resources if topics are triggering.

1. Discuss the power of story-telling and why it is relevant to your class or workshop. One good way to do this is to show Chimamanda Ngozi Adichie's TED Talk: *The Danger of a Single Story.* (20 minutes)

https://www.ted.com/talks/chimamanda_adichie_the_danger_of_a_single_story?language=en

- Pose the following questions to participants:
  - What is the danger of a single story? What does Adichie mean when she says, "the problem with stereotypes is not that they are untrue, but that they are incomplete?"
  - What single stories have been told about you? Have you held about others? Did you/ how did you transform those messages (of self and other)?
  - Think about the "single stories" that exist today. How can we help dispel those dangerous myths and show the rich complexities in our world?
  - Adichie says "Power is the ability not just to tell the story of another person, but to make it the definitive story of that person." What is the role of story-telling in leadership? In power? In identity development? Why start the class this way?

2. Present the prompt for the Personal Narratives as Authentic Expression assignment (consider adapting the prompt to fit the subject of your course, workshop, or learning community).

- Gendered Perspective Story: *Each participant will share a story about a personal experience that made them think or feel deeply about their gender. The story (no more than 5 minutes) will illustrate how your life experiences have shaped your own socially constructed beliefs about how gender shapes opportunities and challenges. These stories will also help participants practice risk-taking and contribute to the development of 'brave space' in our learning community. These stories should be authentic and unrehearsed—no visual materials are needed.*

3. Have participants sign-up for a specific date to present their story. Reserve the first 10 minutes of every class for two participants to share their narratives. Give participants ample time to consider the Personal Narratives as Authentic Expression assignment. It should not be presented as an impromptu activity. Each time someone is about to share their story, remind listeners of the call to be present for their peers, to disconnect from technology, and to respect the confidentiality of the shared space.

Debriefing Questions:

In order to preserve the idea of narrative as gift, do not engage in follow up questions after someone has shared their story. Instead listeners are invited to comment on how the story made them feel, or something it triggered in them, or to thank the sharer. Potential prompts for overall reflection on the power of narratives in learning:

- How do we make explicit the complexities of power within education and prepare individuals and collectives to navigate it?
- How can we interrogate/deconstruct dominant narratives? Whose voices are missing/silenced in classroom content and processes?
- How do we understand intersectional identities (of ourselves and of our participants) in the classroom? To what extent are we engaged in examining our own assumptions, preferences, blind spots, and identities?
- How do our own values/philosophies/identities shape the curriculum and culture of our programs/classes? What are implications for introducing critical perspectives in the classroom as they relate to intersecting identities?
- Do the social locations of those practicing education replicate dominant norms?

Resources:

Adams, M., Bell, L. A., Goodman, D. J., & Joshi, K. Y. (2016). *Teaching for diversity and social justice* (3rd ed.). New York, NY: Routledge.

Arao, B., & Clemens, K. (2013). From safe spaces to brave spaces: A new way to frame dialogue around diversity and social justice. In L. M. Landreman (Ed.), *The art of effective facilitation: Reflections from social justice educators* (pp. 135–150). Sterling, VA: Stylus.

hooks, b. (1994). *Teaching to transgress: Education as the practice of freedom.* New York, NY: Routledge.

Nash, R. J., Bradley, D. L., & Chickering, A. (2008). *How to talk about hot topics on campus: From polarization to moral conversations.* San Francisco, CA: Jossey-Bass.

Reference:

Adichie, C. N. (2009). *The danger of a single story* [Video file]. Retrieved from https://www.ted.com/talks/chimamanda_adichie_the_danger_of_a_single_story

TELLING MY LEADERSHIP STORY
Jane Rodriguez

- 30–45 minutes
- Any size group

Through this reflection, participants will vocalize their own leadership story by reflecting on experiences that led to leadership development. They will be able to reflect on their journey as leaders from when they were very young to their current state through the experiences they had with friends, families, school teachers, peers, mentors, role models, professors, and others. With internal reflection and outward debriefing, participants will be encouraged to take into consideration location, generation, cultural influences, and resource accessibility when it came to their development.

Learning Goals: Participants will have opportunities to:

- analyze how their lived experiences played a role in their leadership identity.
- interpret their identities in relation to leadership development and how this influenced their path as a leader.
- challenge those around them to examine how the presence of their identities, whether marginalized or dominant, contributed to the presence or lack of leadership efficacy.

Materials: writing utensils, paper, and/or electronic device

Process:

Part 1: Internal Reflection (10–15 minutes)

1. Start off by getting participants into a meditative state where they close their eyes, relax, and take deep breaths.
2. Let them know you will be asking a series of questions to initiate reflection. Ask them to think about all of the experiences throughout their life that have contributed to their leadership identity. I would recommend the facilitator give anywhere from 30–60 seconds between questions. Participants are able to take notes on their responses to the questions so they do not forget, but they do not have to. Encourage participants to reflect on their responses to the questions in a way that works for them. Additional questions can be added or personalized.

3. Analyze the different responses and consider how participants' identities play a role in their responses.

4. Have participants think critically about the responses that are being shared and compare and contrast the experiences.

Questions for Internal Reflection:
- Reflect on your leadership journey. What events/moments have influenced your leadership development?
- What is the earliest memory you have of leadership?
- Who in your life do you consider to be a leader?
- What qualities does this individual have that remind you of leadership?
- What aspects within your culture or identity influenced your leadership identity?
- Have you always seen yourself as a leader? Why or why not?
- When you were younger, who did you consider to be leaders?
- When you define leadership, what values or beliefs come to mind?
- What are examples of leadership within your own culture or identity that you have witnessed?
- Who in your life has influenced your leadership learning? This may include family members, teachers, mentors, peers, et cetera.

Part Two: Outward Reflection (15–20 minutes)
5. Ask participants to open their eyes and share any reflections they would like.
6. Ask a series of questions to initiate conversation

Questions for Outward Reflection:
- Based off of the reflections of the peers around you, what similarities or differences do you see in how each individual approached their leadership development journey?
- What resources hindered or helped their leadership identity?
- Do you see any similarities in how different participants developed leadership efficacy?
- How do you differ in who you see as leaders?
- What experiences may have led to these differences?
- At what age did you start seeing yourselves as leaders? Was it when you were younger or older?
- Who or what played a role in when leadership was developed?
- Are there any similarities in how you experienced your leadership journey?

- Did any outside media such as books, TV, movies, music, et cetera influence your leadership development? Why or why not?
- Why do you think there are some differences in the way you developed as leaders?

TESTIMONIO: LEADER PROFILE
Maritza Torres

- 60 minutes–1 hour 15 minutes
- 5–18 participants

Testimonio is a form of storytelling derived from the Latinx culture that intentionally includes affirmation and empowerment (The Latina Feminist Group, 2001; Reyes & Curry Rodríguez, 2012). Testimonio is a form of reflection where individuals share their experiences with others in various forms such as writing, speaking, or visuals (Reyes & Curry Rodríguez, 2012). For this activity, participants will be writing the testimonio of their chosen leader. Participants will be given the opportunity to practice testimonio by creating a leader profile and presenting it in small and large groups.

Learning Goals: Participants will have opportunities to:

- learn the practice of testimonio.
- become knowledgeable of a person's leadership journey.

Materials: computer with Internet access for presentations

Process:

Part 1 (A Week or Month in Advance)

1. Participants will select an individual whom they consider to be a leader. This individual can be anyone or you can designate specific criteria based on your class topic.
2. Participants will construct a leader profile. The key is to have them write the profile as if they were the actual leader. For example, "My name is Sonia Sotomayor and I believe in ...".
3. The leader profile can consist of a written synopsis, spoken word, video, music, drawing, etc. Encourage the use of different mediums (i.e., poetry, spoken word, video, song, art, etc.) when participants present their testimonios. You are also able to designate only one type of medium (i.e. they submit videos only or drawings only).

Topics participants can cover include:

- Background information of the leader.
- Notable moments in the leader's life.
- Connection to key concepts in your class/program.

Part 2 (60 minutes–1 hour 30 minutes)

1. Participants will share their leadership profiles. Break the participants into small groups of 4. Give each participant at least 5–10 minutes to present their profile. Participants can read an excerpt of their testimonio or present it through a visual aid (i.e., PowerPoint, video). Presenters will share their testimonio either in the middle of the circle or from their seat. Encourage questions from other participants. This is meant to be a dialogue.
2. Once everyone has presented their profile, have the chairs of the room set up in a circle. Provide participants the opportunity to share the leader profile they previously shared in their small groups. Use the debrief questions to close the activity with the large group.

Debriefing Questions:
- What qualities do the leaders we learned about today possess and how do those make them leaders?
- What are some similarities amongst the leaders? Differences?
- How do the experiences of these leaders impact the way we understand and practice leadership?

Resources:
Burciaga, R., & Navarro, N. C. (2015). Educational testimonio: Critical pedagogy as mentorship. In C. S. Turner (Eds.), *New Directions for Higher Education: No. 171. Mentoring as transformative practice: Supporting student and faculty diversity* (pp. 33–41). San Francisco, CA: Jossey-Bass.
Delgado Bernal, D., Burciaga, R., & Carmona, J. F. (2012). Chicana/Latina testimonios: Mapping the methodological, pedagogical, and political. *Equity & Excellence in Education, 45*(3), 363–372. doi:10.1080/10665684.2012.698149

References:
The Latina Feminist Group. (2001). *Telling to live: Latina feminist testimonios.* Durham, NC: Duke University Press.
Reyes, K. B., & Curry Rodriguez, J. E. (2012). Testimonio: Origins, terms, and resources. *Equity & Excellence in Education, 45*(3), 525–538. doi: 10.1080/10665684.2012.698571

USING POETRY TO PROMOTE REFLECTION ON EXPERIENTIAL LEARNING
Nicholas F. Mazza and Jane McPherson

- 1 hour 30 minutes
- 5–12 participants

In this exercise drawn from the interdisciplinary field of poetry therapy (Mazza, 2017), reflection on experiential learning will be promoted through the reading, writing, and performance of poetry. Using the elements of poetic inquiry—including, language, symbol, and story—facilitators will promote reflection and the expansion of consciousness. Following Mazza's sequential R.E.S. model, participants will engage their *receptive* (R), *expressive* (E), and *symbolic* (S) selves. In the *receptive phase,* participants are introduced to literature as a practice; in the *expressive* phase, they will experiment with their own creativity in written expression; and in the *symbolic/ceremonial* phase, they will make meaning of their experience through the exploration of metaphor, ritual, performance, and/or ceremony.

Learning Goals: Participants will have opportunities to:

- use poetry to reflect on their personal and experiential learning experiences.
- improve their listening skills and empathic understanding through engaging in this group experience.
- identify the basic principles and techniques of adapting poetry therapy for use in promoting reflection among experiential learners.

Materials: selected poems (poems should be selected by the facilitator to evoke targeted emotions or themes and every participant should receive a copy of all poems used), writing utensils, flip chart or whiteboard (for group poetry composition)

Process:

1. Facilitators should begin by asking about participants' experience with poetry. Participants may be familiar with poetry slams, rap lyrics, and other forms of poetic experience. Encourage some discussion to make poetry seem more familiar.
2. The R.E.S. method for promoting reflection engages participants using a three-phase process that progressively connects with their receptive (R), expressive (E), and symbolic (S) selves

Phase 1: Receptive
In the first phase of R.E.S., participants are introduced to a poem, song, or story. In this example the facilitator will read a poem or perhaps will show a video of someone else reading a poem. Participants are invited to react to the poem as a whole or to

specific lines. For example, Stephen Crane's poem, *If I should cast off this tattered coat,* can be read aloud and used to ask participants to reflect on any number of themes, including decision-making, transitioning to adulthood, identity, human nature, travel, et cetera. The poem, first published in 1905, is available in the public domain.

If I should cast off this tattered coat,
And go free into the mighty sky;
If I should find nothing there
But a vast blue,
Echoless, ignorant—
What then?

Another possibility would be to use the poem *Left* by poet Nikky Finney. The author reads her poem, inspired by the suffering experienced after Hurricane Katrina on YouTube to a backdrop of images of New Orleans (available at https://goo.gl/p9VuBK). This poem is ideal for encouraging participants to reflect on race, poverty, privilege, etc. Any poem may be chosen, and the goal of the activity is to promote reflection and self-disclosure, stimulate group interaction, and universalize or validate feelings. The ideal poem would direct participants' focus to themes they have been processing during their experiential learning experience.

- Before meeting with participants, the facilitator will first want to choose a poem that fits a mood or evokes an emotion, social problem, human experience, et cetera, about which the facilitator intends to promote reflection and connection. There are many good sources for finding poems, but The Poetry Foundation is an excellent place to start: https://www.poetryfoundation.org/poems. Under "Collections," facilitators can find poems grouped together by themes like feminism, civil rights, the environment, and "get well soon." They also have a useful YouTube channel for facilitators who wish to present a visual poem: https://www.youtube.com/watch?v=VMkTo9u0Mjs. The National Association for Poetry Therapy also provides a useful list of links for finding poems: https://poetrytherapy.org/index.php/links-resources/poetry-links/

Phase 2: Expressive/Creative
In this phase, the facilitator or the participants will identify a theme that has emerged from their group experience, perhaps from their guided reflection in Phase 1 (or through their experiential learning) and write a collaborative group poem. Each member of the group will contribute a line to the poem that responds to the previous lines and further develops the themes. The facilitator will repeat the lines and write them down, ideally on a chalk board or flip chart where all participants can see the poem taking shape. When all members have contributed, the group will read the poem. Each line is the contribution of an individual, but as the poem grows the additional lines are chosen by consensus until the poem is complete. When the group decides the poem is complete, the facilitator will record the final product (using a computer or camera) so all members of the group can eventually have a copy.

Phase 3: Symbolic/Ceremonial
This phase can use dance, movement, or performance. Here the group poem may be read aloud–one line at a time or read in harmony. Following the reading, the facilitator will ask the group to engage in poetic enactment. This involves the group working together to express nonverbally what the poem (and therefore the experience) means to them.

Debriefing Questions:
- Would anyone like to share reactions to the specific tasks or the experience as a whole?
- How are you feeling now?
- What was it like when you were asked to perform the poem that you wrote?
- How did you feel with respect to group interaction?
- Did a leader(s) emerge for planning the performance of the poem?
- What will you take with you from this exercise?
- How did this poetry exercise enrich your experiential learning experience?

Resources:
Chavis, G. G. (2011). *Poetry and story therapy: The healing power of creative expression.* London, England: Jessica Kingsley.

Hynes, A. M., & Hynes-Berry, M. (2012). *Biblio/poetry therapy-the interactive process: A handbook.* St. Cloud, MN: North Star Press.

Mazza, N. (Ed.) (2017). *Expressive therapies* (Vols. 1–4). New York, NY: Psychology Press/ Routledge.

Mazza, N. (2017). *Poetry therapy: Theory and practice* (2nd ed.). New York, NY: Routledge

McPherson, J., & Mazza, N. (2014). Using arts activism and poetry to catalyze human rights engagement and reflection in social work education. *Social Work Education: The International Journal, 33,* 944–958. doi:10.1080/02615479.2014.885008

National Association for Poetry Therapy. (n.d.). Retrieved from www.poetrytherapy.org

Poetry Foundation. (n.d.). Retrieved from www.poetryfoundation.org/poems

CHAPTER 7

Written

A classic method for reflection, writing can be an important component of reflection on experiential learning. Fink (2013) recommended writing as a powerful strategy for teaching because the writing process "has a unique ability to develop the interior life or the writer" (p. 129). Fink (2013) also contended "the act of focusing students' attention on the learning process will make them more aware of themselves as learners and will thereby begin the process of developing their ability to create meaning in their lives" (p. 129). Suskie (2018) noted an increasing value on reflection as a strategy for learning assessments. She noted four reasons reflective writing may be gaining interest: reflective writing allows participants to demonstrate learning; it can be a tool to understand attitudes or values; qualitative insight balances quantitative measures of learning; and reflective writing enhances the human dimension of reporting assessment results. Written reflection is powerful on its own, and it also serves as a complement to other reflection strategies.

Journaling. A journal is "a sequential, dated chronicle of events and ideas, which includes the personal responses and reflection of the writer (or writers) on those events and ideas" (Stevens & Cooper, 2009, p. 5) Reflective journaling can include a range of prompted and unprompted writing activities. In an analysis of graduate student journals from a 1-month international service-learning experience, Sturgill and Motley (2014) found guided reflection, including instructor prompts, resulted in more paragraphs that demonstrated analytic and integrative thinking than free writing, which resulted in more descriptive writing. Without guidance, journals may become a place for students to reiterate activities rather than make connections to course concepts or future actions (Ash & Clayton, 2009; Bringle & Hatcher, 1999). In combination with their own research and teaching practice, Dyment and O'Connell (2010) reviewed literature on journaling in higher education to identify factors that limited or enabled highly reflective journaling. They found elements that enabled journaling included clear expectations and an understanding of the purpose for the journals; appropriate training, which may include an introduction to reflection frameworks or samples of writing; feedback from the instructor; graded journals as motivation; trust and a climate that invites honesty; reflection as a habit, which may include devoting class time to journaling; and structured prompts, among others (Dyment & O'Connell, 2010). Like many reflective practices, facilitators' investment and role modeling supports students' engagement in deep reflection.

Portfolios. Both paper and digital portfolios provide platforms to aggregate reflection artifacts including written work, feedback reports, and narratives of learning. Through sustained documentation, portfolios include the process and the products of reflection (Fernsten & Fernsten, 2005). Portfolios can also provide an opportunity for self-assessment. Self-assessment refers to the involvement of learners in making judgments about their own learning: particularly about their achievements and the outcomes of learning (Boud & Falchikov, 1989). Using self-assessment as an instructional strategy promotes skill-building, responsibility for one's own learning, and problem solving (Sluijsmans, Dochy, & Moerkerke, 1999). Conger (1992) described the importance of students learning about themselves; he argued, "we can place more responsibility on students' shoulders for the evaluation of their own performance, attitude, and behavior" (p. 636). Examples of this sentiment from across higher education include portfolios where students report on their own learning through the completion of assignments.

REFERENCES

Ash, S. L., & Clayton, P. H. (2009). Generating, deepening, and documenting learning: The power of critical reflection in applied learning. *Journal of Applied Learning in Higher Education, 1*(1), 25–48.

Boud, D., Falchikov, N. (1989). Quantitative studies of student self-assessment in higher education: A critical analysis of findings. *Higher Education 18,* 529–549.

Bringle, R. G., & Hatcher, J. A. (1999). Reflection in service-learning: Making meaning of experience. *Educational Horizons,* 179–185.

Conger, J. (1992). *Learning to lead: The art of transforming managers into leaders*. San Francisco, CA: Jossey-Bass.

Dyment, J. E., & O'Connell, T. S. (2010). The quality of reflection in student journals: A review of limiting and enabling factors. *Innovative Higher Education, 35*(4), 233–244.

Fernsten, L., & Fernsten, J. (2005). Portfolio assessment and reflection: Enhancing learning through reflective practice. *Reflective Practice, 6*(2), 303–309.

Fink, L. D. (2013). *Creating significant learning experiences*. San Francisco, CA: John Wiley & Sons.

Sluijsmans, D., Dochy, F., & Moerkerke, G. (1999). Creating a learning environment by using self-, peer- and co-assessment. *Learning Environments Research, 1*, 293–319.

Stevens, D. D., & Cooper, J. E. (2009). *Journal keeping: How to use reflective writing for effective learning, teaching, professional insight, and positive change*. Sterling, VA: Stylus.

Sturgill, A., & Motley, P. (2014). Methods of reflection about service learning: Guided vs. free, dialogic vs. expressive, and public vs. private. *Teaching and Learning Inquiry, 2*(1), 81–93.

Suskie, L. (2018). *Assessing student learning: A common sense guide* (3rd ed.). San Francisco, CA: John Wiley & Sons.

THE BIG PICTURE
Danielle Morgan Acosta

- 45–60 minutes
- Any size group

This activity encourages participants to think about how their actions (ex. goals, organization, leadership) are connected to the bigger picture and the world beyond their current reality. By connecting daily actions to larger entities (historical context, social change movements, etc.) and reflecting upon campus culture, organizational goals, and personal goals, participants are able to understand the scope and purpose of their work and realize they are not alone in their efforts.

Learning Goals: Participants will have opportunities to:

- learn about history of their organization(s), including any connections to institutional or social history, movements, other groups, et cetera.
- reflect upon personal goals and link aligned activities and goals to their local and global communities.
- commit to action.

Materials: worksheet, writing utensils, historical/structural understanding of organization(s)/social change movement(s)

Process:

The process of the "Big Picture" includes providing knowledge and context, and having participants write and reflect upon their global and local communities, and themselves individually, before discussing with others and committing to personal action.

1. Provide historical context, mission, and general information. (15–20 minutes)

   - *Positional Leader Training*: Help participants understand the scope of an organization that has existed for decades: there are leaders, advocacy, and victories that have come before the current group of participants. The organization may be tied to national or global social change movements over time. Providing a framework and historical context for participants, then allowing them to reflect upon their goals and how they connect to the organizational mission is critical to helping them positively effect changes in their communities. Include old and current mission statements, photographs, logos, and organization accomplishments.
   - *Connecting to Global Issues:* Perhaps participants are being asked to think about the role they can play in social change (human rights movements, sustainability initiatives, etc.). Share the history of the movement, times young people have made an impact, and the options international associations present as a way to create change.

2. Big Picture Reflections (20–30 minutes)

   - Ask participants to think about their communities on the large scale, including local, state, regional, national, or global level. *What is important for your community? What are people advocating for around the globe? What change has been accomplished over time?*
   - Ask participants to think about the context of their campus community. *How do these issues show up on campus? How do you seem them being addressed?*
   - Ask participants to dig deeper into their own sphere of influence. *How can your organization begin to enact change to address the needs you see and think are important? What can you do to begin to see those changes?*
   - Have participants share their reflections and thoughts in small and large groups.

3.   Commitments (10 minutes)

* Have participants take some time to reflect upon the knowledge they have gained, shared, and reflected upon. *What will you do next?*

Debriefing Questions:
* If you had no restrictions, what changes would you pursue in response to your community's needs?
* What can you do to start creating and supporting change?
* Who do you need to help you? What resources do you need?
* Who has come before you in this work? How do you identify who will continue the work?
* What are you committed to working toward this year?

Resources:
* A university archivist, old school newspapers, yearbooks, or annual reports may be helpful in gathering historical information.
* Briefly researching social change movements, stories, and timelines may provide additional context and help participants reflect upon their current work and purpose.
* Awareness of campus resources and additional organizations and departments to support participants in their future plans can help continue the dialogue.

CAREER READY: IDENTIFYING TRANSFERRABLE SKILLS
Jillian M. Volpe White

* 60 minutes
* Any size group

Experience alone is insufficient for learning; participants need to reflect on experiences for them to be educative. Along the same lines, cultivating a resume full of experiences is not useful if participants cannot describe learning meaningfully. This activity invites participants to consider what they learned and how they will communicate what they learned through a resume.

Learning Goals: Participants will have opportunities to:

* describe knowledge and skills developed during an experience.
* reflect on how knowledge and skills from an experience could transfer to other contexts.

Materials: paper and writing utensils

Process:

As you prepare for this activity, consider inviting someone from career services to talk about resume writing.

1.   Set up the activity for participants. (5 minutes)

You will reflect on how you might share the story of what you learned from this experience. Your resume is one place where you document experiences to tell the story of what you learned. Think about the knowledge you acquired and the skills you developed as a result of your experience. You might also consider how your attitude was shaped. We will also consider how to translate experiences from one context to another. Sometimes your service or work takes places in a different setting than your anticipated career. For example, if you served in a classroom but you want to be a doctor, you might highlight skills that are transferable such as connecting with people or developing empathy.

2.   Give participants time to jot down thoughts in response to these prompts: (5 minutes)

* What did you do as part of your experience? Be specific about the tasks or projects.
* What did you learn as a result of the experience? What knowledge did you acquire? What skills did you develop? How has your attitude been shaped?

3.   Once participants have written down thoughts, share a framework for describing on a resume, perhaps providing a few examples. Introduce taxonomies of learning outcomes and/or the National Association of Colleges and Employers (2019) career readiness competencies as ways to frame their knowledge and skills. (10 minutes)

* It may be useful to pull up or have copies of a learning taxonomy to help participants think of action verbs. Some taxonomies are listed in the resources.

4.   Instruct participants to take their notes and draft entries for their resume. Ask them to be specific regarding knowledge, skills, and attitudes, trying to write down at least a few examples of each (depending upon the duration of the experience). (15 minutes)

5.   After a few minutes, bring the group back together. Invite participants to share some examples. (10 minutes)

6. Have a large group debrief about the activity. (15 minutes)

   • Variation: Resume Exchange—If time allows in your program or class, introduce this activity during one session and ask participants to bring a draft of their resume, including entries about their experience, to the next meeting. Have participants exchange resumes and provide feedback to one another.
   • If your institution has an online or e-portfolio system, participants may consider adding their completed materials to this system.

Debriefing Questions:
• Of knowledge, skills, and attitudes, which was the most challenging to describe? What was the easiest to describe?
• Thinking about the entries you just wrote, what specific story or instance would highlight what you learned or how you developed?
• It is possible you will apply the skills you learned in a different setting. Consider one of your entries—how would this transfer to a different setting?
• Looking at your entries, are there concentrations of knowledge, skills, and attitudes? How would you highlight this or make connections to demonstrate the depth of your knowledge or skill? What knowledge or skills do you still need to develop?

Resources:
Anderson, L. W., & Krathwohl, D. R. (Eds.). (2000). *A taxonomy for learning, teaching, and assessing: A revision of Bloom's taxonomy of educational objectives.* London, England: Pearson.
Fink, L. D. (2013). *Creating significant learning experiences: An integrated approach to designing college courses.* San Francisco, CA: Jossey-Bass.
Marzano, R. J., & Kendall, J. S. (2008). *Designing and assessing educational objectives: Applying a new taxonomy.* Thousand Oaks, CA: Corwin Press.
National Association of Colleges & Employers. (2019). *Career readiness defined.* Retrieved from http://www.naceweb.org/career-readiness/competencies/career-readiness-defined/

CRAFTING A LEADERSHIP PHILOSOPHY STATEMENT
Dawn Morgan

• 30–45 minutes
• Any size group

This activity is designed to capture participants' reflections regarding core leadership concepts utilizing a written personal philosophy statement. Using provided prompts, curriculum materials, and personal experiences, participants will craft their leadership philosophy in multiple edits over the span of the course or program.

Learning Goals: Participants will have opportunities to:

• interpret their understanding of core leadership concepts.
• identify their personal leadership values, attitudes, and behaviors.
• develop a comprehensive leadership philosophy statement.

Materials: curriculum on core leadership concepts, blank paper and writing utensils, printed or digitally displayed prompts

Process:

1. Facilitate a discussion about the importance of understanding one's own leadership philosophy. Discuss the importance of reflecting on personal thoughts, beliefs, and practices. (5 minutes)
2. Communicate expectations of what completion entails and how the philosophies will be used. Philosophy statements could be for personal use, as an assignment to ensure participants are making the appropriate connections to the curriculum. If statements will be used for marketing and promotional purposes, consider providing a branded template and specific guidelines. Make sure to collect a signed consent form from each participant.
3. In a provided journal, have participants draft a leadership philosophy statement. (15 minutes) For context, have them consider what they might include in an elevator pitch or an objective statement on their resume. Participants might include their core or ethical values, leadership style and practices, social identities or other influential factors. Other appropriate insertions might include information about an organization, service project or community effort with which they are involved. They may also mention why they are invested in this activity and how their leadership is demonstrated through this effort.

- Prompting questions (could vary based on curriculum content):
  - What is leadership to you? Do you believe leadership is innate or learned over time? What life experiences have led you to believe this?
  - Do you identify as a leader? If so, what kind of leader are you? How would others describe your leadership? If not, what kind of leader do you want to be?
  - Where do you lead and who benefits from your leadership? If you are not yet involved with a cause, what kind of impact do you hope to make on your campus and community?

4. During the program, design checkpoints for participants to extend and edit their philosophy statements. Incorporate reflections on the various concepts covered in the content material (i.e., their understanding of group development, equity and inclusion, effective communication, etc.). Based on group dynamic and level of trust, have participants switch with a peer to give and receive feedback. Give ample opportunity to reach a "finished" product. Lastly, following their final opportunity to revise and edit their statement, debrief the process of crafting these personal philosophy statements as a group.

Debriefing Questions:
- How has your leadership philosophy statement evolved over time?
- What leadership concepts are incorporated now that were not in your first draft?
- What thoughts, opinions or practices related to leadership were challenged, and how have they changed?
- What parts of your personal statement are you most proud of and why?
- What parts are you still figuring out? What do you think is hindering you from writing about these concepts?

LEADERSHIP DEVELOPMENT: A WRITTEN REFLECTION SERIES
Ashley Curtis and Darren Pierre

- 30 minutes–1 hour 20 minutes
- 3–5 participants per group

This activity includes a written journal that will guide participants through reflection as a means to gain a deeper understanding of themselves and their identities. Through this exercise, participants will understand how their multiple identities impact the way in which they perceive experiences and the world around them.

Learning Goals: Participants will have opportunities to:

- design a written reflection.
- understand the importance of written reflection in the practice of leadership.
- develop self-awareness and self-actualization.
- increase awareness of personal leadership style.
- develop leadership efficacy and capacity.

Process:

Over the course of several months (perhaps an academic term), participants will write six reflections that will be submitted biweekly to a facilitator for review and feedback.

In the content below, the bold text provides a brief topical overview. Facilitators should provide additional readings or other content related to the topics and reflective prompt. Following the bold content is each submission's topical prompt accompanied by an example to understand the context and intention for each prompt. In a free-write, participants will reflect on the following prompts:

Submission 1: **Reflection is an essential component of leadership development as it allows the learner to "promote growth in self-awareness and self-actualization" (Guthrie & Jenkins, 2018, p. 207). An integral part of self-awareness and self-actualization is understanding one's identity.**

Identify your most salient identities. Describe why these identities are most salient to you. (e.g., A student may identify race, gender, age, ability, socioeconomic status as their most salient identities. An identity may be most salient for many reasons. Consider how each identity influences the way the student experiences privilege and oppression.)

Submission 2: **According to Volpe White, Guthrie, and Torres (2019), reflection "requires cognitive and affective complexity to consider past experiences, draw conclusions, infer meaning, and consider applications for the future" (p. 25). The ability to construct and make meaning of our experiences through reflection helps us as individuals understand the factors that influence our decision-making process.**

Describe a leadership experience that has had a significant impact on your life. In what ways did your identities influence the way in which you demonstrated leadership? Consider how your identities influenced your actions as a leader. Are there ways this leadership experience shaped your identities? (e.g., Let's say a student identifies an experience in which the student took on a leadership role in their home growing up. The student states that they were very young when they first took on the leadership role as the primary caretaker for their three younger siblings. In this experience, the student may acknowledge multiple identities. For instance, the student may identify race and socioeconomic status as two prominent identities in this catalyzing experience.)

Submission 3: **Observation plays a central role in adaptive leadership: "Two people observing the same event or situation see different things depending on their previous experiences and unique perspectives ... in exercising adaptive leadership, the goal is to make observing as objective as possible" (Heifetz, Grashow, & Linsky, 2009, p. 32). An essential component to reflection is the ability to objectively observe our experiences. Objective observation removes emotion from the way we process and interpret a situation, allowing us to view the event or situation from multiple lenses and gain a holistic understanding of the experience.**

Using the leadership experience described in submission three, rewrite your experience as objectively as possible. Consider questions such as Who's talking with whom? Who responds to whom? What are the alliances and relationships? What is the history of the challenge we are facing? Utilize objective language, which removes emotion from the experience (e.g., I observed, I noticed, I saw, I heard, etc.) (Using the previous example, as the student writes about their upbringing, and their experience raising three younger siblings, the student may write about a lot of hostility/resentment. The student may feel

anger toward their parent and write something like "I was really angry that my parent was never around while I was growing up. It was their job to do the cleaning and the cooking and instead I had to do everything." Using objective language, the student could rewrite this saying something to the effect of: I often observed that my parent was absent during my childhood. I noticed that this absence makes me feel angry.).

Submission 4: **Discovering multiple interpretations is another essential component to adaptive leadership. "You have to take time to think through your interpretation of what you observe, before jumping into action.... The idea is to make your interpretations as accurate as possible by considering the widest possible array of sensory information" (Heifetz et al., 2009, p. 34). Identifying multiple interpretations is the core of reflective practice. Reflection where we are able to examine and understand the way in which all individuals experience a situation allows a leader to critically identify and understand how both a situation and solution may affect the community. The practice to seek and identify multiple interpretations moves to a framework of transformational, authentic, and team-based leadership.**

Consider the different lenses in which your leadership experience could be perceived. First discuss the experience from the dance floor (your own personal perspective). Next, look at this event from the balcony (someone else's perspective). Are there any other perspectives to consider as you more closely examine this experience? What voices were heard and which voices were silent? (The student who is upset about the absence of their parent during their childhood should consider multiple perspectives. The student may identify one perspective as: perhaps the parent was unable to physically be at home to support the family because the parent needed to work multiple jobs in order to generate enough income to support the family in other ways, like being able to buy food and clothes for their children.)

Submission 5: **"Once you have made an interpretation of the problem-solving dynamics you have observed, what are you going to do about it" (Heifetz et al., 2009, p. 35). An integral component to reflection is both self-awareness and situational awareness so this information can then be utilized as a means to take action.**

As a leader, think about how you responded in this experience. What actions did you take? Using your understanding of your identities and the observations and interpretations made, would you change your actions? If so, what actions would you change and how? If not, discuss why not. (In this scenario, the student may find they would not have taken different actions as the experience provided the opportunity for the student to take a position of leadership and provide for and serve their family.)

Submission 6: "[Critical reflection] *generates* learning (articulating questions, confronting bias, examining causality, contrasting theory with practice, pointing to systemic issues), *deepens* learning (challenging simplistic conclusions, inviting alternative perspectives, asking "why" iteratively), and *documents* learning (producing tangible expressions of new understandings for evaluation)" (Ash & Clayton, 2009, p. 27, emphasis in original). Self-assessment and evaluation are vital to our self-awareness and leadership development. In order for these practices to be most effective, it is imperative that reflection be continuous and ongoing.

Look back at your previous reflections. Describe why you believe reflection is important to leadership. What discoveries have you made in this process? How has this reflection been helpful to you as a leader? Discuss how you can continue to incorporate reflection in your daily life. (The student may find that while they gained valuable experience as a leader, the situation created anger and resentment. Upon reflection, the student may be able to identify this feeling of anger and resentment and consider possible actions to take in future situations. Perhaps the student gains an understanding of the importance of self-advocacy and boundary setting, and describes how they will advocate and set boundaries for themselves in similar situations which might occur in the future.)

Debriefing Questions:
- After each prompt it is important the facilitator incorporate a discussion around impact and benefits of written reflection.
- What was your original perception of reflection?
- Why is reflection important to leadership?
- What did you learn about yourself as a leader?
- What observations were you made aware of through this reflection series?
- How are observations helpful to you as a leader?

- What new perspectives did you gain from this reflection series?
- How does reflection impact the actions you take as a leader?

References

Ash, S. L., & Clayton, P. H. (2009). Generating, deepening, and documenting learning: The power of critical reflection in applied learning. *Journal of Applied Learning in Higher Education, 1*(1), 25–48.

Guthrie, K. L., & Jenkins, D. M. (2018). *The role of leadership educators: Transforming learning.* Charlotte, NC: Information Age.

Heifetz, R. A., Grashow, A., & Linsky, M. (2009). *The practice of adaptive leadership: tools and tactics for changing your organization and the world.* Boston, MA: Harvard Business Press.

Volpe White, J. M., Guthrie, K. L., & Torres, M. (2019). *Thinking to transform: Reflection in leadership learning.* Charlotte, NC: Information Age.

1-MINUTE REFLECTION PAPER
Jillian M. Volpe White

- 5–10 minutes
- Any group size

Sometimes less is more. A brief but useful way for participants to process an experience is a 1-minute written reflection. Brief written reflections can be useful for formative assessment, and they can build toward summative reflection. Clear and compelling prompts are designed to elicit reflection in a short period of time, and these prompts can also be used for other reflection activities.

Learning Goals: Participants will have opportunities to:

- develop ideas in response to a prompt.
- write reflections without filtering their responses.
- revisit responses to engage in a meta-analysis of reflection.

Materials: paper or index card and a writing utensil for each person

Process:

1. Pass out index cards or paper.
2. Tell participants they will have a set amount of time to reflect (you can decide how long this will be—typically between 1 and 5 minutes).
3. Provide a prompt (your familiarity with the group, knowledge of the program or service, or a scan of

the room can help you determine which prompt is the best fit for the group or experience). If you are using index cards, you might ask them to respond to two questions, one on each side of the card.

4. The list provides potential prompts:

   - I believe …
   - What is one thing you learned?
   - What is one question you still have?
   - How will you take action on something you learned?
   - How can you use your knowledge, skills, or abilities to create positive change?
   - Who has influence on your life? How do you influence others?
   - What assumptions are you bringing to this experience?
   - What would happen if I …?
   - How would other people know you care deeply about something?
   - Who do you want to become?
   - I don't think I will ever forget …
   - Leadership is …
   - What do you need from others in order to be your best self?
   - I need to learn more about _____. Explain.
   - What did you expect would happen? What actually happened?
   - I am nervous or anxious about …
   - What are your values? How do you know these are your values?
   - How do you lead?
   - If I could do one thing differently, I would …

5. After participants have written their responses, invite people to share what they wrote. In a larger group, have participants get into pairs or smaller groups to share.

   - Variation—Group Feedback: If the group is going to reconvene (for another session or class period), you could collect the cards and summarize the information for the group at the next meeting. This is an excellent opportunity to address questions people do not feel comfortable voicing in front of the group and to close the loop on an informal assessment of the experience. Even if the group will not meet again in person, you could post a few takeaways to a course website or send a follow up email.
   - Variation—Learning over Time: If the group is going to reconvene regularly over a period of time, you could ask participants to write their name at the top of the card/paper. Keep the cards until the end of the semester or experience. At one of the final meetings, give each person their reflection cards/papers. Invite them to

read over their responses from the semester or experience. Their final reflection can be a meta-reflection of how they have changed or grown over the course of the semester or experience.

Debriefing Questions:
- What did you write in response to the prompts?
- How easy or difficult was it to respond to the prompt(s)?
- What do our collective responses say about what we learned from this experience?
- How will you apply what you learned from this experience going forward?

Resources:
Angelo, T. A., & Cross, K. P. (1993). *Classroom assessment techniques: A handbook for teachers*. San Francisco, CA: Jossey-Bass.
Stead, D. R. (2005). A review of the one-minute paper. *Active Learning in Higher Education, 6*(2), 118–131.

T.I.P.S. FOR LEADERSHIP LEARNING
Kerry L. Priest, Tamara Bauer, and J. Michael Finnegan

- 60 minutes–1 hour 30 minutes
- Any size group

This letter writing exercise is based on Anu Taranath's (2014) book, *T.I.P.S. to Study Abroad: Simple Letters for Complex Engagement*. T.I.P.S. stands for *thing, idea, person,* or *self*. The method was developed by Taranath and her participants at the University of Washington to help global travelers "reflect on how moving from one context to another invites questions about identity, society, and the meaning of travel itself" (p. 3). As faculty in an Introduction to Leadership course, we have adapted the method for a reflection assignment as part of academic service-learning work, in this case around the social issue of food security. However, it can be used more broadly to reflect on experiences that contribute to leadership learning.

Learning Goals: Participants will have opportunities to:

- develop critical reflection skills.
- convey meaning through written communication.
- apply leadership learning to experience.

Materials: reflection guide (as outlined in process instructions below)

Process:

1. This activity is based on a method called T.I.P.S., which stands for *Things, Ideas, People,* or *Self* (Taranath, 2014). Participants will identify one of these lenses and compose a letter that demonstrates their reflection process and articulates learning. Ask participants to choose a thing, idea, person, or self-learning that impacted them. Here are some examples of how the letter might start:

   - **Thing:** An actual physical thing that serves as a representation, metaphor or inspiration for your learning (e.g., Dear Pallet of Expired Food, Dear House on the Corner …)
   - **Idea:** A course-related concept or broader perspective that inspired your learning (e.g., Dear Socially Responsible Leadership, Dear Ethical Leadership …)
   - **Person:** Someone you engaged with or observed during the service-learning experience (e.g., Dear Man Using Food Assistance, Dear Volunteer for Meals on Wheels …)
   - **Self:** Write to yourself

2. The letter should follow this general format: introduction, body, and conclusion. *Your narrative should demonstrate critical reflection and application as they elaborate on 1–3 key points that represent your most significant learning* (e.g., their attitude toward the idea of the service project, how they chose actions steps, their level of investment/engagement, motivation, skepticism, what they learned, how it all made sense or not, how can it make better sense, how this experience helped them make connections with the class concepts, what they are taking away from this experience, challenges of working with a community partner, sense of commitment, ideas for change, sentiments for community service, or purpose to lead).

Debriefing Questions:

If used as an in-class or online activity, you can invite participants to share their letters with a partner, in small groups, or through a discussion board. Allowing participants to voluntarily read their letters aloud allows for the generation of multiple perspectives and deeper conversation and about their shared experience. Some additional reflection questions may include:

- What did you notice about the commonalities and differences between these letters and the choices of to whom/what they were addressed?
- What might this mean about our experience of learning and exercising leadership through this project?

Example 1

Dear Lesly,

Coming into this project, you knew this issue [Food Insecurity] was an important issue that you valued, however, you also saw this as a grade in the grade book which kept you from reaching your full potential. As this project progressed you became engaged and interested in the ways in which you could help, whether it was stepping in when your small group was arguing or picking up cans in the neighborhood.

When first discovering your strengths, you were excited to see the results were ones you could actually see in your life as you exercised leadership. You were able to make connections with the people you engaged with whether you used your strength as an includer or an achiever. Before this class, you had not experienced leadership in the lens of your strengths and it made you happier and more engaged. Your commitment only grew higher with your acknowledgment and awareness of your strengths. Even though you struggled to view this as something outside of a grade, your commitment grew vastly and you began to ask yourself much deeper questions about this experience such as, "How can I leave a meaningful mark on the lives of the people I am asking donations from?"

I am proud of you for learning how to value your strengths and use them in a positive manner toward your leadership exercises. You now have experienced the difference of looking at leadership as a way to improve your weaknesses and looking at leadership as a way to engage your strengths. The attitude you found from both was astonishing and I am happy to see your commitment grow with it. I hope to see you do more projects like this and engage your leadership activities with commitment and a focus on your strengths.

Sincerely,
Myself

Example 2

Dear Social Change,

I will say you were not something I thought about much at all before this project. I never thought of you whenever I had donated food in any of my previous experiences. You completely changed how I will always view service projects, missions trips, or any kind of donations to people who are in need or are underprivileged, or at least if I want to do a good job at volunteering or donating.

Social Change, you have made it so much harder to make a difference whenever I volunteer my time for people in need. It is no longer just helping people and moving on with my life. I actually have to find a way to get to the root causes of the problems and find ways to fix those, too. You say that the things people do when they volunteer are normally just a band aid to the problem and don't actually fix the problem the people in need have in the long term. Social Change, I realize now how important you are and why we need to focus on you when we take our time to volunteer for people. You can turn a small volunteer experience into a meaningful change for the people in need. But I feel you can also be a deterrent to people that want to volunteer. Not everyone can take the time it takes to make a social change but still want to help. I feel that you say these band aids don't create much meaningful change for the people in need, but it is still important for these people to get food until they are able to find a way to provide for themselves.

Overall, I am glad to have gotten to know you throughout this experience. I hope to be able to include you in all of my volunteer experiences from now on. You have really changed my view on helping people and making sure that it is about them and not me.

Sincerely,
Calvin

Reference:

Taranath, A. (2014). *T.I.P.S. to study abroad: Simple letters for complex engagement.* Seattle, WA: Flying Chickadee.

WHAT'S IN MY LEADER HOUSE?
Trisha Teig

- Varies
- Any size group

Guided reflective writing allows learners the opportunity for thinking and processing their leader identity in relationship to interpersonal, intrapersonal, and societal constructs. Participants who progress in ownership of a leader identity require critical reflective processing (Turner Kelly & Bhangal, 2018) to understand their past experiences in learning leadership, how they were framed within historical contexts, and how institutional structures still reify historical legacies of inclusion/exclusion based on identity. In this activity, participants engage in written reflection to consider the formulation of their leader identity through the lens of the culturally relevant leadership learning model (Bertrand Jones, Guthrie, & Osteen, 2016).

Learning Goals: Participants will have opportunities to:

- identify how, where, and why they have been influenced in their understanding of leader and leadership.
- ascertain institutional examples of historically gendered/racialized concepts of leadership.

- recognize institutional examples of reformulation of leadership outside of historically gendered/racialized understandings.
- create action plans to disrupt historically gendered/racialized concepts of leadership in their own organization.

Materials: writing utensils and paper, handout with reflection prompts

Process:

This activity should be employed in relationship to teaching the culturally relevant leadership learning model (Bertrand Jones et al., 2016). The activity can be done in class, but ideally would be completed by participants outside of the group meeting to allow adequate time for thoughtful responses. Give participants the following reflection prompts. Encourage participants to read through the prompts and ask any questions they may have. The facilitator/instructor may choose to give specific guidelines for length of responses to each question. This is intentionally not included in the guide to allow for best interpretation based on circumstances.

1. Historic conceptualization of leader/leadership (historical legacy):

   - What is your first memory of learning about a leader/leadership?
   - How were you taught about being a leader?
   - How were you taught about leadership?
   - Where (location, context) did you learn this?

2. Personal conversations you have had and encouragement toward particular types of leader/leadership (behavioral/psychological):

   - Who taught you about becoming a leader or leadership?
   - Did anyone encourage you to think of yourself as a leader? How? Why?
   - How did this conversation relate to your salient social identities?

3. Experiences with positional leader roles in relation to who else was present (compositional diversity):

   - What positional leader experiences have you had?
   - What were the social identities of others who were in those organizations with you? What about the other positional leaders?

4. Consideration of examples of ways structures in your institution may:

- Still represent leadership as gendered/racialized:
  - Where do you see examples of leadership as gendered or racialized at your institution?
- Be reformulating leadership outside of a binary or construct of Whiteness:
  - Does your institution have examples of conceptualizing leadership outside of the gender binary?
  - Does your institution have examples of recognizing leadership outside of a construct of Whiteness?
- Need to take action/change: (This question may be further utilized to create a personal or group project for institutional/organizational change)
  - How can you take action to begin the conversation about deconstructing/reconstructing leadership outside of the gendered/racialized examples within your institutional structure?

The facilitator should encourage participants in small groups (3–5 participants) to share their responses and compare their experiences in understanding leader/leadership. The written reflection can also be debriefed within a large group after all participants have completed the activity.

Debriefing Questions:
- Share your responses in your small group to questions 1–3.
- What was similar about your experience? What was different?
- What surprised you about what you heard today?
- What did you learn from your peers?
- Share your responses in your small group to the fourth question. Repeat debrief questions.
- Based on your responses to the final question (How can you take action to begin the conversation about deconstructing/reconstructing leadership outside of the gendered/racialized examples within your institutional structure?), identify a change project you would like to implement with your group on campus.

References:
Bertrand Jones, T., Guthrie, K. L., & Osteen, L. (2016). Critical domains of culturally relevant leadership learning: A call to transform leadership programs. In K. L. Guthrie, T. Bertrand Jones, & L. Osteen (Eds.), *New Directions for Student Leadership: No. 152. Developing culturally relevant leadership learning* (pp. 9–21). San Francisco, CA: Jossey-Bass.

Guthrie, K. L., & Chunoo, V. (Eds.). (2018). *Changing the narrative: Socially just leadership education.* Charlotte, NC: Information Age.

Turner Kelly, B., & Bhangal, N. K. (2018). Life narratives as pedagogy for cultivating critical self-reflection. In J. Dugan (Ed.), *New Directions for Student Leadership: No. 159. Integrating critical perspectives into leadership development* (pp. 41–52). San Francisco, CA: Jossey-Bass.

WRITTEN LEADERSHIP PORTFOLIOS: A LONGITUDINAL TOOL FOR REFLECTIVE LEARNING
Stephanie L. Quirk

- Semester–Multiple Years
- Any size group (with appropriate support)

A leadership portfolio is a collection of reflections and artifacts participants curate to demonstrate learning over the course of their participation in leadership activities. They can be created as digital projects on personal websites, within an institutional learning management system, or printed in a binder. Written portfolios are valuable as capstone projects for participants participating in formal programs or courses providing space for participants to reflect on their learning and to see development over time.

Learning Goals: Participants will have opportunities to:

- apply a reflective framework to leadership development experiences.
- explain the value of a living document and commitment to continuous growth.

Materials: a list of portfolio requirements and guided reflection questions

Process:

The design of the portfolio should align with learning outcomes and can be used as part of individual and program (or course) assessment. The format can vary including using a learning management system with portfolio capabilities, a hard copy in a binder or expandable folder, or a free personal website.

1. Introduce the leadership portfolio concept to participants at the beginning of the program or course. Portfolios are living documents that can grow and be modified over time. Hiemstra (2001) recommends including resource materials for participants including write-ups on journaling and samples from previous participants. Provide a list of requirements and prompts to assist participants in staying on track with their portfolio development.

   - Sample portfolio requirements:
     - Cover page
     - Current resume

- o Table of contents
- o Written reflections on program experiences
- o Personal leadership philosophy
- o Written reflection on campus involvement
- o Service-learning and / or community engagement reflection
- o Capstone reflection (completed at the end with the purpose of looking back on the entire course or program experience)
- o Personal additions (leadership assessment results, photos, presentation slides, handouts, or other artifacts that showcase their leadership learning)

2. Educators will want to create the reflection guide and structure the questions using a reflective framework. Borton's (1970) "What," "So What?," "Now What?" reflective framework is ideal. The "Now What" is significant because "reflection in and of itself is not enough: it must always be linked with how the world can be changed" (Brookfield, 1995, p. 217).

Sample reflection guide questions for leadership development experiences including skills workshops, guest speakers, and simulations.

- • What?
  - o Describe the session. Who presented and what was the topic?
  - o What were you hoping to learn through your participation?
- • So What?
  - o Did you get valuable information from the session?
    - * What lessons did you take away?
    - * How did you feel during the session?
    - * Did you feel challenged? How?
  - o Connect the information to something in your own life.
    - * Share a story about something that has happened to you (or that you observed someone else experience) that connects to the topic.
- • Now What?
  - o The most enlightening thing I took away from this session was...
  - o This session will assist me in developing my full leadership potential because…
  - o What is one thing you plan on taking from this session and putting into action?
  - o Concluding thoughts—include anything you would like to add.

Sample reflection guide questions for campus involvement.

- • What?
  - o Why did you join this group and what were your goals for being involved?
  - o In your own words, what is the mission of the group?
- • So What?
  - o What was your unique contribution to the mission?
    - * Give a brief overview of your role within the group.
    - * How did you personally contribute to achieving the mission?
    - * What do you like the most about being a part of this group? The least?
  - o Share a story.
    - * Share a story about something that happened to you or that you observed that you would consider a success in fulfilling the mission of the group.
- • Now What?
  - o After your experience how will you continue your leadership development?
  - o How do you see yourself having a positive impact in your campus community in the future?

Sample reflection guide questions for community engagement experiences.

- • What?
  - o Name of the service organization and length of your service?
  - o What was the community need being met through this service experience?
- • So What?
  - o How did your service contribute to the goals of the organization?
  - o What skills did you develop to assist in meeting the service organization's goals?
  - o What were the best things you learned / did during your service?
  - o What challenges did you have to meet during your service and how did you meet them?
  - o What did you learn about your value to your community?
- • Now What?
  - o Did your service experience change anything in you?
  - o Will you continue to serve the community after this experience? How?
  - o Concluding thoughts—include anything you would like to add.

Debriefing Questions:

If possible, educators should meet with participants individually to discuss the final portfolio and debrief using the sample questions below as a starting point. Debriefing the program (or course) and portfolio experience can prompt additional reflection and reveal transformational moments. Alternatively, if participants are part of a cohort or class they may be paired to debrief using these questions.

- At this point in your leadership journey, what is your personal leadership philosophy in your own words?
- Why did you decide to include these specific reflections in your portfolio?
- Looking back on your program (or course) journey, can you share a highpoint learning experience? What made it a highpoint experience for you?

- Do you feel you have been challenged or changed through the program (or course) experience? How about through the process of creating your leadership portfolio? How so?

References:
Borton, T. (1970). *Reach, touch and teach*. New York, NY: McGraw-Hill Paperbacks.
Brookfield, S. D. (1995). *Becoming a critically reflective teacher*. San Francisco, CA: Jossey-Bass.
Hiemstra, R. (2001). Uses and benefits of journal writing. *New Directions for Adult and Continuing Education, 2001*(90), 19–26. doi:10.1002/ace.17

About the Editors and Contributors

Danielle Morgan Acosta supports student leadership, governance, advocacy, and community development at Florida State University and is an active member of ACPA, College Student Educators International. Danielle, who wrote her dissertation on the college student leadership experiences of female undergraduate students who experienced divorce in childhood, has a passion for student learning and development, training and facilitation, and advising students and organizations.

Jennifer Batchelder is a doctoral research assistant for the Leadership Learning Research Center at Florida State University where she serves as an instructor for the undergraduate leadership certificate program and contributes to research on leadership programs across the United States and internationally. She has served as a passionate leadership educator in practitioner roles on Semester at Sea, at Austin College, and at St. Mary's University.

Tamara Bauer is an instructor at the Staley School of Leadership Studies, Kansas State University. She teaches several leadership studies classes ranging from 20 to 165 students and uses experiential learning opportunities, including service-learning, with her students to actively apply leadership concepts to their lives. Tamara's experience focuses on creating asset-based processes to learn about social challenges and apply leadership concepts throughout the process.

Cameron C. Beatty is an assistant professor at Florida State University in the undergraduate leadership studies program and the higher education graduate program. Cameron's research and teaching is rooted in liberatory pedagogy and other critical perspectives when exploring leadership education for undergraduate students.

Break Away was established in 1991 and is a national nonprofit that supports thoughtful and ethical community-based learning through training, assisting, and connecting campuses and communities. They work to create a society of active citizens—people who make community a priority in their values and life choices.

Ashley M. Brown is a doctoral student in higher education at Loyola University Chicago and serves as a research assistant in the School of Education. In previous professional roles, Ashley worked to integrate critical pedagogy into undergraduate curricular programs, including first-year seminar and intergroup dialogue courses.

Virginia L. Byrne, is a doctoral candidate in technology, learning and leadership at the University of Maryland, College Park's Department of Teaching and Learning, Policy, and Leadership. Virginia is an experienced leadership and education researcher and teacher, who specializes in how technology can be used for learning, community building, and positive social change.

Natasha H. Chapman is a lecturer for the Minor in Global Engineering Leadership in the A. James Clark School of Engineering at the University of Maryland, College Park. Natasha's scholarly interests include critical perspectives in leadership, leadership educator identity, and transforming learning.

Jessica Chung serves as the curriculum and instruction coordinator for the Undergraduate Leadership Minor at the University of Minnesota Twin Cities. Jessica has spent years studying and practicing leadership education and development pedagogies to better serve all students through continually refining course curriculum and instructor training.

Ashley Curtis is a graduate student in the Higher Education program at Loyola University Chicago. Passionate about leadership, she has utilized critical reflection pedagogy in her work with students in the leadership minor at the University of Minnesota, and as a staff instructor at Loyola University Chicago.

Thinking to Transform: Facilitating Reflection in Leadership Learning (Companion Manual), pp. 97–100

June Dollar is an arts administrator who has worked in theater for the last 20 years as a coach, accompanist, and performer. June also serves as a leadership educator at Florida State University, teaching *LDR 2560: Leadership in Film*.

Grady K. Enlow serves as interim associate dean for community engagement and entrepreneurship for the College of Music at Florida State University. In this capacity, Grady also serves as Entrepreneur in Residence for the college, preparing music students for successful careers in music entrepreneurship whether their primary career is performance, research or pedagogy.

Chris Ruiz de Esparza is the director of diversity, inclusion, and leadership development at the University of Oregon's School of Law. Chris was introduced to improvisational theater over 25 years ago, performed with the Stanford Improvisors troupe for 4 years, and has since continued learning and teaching others about the applications of improv's key principles to life and leadership.

J. Michael Finnegan is an assistant professor at the Staley School of Leadership Studies, Kansas State University. Mike teaches undergraduate leadership courses at the Staley School of Leadership Studies and consults for local, state, and regional organizations focused on leadership education and development.

Jesse Ford is a doctoral student in the higher education program at Florida State University. His research examines the connections between leadership and multicultural pedagogy, particularly in the experiences of Black males.

Gabrielle Garrard is the assistant director for Student Leadership in the Center for Student Involvement at Santa Clara University. Gabrielle teaches a class on leadership and social change for first-year students in the Emerging Leaders Program and plans and implements leadership retreats and workshops.

Patrick M. Green is the (founding) executive director of the Center for Experiential Learning at Loyola University Chicago and a clinical instructor of experiential learning. Patrick received his doctorate in Educational Leadership and Organizational Change from Roosevelt University (Chicago, IL), and has published, presented, and consulted with institutions on topics of reflection, leadership, and service-learning/community engagement.

Kathy L. Guthrie is an associate professor in the higher education program, director of the Leadership Learning Research Center, and coordinator of the Undergraduate Certificate in Leadership Studies at Florida State University. Kathy's research focuses on leadership learning outcomes, environment of leadership and civic education, and technology in leadership education.

Tristen Hall is a second-year master's student in higher education and a graduate assistant in student diversity and multicultural affairs at Loyola University of Chicago. Tristen uses reflection practices as a framework for identity-based programming, retreats and intragroup dialogue in her current role.

Amber E. Hampton is an associate director for assessment and research at George Mason University and a doctoral candidate at Florida State University. Amber's development of the Leadership through Intergroup Dialogue (IGD) course, IGD facilitator training, faculty/staff workshop, and numerous dialogue-based programs at Florida State University has helped to advance the need for more dialogue across difference in higher education.

Courtney Holder is the coordinator for the Maryland LEAD Program and National Clearinghouse for Leadership Programs as well as an instructor in the Leadership Studies Program at the University of Maryland. Her professional and pedagogical focus centers on critical reflection and community-based learning as tools for socially responsible leadership and active citizenship.

Melissa Jarrell is the veteran retention specialist at Florida State University's Student Veteran Center. Melissa is a part time doctoral student in the higher education program at Florida State University.

Naliyah Kaya is an assistant professor of sociology at Montgomery College and facilitates TOTUS Spoken Word Experience at the University of Maryland. As a public sociologist, through artistic projects and assignments, she encourages students to engage in the sociological practice of reflexivity to better understand how external social factors influence and impact them and the ways in which they can utilize agency to address oppression.

Julie LeBlanc is a doctoral student in the higher education program at Florida State University. She works in the Leadership Learning Research Center as an instructor for the Undergraduate Certificate in Leadership Studies program. Julie has over 5 years of experience designing community engagement and leadership education programs and integrates reflective practices in curriculum for undergraduate students.

Daniel Marshall is a doctoral candidate in the higher education program at Florida State University and works as the assistant director of assessment at Virginia Military Institute. Daniel is a certified group exercise instructor who has led numerous stretching and relaxation focused classes, and his research interests focus on undergraduate student leadership development.

Nicholas F. Mazza is dean and the Patricia V. Vance professor emeritus in the College of Social Work at Florida State University. He also serves as the editor of *Journal of Poetry Therapy*, author of *Poetry Therapy: Theory and Practice* (2nd ed.), and editor of a four-volume series, *Expressive Therapies*.

Jane McPherson is an assistant professor and director of global engagement at the University of Georgia's School of Social Work. Jane is interested in reflection as a tool for promoting learning and self-awareness, and also as a necessary component of ethical practice for social workers.

Juan Cruz Mendizabal is the assistant director for leadership education and development at Appalachian State University. Juan previously facilitated reflective experiences as coordinator of the Spiritual Life Project at Florida State University and currently teaches leadership studies courses using contemplative inquiry, pedagogy, and practices.

Steven D. Mills holds a courtesy appointment with Florida State University's Center for Leadership and Social Change. Steve is a licensed psychotherapist and experienced leadership educator with a specialty in group socialization.

Carlo Morante is the leadership engagement coordinator for the Office of Residential Life at the University of California, Los Angeles (UCLA). Carlo currently coordinates a leadership certificate and workshop series for UCLA residents and oversees the planning and implementation of leadership initiatives relating to civic engagement and sustainability for residential life.

Dawn Morgan is the coordinator for student leadership programs at Auburn University where she is also pursuing her PhD in higher education administration. Her research interests include the self-efficacy of student leaders of color, student affairs practitioners engaging in equity and inclusion work, and the intersection of leadership and social justice education.

Laura Osteen serves as the director of Florida State University's Center for Leadership and Social Change. Laura envisions a world where everyone is enabled and empowered to create positive sustainable change in their community.

Julie E. Owen is an associate professor of leadership studies and coordinator of the leadership major and minor at the School of Integrative Studies, George Mason University. Julie frequently publishes on the value of critical reflection in leadership learning and is author of the forthcoming book, *Women's Leadership Development in College: Counter-Narratives & Critical Considerations* (Stylus).

Courtney "Pearson" Pearson is a doctoral student in the higher education program and assistant director for new student and family programs at Florida State University. Pearson is a member of the Digital Leadership Network and her research interests include students' engagement with their institution in online spaces such as Twitter.

Joi N. Phillips serves as an associate director at the Center for Leadership & Social Change at Florida State University. Dr. Phillips' work centers on education and civic participation with an emphasis on community engagement to understand how communities and institutions of higher education develop and sustain partnerships.

Darren Pierre is a clinical assistant professor in the higher education program at Loyola University Chicago where he teaches courses on student development, leadership in higher education, and oversees the undergraduate leadership minor. Darren has over 15 years of experience as a leadership educator serving in various roles within student activities and leadership programs.

Kerry L. Priest is an associate professor in the Staley School of Leadership Studies at Kansas State University. Kerry's teaching and scholarship integrates critical perspectives and engaged pedagogies that create the conditions for people to develop leadership through practice.

Stephanie L. Quirk is coordinator of student life responsible for overseeing cocurricular leadership development programs at College of DuPage. Since 2010, over 2,300 students have participated in program offerings with approximately 235 students engaging in reflective practice to complete written leadership portfolios.

María Rivera serves as strategic projects director for the leadership institute at Tecnológico de Monterrey. Maria is currently a doctoral candidate in Leadership Studies at Gonzaga University and has more than 10 years of experience in student development work in cocurricular and curricular programs.

Jane Rodriguez currently works as a student engagement coordinator for clubs and organizations at California State University, San Bernardino. She has worked with Latinx students in helping them discover their leadership identity through reflection and realization of their own cultural values and hopes to continue her work with this student population at her current institution.

Kimberly Sluis serves as the vice president for student affairs and strategic initiatives at North Central College in Illinois. Kimberly has over 15 years of experience working in student development and leadership learning.

Elizabeth Swiman is the director of campus sustainability at Florida State University. For the past 9 years she has taught leadership in sustainability, an introductory course connecting applicable leadership theories to the interconnected work of sustainability issues.

Brody C. Tate is the learning portfolio program manager in the Center for Experiential Learning at Loyola University Chicago. He uses his background in leadership theory in his work with faculty to develop and implement digital learning portfolios and present and host trainings on leadership.

Trisha Teig is a teaching assistant professor in leadership studies at the University of Denver. She is the faculty director for the Colorado Women's College Leadership Scholars Program. She focuses on research regarding gender and leadership, leadership development for college students, and leadership education professional training.

Maritza Torres is the assistant director for LEAD Scholars Academy at the University of Central Florida. Maritza teaches, advises, and facilitates leadership learning and scholarship to undergraduate and graduate students. Maritza's research centers on Latina undergraduate leader identity development, culturally relevant leadership learning and identity based leadership courses.

Rolando Torres is a senior college life coach at Florida State University's Centers for College Life Coaching.

Rolando has 5 years of experience coaching college students through a multitude of topics such as developing their visions, leader development, college success, and critical thinking. Rolando has also developed and taught 3 years of empowerment strategies for the 21st century leaders at Florida State University.

Jillian M. Volpe White serves as director of strategic planning and assessment in the office of the vice president for student affairs at Florida State University. Jillian has more than 10 years of experience in community engagement and leadership development.

Ana Maia Wales is the associate director of leadership engagement, adjunct faculty for the Leadership Studies Minor, and chair for the Student Affairs Strategic Planning and Assessment Team at The University of Tampa. She oversees the President's Leadership Fellows program and her research and professional experience is focused on global leadership, inclusion, and the holistic development of college students.

Sally R. Watkins is a teaching faculty in leadership studies at Florida State University. Sally enjoys reflecting on her 20 years of professional work in student affairs and time spent teaching at the K–12 level as an art educator to identify ways to incorporate her learning in those arenas into the leadership studies classroom.

Shane Whittington is a coordinator within the Center for Leadership and Social Change at Florida State University where he focuses on multiculturalism, social justice, and leadership. The activity he has shared is one of his more potent leadership tools for group growth in that it helps develop a team of leaders into a family. He is intentional about honoring external/visible leadership efforts while simultaneously addressing internal/invisible values.

Erica Wiborg is a graduate assistant in the Leadership Learning Research Center and a doctoral student in the higher education program at Florida State University. Erica teaches in the undergraduate certificate in leadership studies program and has served on multiple university committees to create spaces and programs for reflection, including the development and building of the Labyrinth at Florida State University.

FREE Test Taking Tips DVD Offer

To help us better serve you, we have developed a Test Taking Tips DVD that we would like to give you for FREE. **This DVD covers world-class test taking tips that you can use to be even more successful when you are taking your test.**

All that we ask is that you email us your feedback about your study guide. Please let us know what you thought about it – whether that is good, bad or indifferent.

To get your **FREE Test Taking Tips DVD**, email freedvd@studyguideteam.com with "FREE DVD" in the subject line and the following information in the body of the email:

    a. The title of your study guide.

    b. Your product rating on a scale of 1-5, with 5 being the highest rating.

    c. Your feedback about the study guide. What did you think of it?

    d. Your full name and shipping address to send your free DVD.

If you have any questions or concerns, please don't hesitate to contact us at freedvd@studyguideteam.com.

Thanks again!

AP Calculus AB
2021 & 2022

AP Calc Exam Review Book
with Practice Test Questions
[Includes Detailed Answer Explanations]

Joshua Rueda

Interested in buying more than 10 copies of our product? Contact us about bulk discounts:
bulkorders@studyguideteam.com

ISBN 13: 9781628459623
ISBN 10: 162845962X

Table of Contents

Quick Overview

As you draw closer to taking your exam, effective preparation becomes more and more important. Thankfully, you have this study guide to help you get ready. Use this guide to help keep your studying on track and refer to it often.

This study guide contains several key sections that will help you be successful on your exam. The guide contains tips for what you should do the night before and the day of the test. Also included are test-taking tips. Knowing the right information is not always enough. Many well-prepared test takers struggle with exams. These tips will help equip you to accurately read, assess, and answer test questions.

A large part of the guide is devoted to showing you what content to expect on the exam and to helping you better understand that content. In this guide are practice test questions so that you can see how well you have grasped the content. Then, answer explanations are provided so that you can understand why you missed certain questions.

Don't try to cram the night before you take your exam. This is not a wise strategy for a few reasons. First, your retention of the information will be low. Your time would be better used by reviewing information you already know rather than trying to learn a lot of new information. Second, you will likely become stressed as you try to gain a large amount of knowledge in a short amount of time. Third, you will be depriving yourself of sleep. So be sure to go to bed at a reasonable time the night before. Being well-rested helps you focus and remain calm.

Be sure to eat a substantial breakfast the morning of the exam. If you are taking the exam in the afternoon, be sure to have a good lunch as well. Being hungry is distracting and can make it difficult to focus. You have hopefully spent lots of time preparing for the exam. Don't let an empty stomach get in the way of success!

When travelling to the testing center, leave earlier than needed. That way, you have a buffer in case you experience any delays. This will help you remain calm and will keep you from missing your appointment time at the testing center.

Be sure to pace yourself during the exam. Don't try to rush through the exam. There is no need to risk performing poorly on the exam just so you can leave the testing center early. Allow yourself to use all of the allotted time if needed.

Remain positive while taking the exam even if you feel like you are performing poorly. Thinking about the content you should have mastered will not help you perform better on the exam.

Once the exam is complete, take some time to relax. Even if you feel that you need to take the exam again, you will be well served by some down time before you begin studying again. It's often easier to convince yourself to study if you know that it will come with a reward!

Test-Taking Strategies

1. Predicting the Answer

When you feel confident in your preparation for a multiple-choice test, try predicting the answer before reading the answer choices. This is especially useful on questions that test objective factual knowledge. By predicting the answer before reading the available choices, you eliminate the possibility that you will be distracted or led astray by an incorrect answer choice. You will feel more confident in your selection if you read the question, predict the answer, and then find your prediction among the answer choices. After using this strategy, be sure to still read all of the answer choices carefully and completely. If you feel unprepared, you should not attempt to predict the answers. This would be a waste of time and an opportunity for your mind to wander in the wrong direction.

2. Reading the Whole Question

Too often, test takers scan a multiple-choice question, recognize a few familiar words, and immediately jump to the answer choices. Test authors are aware of this common impatience, and they will sometimes prey upon it. For instance, a test author might subtly turn the question into a negative, or he or she might redirect the focus of the question right at the end. The only way to avoid falling into these traps is to read the entirety of the question carefully before reading the answer choices.

3. Looking for Wrong Answers

Long and complicated multiple-choice questions can be intimidating. One way to simplify a difficult multiple-choice question is to eliminate all of the answer choices that are clearly wrong. In most sets of answers, there will be at least one selection that can be dismissed right away. If the test is administered on paper, the test taker could draw a line through it to indicate that it may be ignored; otherwise, the test taker will have to perform this operation mentally or on scratch paper. In either case, once the obviously incorrect answers have been eliminated, the remaining choices may be considered. Sometimes identifying the clearly wrong answers will give the test taker some information about the correct answer. For instance, if one of the remaining answer choices is a direct opposite of one of the eliminated answer choices, it may well be the correct answer. The opposite of obviously wrong is obviously right! Of course, this is not always the case. Some answers are obviously incorrect simply because they are irrelevant to the question being asked. Still, identifying and eliminating some incorrect answer choices is a good way to simplify a multiple-choice question.

4. Don't Overanalyze

Anxious test takers often overanalyze questions. When you are nervous, your brain will often run wild, causing you to make associations and discover clues that don't actually exist. If you feel that this may be a problem for you, do whatever you can to slow down during the test. Try taking a deep breath or counting to ten. As you read and consider the question, restrict yourself to the particular words used by the author. Avoid thought tangents about what the author *really* meant, or what he or she was *trying* to say. The only things that matter on a multiple-choice test are the words that are actually in the question. You must avoid reading too much into a multiple-choice question, or supposing that the writer meant something other than what he or she wrote.

5. No Need for Panic

It is wise to learn as many strategies as possible before taking a multiple-choice test, but it is likely that you will come across a few questions for which you simply don't know the answer. In this situation, avoid panicking. Because most multiple-choice tests include dozens of questions, the relative value of a single wrong answer is small. As much as possible, you should compartmentalize each question on a multiple-choice test. In other words, you should not allow your feelings about one question to affect your success on the others. When you find a question that you either don't understand or don't know how to answer, just take a deep breath and do your best. Read the entire question slowly and carefully. Try rephrasing the question a couple of different ways. Then, read all of the answer choices carefully. After eliminating obviously wrong answers, make a selection and move on to the next question.

6. Confusing Answer Choices

When working on a difficult multiple-choice question, there may be a tendency to focus on the answer choices that are the easiest to understand. Many people, whether consciously or not, gravitate to the answer choices that require the least concentration, knowledge, and memory. This is a mistake. When you come across an answer choice that is confusing, you should give it extra attention. A question might be confusing because you do not know the subject matter to which it refers. If this is the case, don't eliminate the answer before you have affirmatively settled on another. When you come across an answer choice of this type, set it aside as you look at the remaining choices. If you can confidently assert that one of the other choices is correct, you can leave the confusing answer aside. Otherwise, you will need to take a moment to try to better understand the confusing answer choice. Rephrasing is one way to tease out the sense of a confusing answer choice.

7. Your First Instinct

Many people struggle with multiple-choice tests because they overthink the questions. If you have studied sufficiently for the test, you should be prepared to trust your first instinct once you have carefully and completely read the question and all of the answer choices. There is a great deal of research suggesting that the mind can come to the correct conclusion very quickly once it has obtained all of the relevant information. At times, it may seem to you as if your intuition is working faster even than your reasoning mind. This may in fact be true. The knowledge you obtain while studying may be retrieved from your subconscious before you have a chance to work out the associations that support it. Verify your instinct by working out the reasons that it should be trusted.

8. Key Words

Many test takers struggle with multiple-choice questions because they have poor reading comprehension skills. Quickly reading and understanding a multiple-choice question requires a mixture of skill and experience. To help with this, try jotting down a few key words and phrases on a piece of scrap paper. Doing this concentrates the process of reading and forces the mind to weigh the relative importance of the question's parts. In selecting words and phrases to write down, the test taker thinks about the question more deeply and carefully. This is especially true for multiple-choice questions that are preceded by a long prompt.

9. Subtle Negatives

One of the oldest tricks in the multiple-choice test writer's book is to subtly reverse the meaning of a question with a word like *not* or *except*. If you are not paying attention to each word in the question, you can easily be led astray by this trick. For instance, a common question format is, "Which of the following is...?" Obviously, if the question instead is, "Which of the following is not...?," then the answer will be quite different. Even worse, the test makers are aware of the potential for this mistake and will include one answer choice that would be correct if the question were not negated or reversed. A test taker who misses the reversal will find what he or she believes to be a correct answer and will be so confident that he or she will fail to reread the question and discover the original error. The only way to avoid this is to practice a wide variety of multiple-choice questions and to pay close attention to each and every word.

10. Reading Every Answer Choice

It may seem obvious, but you should always read every one of the answer choices! Too many test takers fall into the habit of scanning the question and assuming that they understand the question because they recognize a few key words. From there, they pick the first answer choice that answers the question they believe they have read. Test takers who read all of the answer choices might discover that one of the latter answer choices is actually *more* correct. Moreover, reading all of the answer choices can remind you of facts related to the question that can help you arrive at the correct answer. Sometimes, a misstatement or incorrect detail in one of the latter answer choices will trigger your memory of the subject and will enable you to find the right answer. Failing to read all of the answer choices is like not reading all of the items on a restaurant menu: you might miss out on the perfect choice.

11. Spot the Hedges

One of the keys to success on multiple-choice tests is paying close attention to every word. This is never truer than with words like almost, most, some, and sometimes. These words are called "hedges" because they indicate that a statement is not totally true or not true in every place and time. An absolute statement will contain no hedges, but in many subjects, the answers are not always straightforward or absolute. There are always exceptions to the rules in these subjects. For this reason, you should favor those multiple-choice questions that contain hedging language. The presence of qualifying words indicates that the author is taking special care with his or her words, which is certainly important when composing the right answer. After all, there are many ways to be wrong, but there is only one way to be right! For this reason, it is wise to avoid answers that are absolute when taking a multiple-choice test. An absolute answer is one that says things are either all one way or all another. They often include words like *every*, *always*, *best*, and *never*. If you are taking a multiple-choice test in a subject that doesn't lend itself to absolute answers, be on your guard if you see any of these words.

12. Long Answers

In many subject areas, the answers are not simple. As already mentioned, the right answer often requires hedges. Another common feature of the answers to a complex or subjective question are qualifying clauses, which are groups of words that subtly modify the meaning of the sentence. If the question or answer choice describes a rule to which there are exceptions or the subject matter is complicated, ambiguous, or confusing, the correct answer will require many words in order to be expressed clearly and accurately. In essence, you should not be deterred by answer choices that seem excessively long. Oftentimes, the author of the text will not be able to write the correct answer without

offering some qualifications and modifications. Your job is to read the answer choices thoroughly and completely and to select the one that most accurately and precisely answers the question.

13. Restating to Understand

Sometimes, a question on a multiple-choice test is difficult not because of what it asks but because of how it is written. If this is the case, restate the question or answer choice in different words. This process serves a couple of important purposes. First, it forces you to concentrate on the core of the question. In order to rephrase the question accurately, you have to understand it well. Rephrasing the question will concentrate your mind on the key words and ideas. Second, it will present the information to your mind in a fresh way. This process may trigger your memory and render some useful scrap of information picked up while studying.

14. True Statements

Sometimes an answer choice will be true in itself, but it does not answer the question. This is one of the main reasons why it is essential to read the question carefully and completely before proceeding to the answer choices. Too often, test takers skip ahead to the answer choices and look for true statements. Having found one of these, they are content to select it without reference to the question above. Obviously, this provides an easy way for test makers to play tricks. The savvy test taker will always read the entire question before turning to the answer choices. Then, having settled on a correct answer choice, he or she will refer to the original question and ensure that the selected answer is relevant. The mistake of choosing a correct-but-irrelevant answer choice is especially common on questions related to specific pieces of objective knowledge. A prepared test taker will have a wealth of factual knowledge at his or her disposal, and should not be careless in its application.

15. No Patterns

One of the more dangerous ideas that circulates about multiple-choice tests is that the correct answers tend to fall into patterns. These erroneous ideas range from a belief that B and C are the most common right answers, to the idea that an unprepared test-taker should answer "A-B-A-C-A-D-A-B-A." It cannot be emphasized enough that pattern-seeking of this type is exactly the WRONG way to approach a multiple-choice test. To begin with, it is highly unlikely that the test maker will plot the correct answers according to some predetermined pattern. The questions are scrambled and delivered in a random order. Furthermore, even if the test maker was following a pattern in the assignation of correct answers, there is no reason why the test taker would know which pattern he or she was using. Any attempt to discern a pattern in the answer choices is a waste of time and a distraction from the real work of taking the test. A test taker would be much better served by extra preparation before the test than by reliance on a pattern in the answers.

FREE DVD OFFER

Don't forget that doing well on your exam includes both understanding the test content and understanding how to use what you know to do well on the test. We offer a completely FREE Test Taking Tips DVD that covers world class test taking tips that you can use to be even more successful when you are taking your test.

All that we ask is that you email us your feedback about your study guide. To get your **FREE Test Taking Tips DVD**, email freedvd@studyguideteam.com with "FREE DVD" in the subject line and the following information in the body of the email:

- The title of your study guide.
- Your product rating on a scale of 1-5, with 5 being the highest rating.
- Your feedback about the study guide. What did you think of it?
- Your full name and shipping address to send your free DVD.

Introduction to the AP Calculus AB Exam

Function of the Test

The Advanced Placement (AP) Calculus AB Exam, created by the College Board, is an exam designed to offer college placement for high school students. The AP program allows students to earn college credit, advanced placement, or both, through the program's offering of the course and end-of-course exam. Sometimes universities may also look at AP scores to determine college admission. This guide gives an overview of the exam along with a condensed version of what might be taught in the AP Calculus AB course, and a practice test.

The AP program creates multiple versions of each AP exam to be administered within various U.S. geographic regions. With these exams, schools can offer late testing and discourage sharing questions across time zones. The AP exam is given in the U.S. nationwide; outside of Canada and the U.S., credits are only sometimes accepted in other countries. The College Board website has a list of universities outside of the U.S. that recognize AP for credit and admission.

Test Administration

On their website, the College Board provides a specific day that the AP Calculus AB exam is given. Because the exam is a culminating exam for a year-long course, the date is usually in mid-May. Coordinators should notify students when and where to report.

Students may take the exam again if they are not happy with their results. However, since the exam is given one day per year, students must wait until the following year to retake the exam. Both scores will be reported unless the student cancels or withholds one of the scores.

A wide range of accommodations are available to students who live with disabilities. Students will work with their school to request accommodations. If students or parents do not request accommodations through their school, disabilities must be appropriately documented, and accommodations requested in advance via the College Board website.

Test Format

The AP Calculus AB exam is three hours and fifteen minutes long and contains a multiple-choice section and a free-response section. The multiple-choice section contains 45 questions and lasts one hour and forty-five minutes. It comprises 50% of the test taker's score. Part A makes up 33.3% of the total exam score; graphing calculators are not permitted on this section. Part B requires the use of the graphing calculator on some questions and contributes 16.7% of the total score.

The free-response section comprises the other 50% of the test taker's score. It contains six questions and lasts ninety minutes. Part A contains two problems. Graphing calculators are used for this section, and it comprises 16.7% of the total score. Part B contains four questions. Graphing calculators are not permitted, and it comprises 33.3% of the total score.

Topics include limits and continuity, differentiation, and integration.

Scoring

Scoring on the AP exam is similar to that of a college course. The table below shows an outline of scores and what they mean:

Score	Recommendation	College Grade
5	Extremely well qualified	A
4	Well qualified	A-, B+,B
3	Qualified	B-,C+,C
2	Possibly qualified	n/a
1	No recommendation	n/a

While multiple-choice questions are graded via machine, the short-answer and free-response questions are graded by AP Readers. Scores on the free-response section are weighted and combined with the scores from the multiple-choice questions. The raw score from these two sections is converted into a 1–5 scale, as explained in the table above.

In 2019, 300,659 students took the AP Calculus AB exam worldwide. In this cohort of test takers, 19.1% earned a 5, 18.7% earned a 4, 20.6% earned a 3, 23.3% earned a 2, and 18.3% of test takers earned a 1. The mean score was 2.97, and 58.4% of test takers achieved a 3 or higher.

Colleges are responsible for setting their own criteria for placement and admissions, so check with specific universities to assess their criteria concerning the AP exam.

Unit 1: Limits and Continuity

Introducing Calculus: Can Change Occur at an Instant?

Limits of Functions Model Dynamic Change

The **limit** of a function can be described as the output that is approached as the input approaches a certain value. Written in function notation, the limit of $f(x)$ as x approaches a is:

$$\lim_{x \to a} f(x) = B$$

As x draws near to some value a, represented by $x \to a$, then $f(x)$ approaches some number B. In the graph of the function $f(x) = \frac{x+2}{x+2}$, the line is continuous except where $x = -2$. Because $x = -2$ yields an undefined output and a hole in the graph, the function does not exist at this value. The limit, however, does exist. As the value $x = -2$ is approached from the left side, the output is getting very close to 1. From the right side, as the x-value approaches -2, the output gets close to 1 also. Because the function value from both sides approaches 1, then:

$$\lim_{x \to -2} \frac{x+2}{x+2} = 1$$

Limits of functions can be used to model and understand dynamic change.

Instances Where A Limit of a Function Does Not Exist

For the limit of a function to exist, it must approach the same value from the left and right side of a given value for the domain. The limit does not exist for $\lim_{x \to 4} \left(\frac{x-4}{x^2-8x+16} \right)$ for the domain $x = 4$. The expression can be simplified to $\frac{x-4}{(x-4)(x-4)}$, where the two binomials on top and bottom can cancel and leave the expression $\frac{1}{(x-4)}$. When $x = 4$, the function does not exist because it approaches infinity. When the limit is not equal to a finite value, then the limit does not exist.

Another example where the limit does not exist is the function $\lim_{x \to 0} \sqrt{x}$. The domain for this function is defined as all numbers greater than or equal to zero. For the limit to exist at a given value in the domain, the limit must converge to the same y-value. Because the domain for this function does not include values less than zero, the limit cannot exist. There are no values less than zero that are found in this function.

One other example of when limits do not exist is when the function oscillates near a given x-value. For the function $f(x) = \sin\frac{1}{x}$, the limit does not exist when x is approaching zero. When looking at the

range when x approaches zero, the values are oscillating between -1 and 1. A picture of this graph may help explain the oscillating range. The following picture is an example of this type of function.

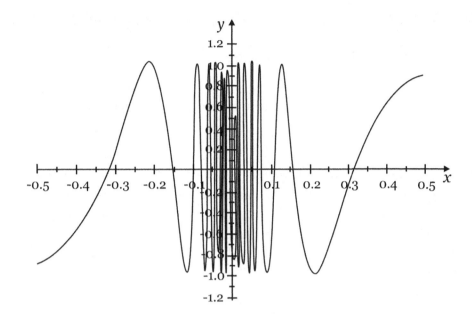

Defining Instantaneous Rate of Change

Given a function $f(x)$, its average rate of change with respect to x over the interval $[a, b]$ is equal to:

$$\frac{\Delta y}{\Delta x} = \frac{f(b) - f(a)}{b - a} = \frac{f(a + h) - f(a)}{h}, h \neq 0$$

This expression is the same as calculating the slope of the line through the points $(a, f(a))$ and $(b, f(b))$, which is referred to as the **secant line**. Therefore, the average rate of change of the function $f(x)$ from $x = a$ to $x = b$ is equal to the slope of the secant line connecting those two points. If the secant line is calculated over smaller and smaller intervals that start at $x = a$, the average rate of change calculations approach the instantaneous rate of change of the function $f(x)$ at $x = a$. In this case, smaller and smaller values of h would be used, which is the same as taking the limit as $h \to 0$. Therefore, the instantaneous rate of change is equal to the limit of the average rate of change as $h \to 0$, or:

$$\lim_{h \to 0} \frac{f(a + h) - f(a)}{h}$$

Defining Limits and Using Limit Notation

Representing Limits Analytically

The function $f(x)$ is defined on an open interval that includes c, however, it does not necessarily have to be defined at c. Therefore, the limit does not actually depend on the function definition at c. The function's behavior near the point is what is important. For example, $f(c)$ might be equal to 2, but the limit of the function at c could be a value other than 2. For instance, $f(c)$ could be equal to 3. $f(x)$

approaches arbitrarily close to 2 as x approaches c. Therefore, the limit notation in this example would be $\lim_{x \to c} f(x) = 2$. Note that this notation would be different than the function notation, which states $f(x) = 3$.

The formal definition of a limit states the same idea in more exact mathematical terms. Let the function $f(x)$ be defined on an open interval containing c, except possibly at c itself. $f(x)$ approaches the limit R as x approaches c, which gives the notation:

$$\lim_{x \to c} f(x) = R$$

This limit exists if for every value $\varepsilon > 0$, there exists a corresponding value $\delta > 0$ such that for all x,

$$0 < |x - c| < \delta$$

implying

$$|f(x) - R| < \varepsilon$$

In other words, the closer that x gets to c, the closer $f(x)$ gets to R.

For instance, the formal definition can be used to show that:

$$\lim_{x \to 1} 2x + 2 = 4.$$

In this scenario,

$$c = 1, f(x) = 2x + 2$$

and $R = 4$. For any $\varepsilon > 0$, a $\delta > 0$ must be found such that if

$$0 < |x - 1| < \delta$$

then

$$|f(x) - 4| < \varepsilon$$

Therefore, the following must be true:

$$|2x + 2 - 4| = |2x - 2| = 2|x - 1| < \varepsilon$$

Or

$$|x - 1| < \frac{\varepsilon}{2}. \delta = \frac{\varepsilon}{2}$$

is chosen to satisfy the limit definition.

Expressing Limits Graphically, Numerically, and Analytically

When determining a limit, it is important to note that the function is being observed close to the given value in which we are finding the limit, and not at the given value. For instance, for $\lim_{x \to a} f(x)$, the function's behavior will be observed close to a but not at a itself. This observation can be performed visually by graphing the function and observing the function's behavior from the right-hand and left-

hand sides of $x = a$. The observation can also be performed numerically by building a table and plugging values close to $x = a$ into the function on either side of a to see if a finite limit exists. Thirdly, this observation can be performed analytically by algebraic methods such as direct substitution to determine if a finite limit approach. If an analytical method is available, this approach gives the exact limit every time.

Estimating Limit Values from Graphs

One-Sided Limits

One special type of function, the **step function** $f(x) = [x]$, can be used to define right- and left-hand limits. The graph is shown below. The left-hand limit as x approaches 1 is $\lim_{x \to 1^-}[x]$. From the graph, as x approaches 1 from the left side, the function approaches 0. For the right-hand limit, the expression is $\lim_{x \to 1^+}[x]$. The value for this limit is one. Because the function does not have the same limit for the left and right side, the limit does not exist at $x = 1$. From that same reasoning, the limit does not exist for any integer for this function.

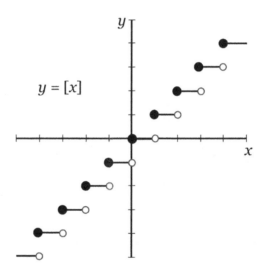

Using Graphical Information to Estimate Limits

The graph of a function will often make estimating a limit fairly simple. Given a graph like the one below:

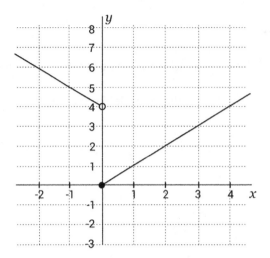

To evaluate the limit as x approaches 0 from the left side, the branch of the graph to the left of $x = 0$ has values that approach $y = 4$. The conclusion is made that the limit as x approaches 0 from the left is 4. Even though there is a whole in the graph at $x = 0$, the limit still exists because it approaches the value $y = 4$ from the left side.

In this same manner, to evaluate the limit as x approaches 0 from the right side, find the branch to the right of $x = 0$ and follow this branch as x gets closer and closer to where $x = 0$. It is seen that the value of the function (the y-value) is getting closer and closer to 0. This indicates that the limit as x approaches 0 from the right is 0.

Now, since the limit from the left of 0 is not equal to the limit from the right of 0, the two-sided limit, the limit as x approaches 0, does not exist. The two-sided limit exists when the limit from the left side and the limit from the right side approach the same point. Above, there is a jump in the graph, so the two-sided limit does not exist as x approaches 0.

The limit can be numerically evaluated using the function as well. Suppose that we are given an equation for the piecewise function graphed above.

$$-x + 4, x < 0$$

$$F(x) = x, x \geq 0$$

Because we are interested in the limit of the function as x approaches 0, we notice that the function changes at $x = 0$. This indicates that the limit from the left of 0 and the limit from the right of 0 must be calculated to see if they are equal. Noticing the domain of the function, you should decide to use the top equation, $-x + 4$, to evaluate the limit as x approaches 0 from the left. Doing this we find that:

$$\lim_{x \to 0-} f(x) = 4$$

Then to evaluate the limit as x approaches 0 from the right, we will use the bottom equation as this is where $x \geq 0$. We find that:

$$\lim_{x \to 0+} f(x) = 0$$

Now we see that just as before,

$$\lim_{x \to 0-} f(x) \neq \lim_{x \to 0+} f(x), \text{ so } \lim_{x \to 0} f(x) \text{ does not exist.}$$

For a polynomial function, like $y = x^2 + 3$, the graph looks like this:

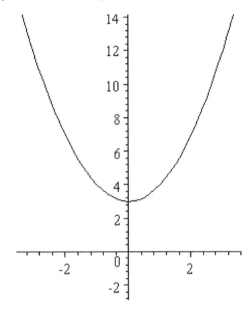

To find the two-sided limit, or the limit as x approaches 0, from this graph, choose the branch to the left of $x = 0$ and see that the graph approaches 3, then choose the branch to the right of $x = 0$ and see that the graph also approaches 3. Because the limit from the left and the right are equivalent, the limit as x approaches 0 for $f(x)$ is 3.

Now this limit as x approaches 0 for $f(x)$ can also be evaluated numerically by using the equation. Since this graph represents a polynomial function, $y = x^2 + 3$, it is seen that this function is continuous and that this is not a piecewise function. To evaluate $\lim_{x \to 0} f(x)$, use direct substitution to evaluate the equation at $x = 0$ to find that:

$$\lim_{x \to 0} f(x) = (0)^2 + 3 = 3$$

Issues with Graphical Representations of Functions

From the definition of limits, the limit of a function at a point in its domain can be found by looking at the behavior of the function by getting closer and closer to that given value. Therefore, limits can be found by looking at the graph of functions near the point of interest. Note that what happens to the

function exactly at the given point of interest is not of concern. What is of concern is what is happening close to that point. Consider the following graph of $f(x)$:

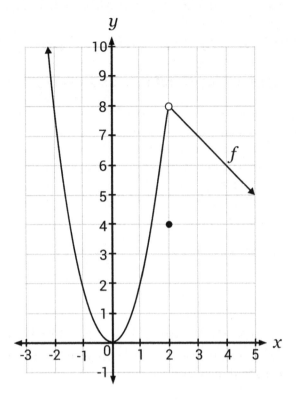

The limit of the function at 0 is equal to 0 and

$$\lim_{x \to 0} f(x) = 0$$

This is true because as 0 is approached along the x-axis from both sides, the function approaches 0 as well.

Now, consider what happens at $x = 2$. Note that there is a jump discontinuity that occurs at this point, and it is true that $f(2) = 4$. However, this value does not define the limit. As 2 approached along the x-axis from both sides, the function approaches 8. Therefore, it is true that:

$$\lim_{x \to 2} f(x) = 8$$

even though $f(2) = 8$. The limit of a function at a point does not have to equal the function value at that point.

Therefore, using graphs is not a preferred method of determining limits. If the actual formula for the function is known, analytical methods are the best method to obtain an exact result. Another method that tends to be more precise is using a table to find a limit.

Instances Where A Limit of a Function Does Not Exist

As mentioned previously, for the limit of a function to exist, it must approach the same value from the left and right side of a given value for the domain. Therefore, for some particular values of x, a limit may

not exist for a function. Recall that some of the instances where a limit might not exist are if the function is unbounded and/or oscillating near this value, if the limit from the left does not equal the limit from the right, or if the limit is not equal to a finite value, then the limit does not exist.

Estimating Limit Values from Tables

Using Numerical Information from Tables to Estimate Limits

In addition to graphs, tables can be used to estimate limits. If used correctly, tables can obtain a more exact estimation than by using graphs. Based on the definition of a limit, tables can be built that create ways to get closer and closer to the desired value in the domain of the function without using the exact value itself. A table used to determine a limit is built out of two columns. One column consists of values in the domain that get closer and closer to the limiting point, and the other column consists of the outputs of the function at those domain values. If the function values are approaching a real number, then that value is the estimation of the limit.

For instance, consider the function:

$$f(x) = \frac{x-1}{x^2-1}$$

The limit of this function as $x \to 1$, or in other words, $\lim_{x\to 1} \frac{x-1}{x^2-1}$, can be found by using a table. Notice the value of 1 cannot be directly plugged into the function because it is undefined at that point. In order to use the table, values will be chosen to plug into the function that is closer and closer to 1 on either side.

Here is the table:

x	$f(x)$
.99	0.502513
.999	0.50025
.9999	0.500025
1.0001	0.499975
1.001	0.49975
1.01	0.497512

Note that as the x-value approaches 1, the function values are approaching 0.5. Therefore, it is estimated that:

$$\lim_{x\to 1} \frac{x-1}{x^2-1} = \frac{1}{2}$$

n this example, the table approach results in finding the exact limit of the function at 1. Notice how close the chosen x-values were to 1. Plugging in values such as 1.5, 1.25, etc. would not have resulted in such precise results.

Determining Limits Using Algebraic Properties of Limits

Determining One-sided Limits Analytically or Graphically

There are many limit rules that allow limits to be calculated analytically. They are built on the following two ideas: The limit of a constant function at any x is the constant itself, and the limit of the identity function at $x = c$ is equal to the value of c. In other words, $\lim_{x \to c} a = a$ and $\lim_{x \to c} x = c$. Here is the list of the limit laws:

1. **Sum Rule**: The limit of the sum of two functions is equal to the sum of the individual limits:

$$\lim_{x \to c}(f(x) + g(x)) = \lim_{x \to c} f(x) + \lim_{x \to c} g(x)$$

2. **Difference Rule**: The limit of the difference of two functions is equal to the difference of the individual limits:

$$\lim_{x \to c}(f(x) - g(x)) = \lim_{x \to c} f(x) - \lim_{x \to c} g(x)$$

3. **Product Rule**: The limit of the product of two functions is equal to the product of the individual limits:

$$\lim_{x \to c}(f(x) \cdot g(x)) = \lim_{x \to c} f(x) \cdot \lim_{x \to c} g(x)$$

4. **Constant Multiple Rule**: The limit of a constant times a function is equal to the constant times the limit of that function:

$$\lim_{x \to c}(k \cdot g(x)) = k \cdot \lim_{x \to c} g(x)$$

5. **Quotient Rule**: The limit of the quotient of two functions is equal to the quotient of the individual limits. Note that the limit of the function in the denominator cannot be equal to 0:
$\lim_{x \to c}(f(x)/g(x)) = \lim_{x \to c} f(x)/\lim_{x \to c} g(x)$, provided $\lim_{x \to c} g(x) \neq 0$.

6. **Root Rule**: The limit of the nth root of a given function $f(x)$ is equivalent the nth root of the limit of $f(x)$:

For a positive integer n, $\lim_{x \to c}(f(x))^{1/n} = \left(\lim_{x \to c} f(x)\right)^{1/n}$. If n is an even integer, the limit is positive.

These limit rules limit polynomials to be evaluated using direct substitution. For instance, consider the polynomial function:

$$f(x) = 5x^2 + 4x + 1$$

Its limit at any x-value is found by directly plugging in that value. For instance:

$$\lim_{x \to 2} f(x) = 5(2)^2 + 4(2) + 1 = 29$$

All the limits that have been discussed so far have been defined on both sides of c, and the limit has been the same as x approaches c from either side. Therefore, these limits are referred to as **two-sided**.

If a two-sided limit does not exist, a **one-sided** limit might exist if a limit can be obtained from only one side. If a limit is reached from the right, a right-hand limit exists, which is written as:

$$\lim_{x \to c^+} f(x) = R$$

If a limit is reached from the left, a left-hand limit exists, and $\lim_{x \to c^-} f(x) = R$ is written.

Consider the following graph of the function $f(x)$. A two-sided limit does not exist at 3. However, it is true that $\lim_{x \to 3^+} f(x) = 3$ and $\lim_{x \to 3^-} f(x) = 2$.

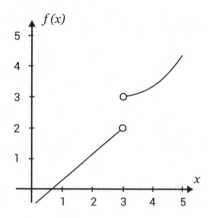

In order for a two-sided limit to exist, both the left-hand and right-hand limit must be equivalent.

Evaluating Limits of Sums, Differences, Products, Quotients, and Composite Functions

To evaluate the limits of sums, differences, products, and quotients, we can just split the terms to find the limit of each and then combine using the indicated operations. In other words, the **limit of a sum** is just the sum of the limits of each term. For example,

$$\lim_{x \to 2} x^2 - 7x + 14 = \lim_{x \to 2}(2)^2 - \lim_{x \to 2} 7(2) + \lim_{x \to 2} 14 = 4 - 14 + 14 = 4$$

This works the same for differences, products, and quotients, so the difference, product, or quotient of a limit is the limit of the difference, product, or quotient.

Given a limit of a quotient, say $\lim_{x \to -4} \frac{x^3 - 17}{x + 13}$, find the limit of the numerator and divide it by the limit of the denominator, like this:

$$\frac{\lim_{x \to -4} x^3 - \lim_{x \to -4} 17}{\lim_{x \to -4} x + \lim_{x \to -4} 13} = \frac{-64 - 17}{-4 + 13} = \frac{-81}{9} = -9$$

For composite functions, given by $f(g(x))$, it can be more difficult. Given $f(x) = \sin x$ and $g(x) = \frac{x}{2}$. Now to evaluate the limit of $f(g(x))$ as x approaches infinity, find the following: $\lim_{x \to \pi} \sin(\frac{x}{2})$.

By direct substitution it is seen that:

$$\lim_{x \to \pi} sin(\frac{x}{2}) = sin\left(\frac{\pi}{2}\right) = 1$$

Notice now that this same result would be achieved if it were evaluated using the following equations:

$$\lim_{x \to \pi} sin(\frac{x}{2}) = sin\left(\lim_{x \to}(\frac{x}{2})\right) = sin\left(\frac{\pi}{2}\right) = 1$$

It follows that $\lim_{x \to a} f\big(g(x)\big) = f\lim_{x \to a}\big(g(x)\big) = f(g(a))$, as long as $g(a)$ is in the domain of f.

Determining Limits Using Algebraic Manipulation

Rearranging Expressions into Equivalent Forms Before Evaluating Limits

When finding the limit of a rational function like this,

$$\lim_{x \to 3} \frac{x^2 - 9}{x - 3}$$

begin by using direction substitution to get:

$$\lim_{x \to 3} \frac{(3)^2 - 9}{(3) - 3} = \frac{0}{0}$$

This is called an **indeterminate form of a limit** because the limit cannot be determined without doing more to the function algebraically. One method of manipulation is to factor the numerator and denominator, if possible, and then simplify the function. In this particular case we can factor and simplify to get

$$\lim_{x \to 3} \frac{(x-3)(x+3)}{x-3} = \lim_{x \to 3}(x + 3)$$

then by direct substitution we see that:

$$\lim_{x \to 3}(x + 3) = 6$$

In some cases, other algebraic methods of manipulation are necessary to evaluate limits of an indeterminate form. Given the example,

$$\lim_{x \to 25} \frac{\sqrt{x} - 5}{x - 25}$$

by substitution we find

$$\lim_{x \to 25} \frac{\sqrt{25} - 5}{25 - 25} = \frac{0}{0}$$

the indeterminate form. Multiplying the numerator and denominator of the function by the conjugate of the numerator, we find:

$$\lim_{x \to 25} \frac{(\sqrt{x} - 5)(\sqrt{x} + 5)}{(x - 25)(\sqrt{x} + 5)} = \lim_{x \to 25} \frac{(x - 25)}{(x - 25)(\sqrt{x} + 5)}$$

$$\lim_{x \to 25} \frac{1}{(\sqrt{x} + 5)} = \lim_{x \to 25} \frac{1}{(\sqrt{25} + 5)} = \frac{1}{10}$$

Determining Limits Using the Squeeze Theorem

Using the Squeeze Theorem

An important theorem that helps to determine limits in calculus is the squeeze theorem, which is also known as the sandwich theorem. Suppose that there exist three functions that satisfy the following inequality in some open interval containing c, except possibly at the value of c itself:

$$g(x) \le f(x) \le h(x)$$

Suppose also that the two functions $g(x)$ and $h(x)$ have the same limit, and:

$$\lim_{x \to c} g(x) = \lim_{x \to c} h(x) = R$$

Then, the limit of the inside function is "squeezed" because according to the squeeze theorem, $\lim_{x \to c} f(x) = R$ as well.

The squeeze theorem can be used to determine the limit of the function $f(x)$ at $x = 0$ that exists within the following inequality:

$$1 - \frac{x^3}{3} \le f(x) \le 1 + \frac{x^3}{3}$$

Consider an open interval around the point $x = 0$. By direct substitution, the limits of both functions on the outer sides of the inequality are equal to 1. Therefore, by the squeeze theorem:

$$\lim_{x \to 0} f(x) = 1$$

In other words, any function that lies between the functions:

$$g(x) = 1 - \frac{x^3}{3}$$

and

$$h(x) = 1 + \frac{x^3}{3}$$

on an open interval around $x = 0$ has a limit equal to 1 as $x \to 0$.

A famous limit that the squeeze theorem is used to prove is the following:

$$\lim_{\theta \to 0} \frac{\sin \theta}{\theta} = 1$$

where θ is measured in radians. The following inequality is built in the proof:

$$\cos \theta < \frac{\sin \theta}{\theta} < 1$$

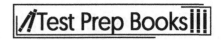

Both of the functions $g(\theta) = \cos\theta$ and $h(\theta) = 1$ have a limit of 1 as $\theta \to 0$. Therefore, by the squeeze theorem:

$$\lim_{\theta \to 0} \frac{\sin\theta}{\theta} = 1$$

Exploring Types of Discontinuities

Types of Discontinuities

Discontinuities are those places where the functions skip from one place to another on the graph. They are breaks in the line. These jumps or steps in the graph come from functions where the limit when approaching from different sides of an x-value has a range of two different y-values. For example, the function:

$$f(x) = \begin{cases} \sqrt{x}, & 0 \le x < 9 \\ 6, & x = 9 \\ x - 2, & x > 9 \end{cases}$$

has a discontinuity at $x = 9$. The left-hand limit approaching 9 is 3. The value of the function at $x = 9$ is 6. The right-hand limit as x approaches 9 is 7. Because the graph is a continuous line until 9, then jumps to a range of 6, then jumps up to 7, the function is discontinuous at the input value of nine. This type of discontinuity is a **jump discontinuity**.

A **discontinuity due to a vertical asymptote** can be seen in the function:

$$f(x) = \frac{x^2 + x - 12}{x - 3}$$

The range of this function is continuous for all values except $x = 3$. The function value for $f(3)$ does not exist because when it is plugged into the function, it results in a zero in the denominator. Since zero cannot be in the denominator of the fraction, there is a vertical asymptote. The limit when approaching $x = 3$ from the left is positive infinity, while the limit when approaching from the right is negative infinity.

A **removable discontinuity** occurs when there is a hole in the graph. This occurs in the following function:

$$f(x) = \begin{cases} x + 4, & x \ne 3 \\ 5, & x = 3 \end{cases}$$

This function is a continuous line at all points in the domain except for $x = 3$. When the domain gets to 3, the point is removed from the continuous line and put at the point $(3, 5)$. This is called a removable discontinuity because it occurs as a hole in the graph where one point is removed and replaced at another place on the graph.

Defining Continuity at a Point

Continuity

A function is **continuous at a point** if the point is neither a hole nor jump discontinuity. The **limit definition of continuity** states that a function is continuous at a point if its limit at that point is equal to the function value at that point. A function is **differentiable** at a point if a vertical tangent, a cusp, or corner does not exist at that point. Basically, the function must have a nonvertical tangent at the point, and the function must also be continuous at the point.

To find if a function is continuous, the definition consists of three steps. These three steps include finding $f(a)$, finding $\lim_{x \to a} f(x)$, and finding:

$$\lim_{x \to a} f(x) = f(a)$$

If the limit of a function equals the function value at that point, then the function is continuous at $x = a$.

For example, the function $f(x) = \frac{1}{x}$ is continuous everywhere except $x = 0$. The function $f(0) = \frac{1}{0}$ is undefined; therefore, the function is discontinuous at 0. Second, to determine if the function $f(x) = \frac{1}{x-1}$ is continuous at 2, its function value must equal its limit at 2. First,

$$f(2) = \frac{1}{2-1} = 1$$

Then the limit can be found by direct substitution:

$$\lim_{x \to 2} \frac{1}{x-1} = 1$$

Because these two values are equal, then the function is continuous at:

$$x = 2$$

Differentiability and continuity are related in that if the derivative can be found at $x = c$, then the function is continuous at $x = c$. If the slope of the tangent line can be found at a certain point, then there is no hole or jump in the graph at that point. Some functions, however, can be continuous while not differentiable at a given point. An example is the graph of the function $f(x) = |x|$. At the origin, the derivative does not exist, but the function is still continuous. Points where a function is discontinuous are where a vertical tangent exists and where there is a cusp or corner at a given x-value.

Confirming Continuity over an Interval

Determining If a Function is Continuous on an Interval

Just as a function is continuous at a point if the point is neither a hole nor jump discontinuity, a function is continuous over a given interval if there are no holes or jumps within that interval. The same steps in determining continuity as just described apply when moving beyond just investigating a point into examining an interval of a function.

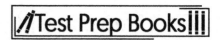

Functions that are Continuous at All Points in Their Domains

Polynomial functions are those functions where the exponent on the independent variable, or x, is always positive. Because the power of x is positive, the function is continuous for all x-values, or the domain. For example, the function $y = 3x - 4$ is a **linear function** because the power of x is 1 and the graph is a straight line that is continuous. As x approaches 0, the y-value approaches -4, both from the left and the right on the graph. Another example is the function:

$$y = x^3 - 2x + 3$$

This is a **cubic function** where the domain is continuous for all points. Any input value that is chosen within the given domain for x will yield an output value, or y where the values converge when approaching from the left and right of any number.

Rational functions are those functions where the power of x is at least 1 in the denominator. An example of this is the function $y = \frac{1}{x}$. The graph of this function follows.

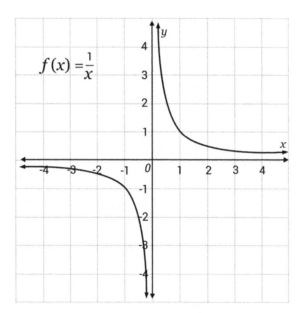

The domain for this function is all real numbers except $x = 0$. For any value of x other than 0, there is a corresponding y-value. The reason that $x = 0$ is not in the domain is because there is an asymptote there. The value does not exist on this graph.

Power functions are those monomials where the independent variable, x, is raised to a constant power. Examples of power functions are $y = \frac{4}{3}x^3$ and $y = \sqrt[4]{x}$.

A power function can take the form $y = kx^p$. When the value of p is positive, the domain for the function is all real numbers. For every value in the domain, the function is continuous over all real numbers. For some power functions, the domain is not continuous over all real numbers; there are certain values of the domain that do not exist. Take for example the following function: $y = 3x^{-2}$. This

function can be rewritten as $y = \frac{3}{x^2}$. The input, or domain, can be any value that is not equal to zero. Since this is a fraction you cannot divide by zero; therefore, this function is not continuous when $x = 0$.

Exponential functions are those where the independent variable is in the exponent. For example, the function $y = 3^x$ is an exponential function because the input values are those that replace the exponent. For this exponential function, the domain is all real numbers, but the range contains only values that are greater than or equal to zero. The function is continuous for all values in the domain because there are no values for the independent variable that will not return a corresponding output for the dependent variable. The following table shows possible input and output values for the function $y = 3^x$. For each value in the domain, or x, there is a corresponding y-value, with no discontinuity between values.

X	Y
-3	$\frac{1}{27}$
-1	$\frac{1}{3}$
0	1
1	3
3	27

A **logarithmic function** can be stated in the form $y = \log_b x$, where $b > 0$ and $b \neq 1$. A logarithmic function is the inverse of an exponential function. An example of this can be seen through a graph of these two types. The following graph shows two general functions, where one is exponential, and one is logarithmic. As with exponential functions, log functions are continuous for all values inside the domain. The domain of log functions is limited, while the range is all real numbers. For all values of x greater

than zero, there is a corresponding *y*-value, without steps or jumps in the graph. The line is continuous; therefore, the range is continuous for all values in the domain.

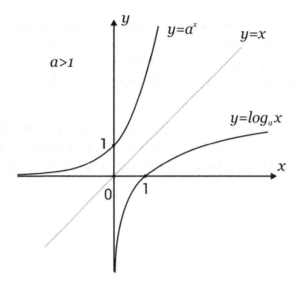

Trigonometric functions are those that use the trig ratios and put them into equations using an input of *x* and an output of *y*. The following is a graph of the function $y = \cos(x)$. As seen in the graph, for every value of *x* that exists, there is a *y*-value that exists with values in a continuous line. For the following graph, the domain is all real numbers and the range is any value from −1 to 1. There are no skips or jumps in values for the functions of trigonometric ratios. As the value of *x* approaches 2π, the range is approaching 1.

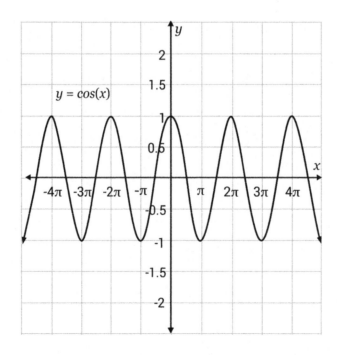

Removing Discontinuities

Removing Discontinuity by Defining or Redefining Values of the Function

If a function has a discontinuity at a point, and if the discontinuity is removed, the function is said to be continuous at that point. A function is continuous at a point if its two-sided limit is equal to its function value. A function is continuous over its entire domain if it is continuous at every point within its domain. Therefore, when sketching a graph that is continuous over its entire domain, one would never need to pick up their pencil.

For example, the following graph shows a jump discontinuity at x_0. Note that the two-sided limit does not equal the function value at that point. In order to remove the discontinuity, the hole at x_0 would need to be filled in. This process would create a continuous graph, and the function value would equal the two-sided limit at x_0.

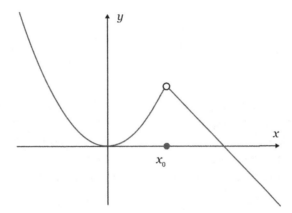

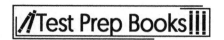

Continuous Piecewise-Defined Functions

The following graph shows a continuous piecewise defined function:

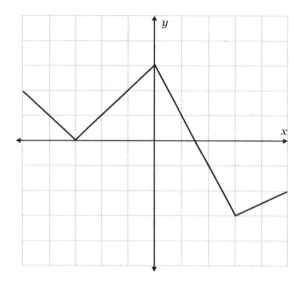

Note that every point within the domain of the function has a two-sided limit that exists. For instance, at $x = 0$, even though a different function is defined over the interval [-3, 0] than the one defined over the interval [0, 4], the limit at 0 exists and is equal to the function value at that point. Therefore, this piecewise defined function is continuous. At each point where the function changes, the value on one side of the boundary is equal to the value on the other side of the boundary.

Connecting Infinite Limits and Vertical Asymptotes

Infinite Limits

Sometimes a function approaches infinity as it draws near to a certain x-value. For example, the following graph shows the function:

$$f(x) = \frac{2x}{x - 3}$$

There is an **asymptote** at $x = 3$. The limit as x approaches 3:

$$\lim_{x \to 3} \frac{2x}{x - 3}$$

does not exist. The right- and left-hand side limits at 3 do not approach the same output value. One approaches positive infinity, and the other approaches negative infinity. **Infinite limits** do not satisfy the definition of a limit.

The limit of the function as x approaches a number must be equal to a finite value.

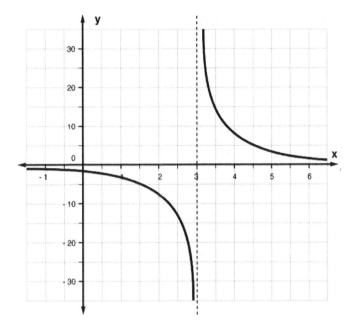

Horizontal asymptotes can be found using limits. Horizontal asymptotes are limits as x approaches either ∞ or $-\infty$. For example, to find;

$$\lim_{x \to \infty} \frac{2x}{x - 3}$$

the graph can be used to see the value of the function as x grows larger and larger. For this example, the limit is 2, so it has a horizontal asymptote of $y = 2$. In considering,

$$\lim_{x \to -\infty} \frac{2x}{x - 3} = 2$$

the limits can also be seen on a graphing calculator by plotting the equation $y = \frac{2x}{x-3}$. Then the table can be brought up. By scrolling up and down, the limit can be found as x approaches any value.

In the following equation, the constant and multiplication properties can be used together, and the problem can be rewritten:

$$\lim_{x \to 2} 4x^2 - 3x + 8$$

$$4\lim_{x \to 2} x^2 - \lim_{x \to 2} 3x + \lim_{x \to 2} 8$$

Because this is a continuous function, direct substitution can be used. The value of 2 is substituted in for x and evaluated as $4(2^2) - 3(2) + 8$, which yields a limit of 18. These properties allow functions to be rewritten so that limits can be calculated.

Using Limits to Explain Asymptotic Behavior

The graph of a function has a horizontal asymptote at $y = L$ when the limit as x approaches positive infinity or negative infinity is L. This occurs in a function like:

$$f(x) = \frac{x^2 - 5}{2x^2 + 3}$$

Evaluating the limit of f as x approaching infinity, divide each term by x^2 because this is the highest power of x to get:

$$f(x) = \lim_{x \to \infty} \frac{\frac{x^2}{x^2} - \frac{5}{x^2}}{\frac{2x^2}{x^2} + \frac{3}{x^2}} = \lim_{x \to \infty} \frac{1 - \frac{5}{x^2}}{2 + \frac{3}{x^2}} = \frac{1}{2}$$

so the limit is found to be $\frac{1}{2}$ and the graph of f has a horizontal asymptote at $y = \frac{1}{2}$. With a horizontal asymptote at $y = \frac{1}{2}$, it is seen that moving to the right, the graph will approach a y-value of $\frac{1}{2}$. Likewise, the limit as x approaches negative infinity will be the same, $\frac{1}{2}$. On the graph the function value approaches $\frac{1}{2}$ as the x values move to the left toward negative infinity.

Consider the following function:

$$f(x) = \frac{x + 7}{x^2 - 5}$$

To discover any horizontal asymptotes, evaluate the limit as x approaches positive and negative infinity. Noticing that this is a rational function with the highest power of x being x^2, divide every term by x^2 to get:

$$f(x) = \lim_{x \to \infty} \frac{\frac{x}{x^2} + \frac{7}{x^2}}{\frac{x^2}{x^2} - \frac{5}{x^2}} = \lim_{x \to \infty} \frac{\frac{1}{x} + \frac{7}{x^2}}{1 - \frac{5}{x^2}} = \frac{0}{1} = 0$$

It is found that there is a horizontal asymptote at $y = 0$, and as x approaches infinity, the function values are moving closer and closer to 0. The limit as x approaches negative infinity will be the same, so the graph also approaches $y = 0$ as x moves toward negative infinity.

Take the following function as a final example:

$$f(x) = \frac{x^3 - x + 2}{x^2 + x + 1}$$

Evaluating the limit as x approaches positive or negative infinity, we see that we should divide every term by x^3. Doing this as above, we find the limit:

$$\lim_{x \to \infty} \frac{1 - \frac{1}{x^2} + \frac{2}{x^3}}{\frac{1}{x} + \frac{1}{x^2} + \frac{1}{x^3}} = \frac{1}{0}$$

so the limit does not exist. This indicates that there is no horizontal asymptote for this function.

The three examples above fall into the following three categories:

- Rational functions where the degree of the numerator is equal to the degree of the denominator: In this case, the limit of the function is the ratio of the coefficients of the leading coefficients in the numerator and denominator. The horizontal asymptote will be $y = $ ratio of the coefficients.

- Rational functions where the degree of the numerator is one less than the degree of the denominator: In this case, the limit of the function is 0. The horizontal asymptote will be $y = 0$.

- Rational functions where the degree of the numerator is greater than the degree of the denominator: In this case, the limit of the function does not exist as x approaches infinity. For this example, there will be no horizontal asymptotes.

Connecting Limits at Infinity and Horizontal Asymptotes

Limits at Infinity

If a function approaches a real number as x approaches either positive or negative infinity, the function has a finite limit as $x \to \pm\infty$. If the function $f(x)$ has the limit R as x approaches infinity, the notation is:

$$\lim_{x \to \infty} f(x) = R$$

If the function $f(x)$ has the limit R as x approaches negative infinity, the notation:

$$\lim_{x \to -\infty} f(x) = R$$

Basically, in order to find a finite limit at infinity, the behavior of a function as x either gets very large or very small is observed. This process is known as determining the end behavior of a function, and it is the same as determining if a horizontal asymptote exists. A line $y = b$ is a horizontal asymptote of the function $f(x)$ if either:

$$\lim_{x \to \infty} f(x) = b$$

or

$$\lim_{x \to -\infty} f(x) = b$$

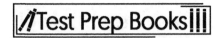

Here is the graph of a function with finite limits at both positive and negative infinity:

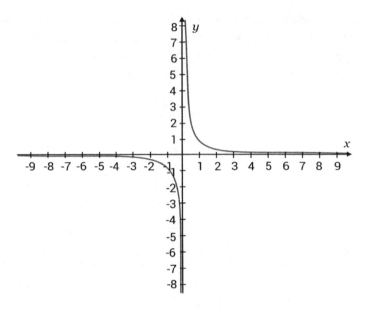

As x approaches both positive and negative infinity, the function approaches 0. Therefore, the line $y = 0$ is a horizontal asymptote on both sides of the graph, and $\lim_{x \to \infty} f(x) = 0$ and $\lim_{x \to -\infty} f(x) = 0$.

Limits at Infinity and End Behavior

A function can also have an infinite limit at infinity or negative infinity. In this case, the function would not approach a finite value and would blow up graphically. Therefore, $\lim_{x \to \infty} f(x) = \pm\infty$ or $\lim_{x \to -\infty} f(x) = \pm\infty$. Again, the end behavior of a function would be observed, and in this scenario, the function would grow without bound on at least one side of its domain. Here is a function whose graph has infinite limits at infinity:

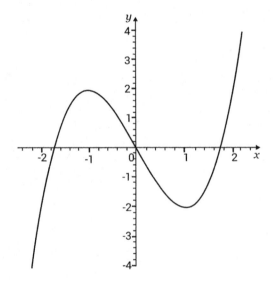

For this function, $\lim_{x \to \infty} f(x) = \infty$ and $\lim_{x \to -\infty} f(x) = -\infty$.

Using Limits to Compare the Relative Magnitudes of Functions

A **vertical asymptote** occurs when the magnitude of a function increases or decreases without bound as the input values approach a certain value of x from one or both sides. That is, if the limit as x approaches a number, a, from the left and/or right side is found to be positive or negative infinity, then there is a vertical asymptote at $x = a$. Take the following function,

$$f(x) = \frac{1}{x + 5}.$$

First, notice that at $x = -5$, the function is undefined because:

$$f(-5) = \frac{1}{0}$$

To see what happens to the graph as x approaches $x = -5$, investigate the limit as x approaches -5 from left and from the right. To do this, take a look at the table of values below and notice that at $x = -6$, moving closer to $x = -5$ from the left side, the function values are decreasing. This indicates that the limit as x approaches -5 from the left is negative infinity, so the graph will be decreasing on the left side of the vertical asymptote. Then on the right side of the graph, beginning at $x = -4$, move closer to $x = -5$ and see that the function values are increasing, so the limit as x approaches -5 from the right side is positive infinity. (Notice that the two-sided limit, $\lim_{x \to -5} f(x)$ does not exist because the one-sided limits are not equal.) Take a look at the graph below for a visual of what is indicated by our work.

x	$\dfrac{1}{(x + 5)}$
-6	-1
-5.7	-1.4285714
-5.5	-2
-5.3	-3.3333333
-5.3	-10
-5	undefined
-4.9	10
-4.6	2.5
-4.2	1.25
-4	1

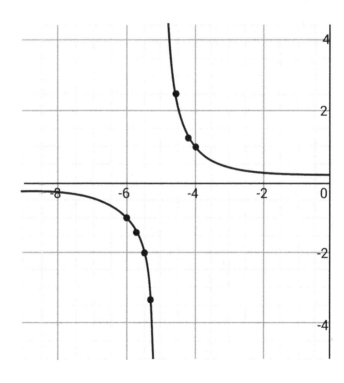

Working with the Intermediate Value Theorem (IVT)

Intermediate Value Theorem

If a function is continuous on a given interval over its domain, it has what is known as the **Intermediate Value Property**. Basically, a continuous function has to take on the values between two other values. Here is the actual theorem:

Given a function $y = f(x)$ that is continuous on the closed interval $[a, b]$, the function takes on every value between $f(a)$ and $f(b)$, the function evaluated at both endpoints. Therefore, if c is any value in the open interval (a, b), then the graph reaches the point $f(c)$ between $f(a)$ and $f(b)$. If the function is discontinuous at any x-value in between a and b, the theorem fails. Here is a diagram that represents the property:

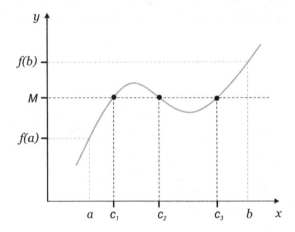

Note that the diagram shows three points, c_1, c_2, and c_3, which satisfy the theorem, and the function evaluated at all three points results in an output of M.

This property is useful to determine if functions have zeros or roots (points in which the graph crosses the x-axis). If a function is continuous over an interval $[a, b]$ and $f(a)$ and $f(b)$ are opposite in sign, then the function must cross the x-axis at a minimum of one point between a and b. Therefore, the function has at least one zero or root. An example of this is the function:

$$f(x) = -x^2 + x + 3$$

Because it is a polynomial, it is continuous over all real numbers. However, specifically, it is continuous over the interval $[-4, 0]$.

$$f(-4) = -17 \text{ and } f(0) = 3$$

Because these two values are opposite in sign, the graph of the function must cross the x-axis at least one time between $x = 0$ and $x = -4$.

Unit 2: Differentiation: Definition and Fundamental Properties

Defining Average and Instantaneous Rates of Change at a Point

Expressing the Average Rate of Change of a Function Over an Interval

The secant line to a graph of the function $f(x)$ on the interval $[a, b]$, where $a < b$, passes through the points $(a, f(a))$ and $(b, f(b))$. The rate of change for this interval is found by calculating the slope using the two given points. The slope of a line is how much the y-values change with respect to the corresponding x-values. For two given points, a straight line is drawn between them, called the **secant line**, and the slope is calculated based on the change in y divided by the change in x.

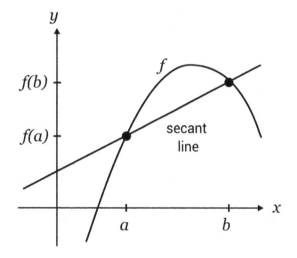

The slope of this secant line is found using the formula:

$$\text{Slope} = \frac{\Delta y}{\Delta x} = \frac{f(b) - f(a)}{b - a}$$

We call this quotient, $\frac{Difference\ in\ outputs}{Difference\ in\ inputs}$, the **difference quotient**.

The **average rate of change of a function**, $f(x)$, is equal to the difference quotient. It is called the average because it uses two points on a line that is curved, where rate of change is constantly changing. The average rate of change of the function, $f(x)$, on the interval $[a, b]$, where $a < b$, is given by:

$$\frac{f(b) - f(a)}{b - a}$$

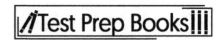

Expressing the Instantaneous Rate of Change of a Function at a Point

The **instantaneous rate of change of a function**, $f(x)$, at the point, $(c, f(c))$, in its domain can be found by evaluating the limit of the difference quotient as x approaches c, provided that limit exists. This is known as the **derivative** of the function at the point where $x = c$ and is denoted by $f'(c)$,

$$f'(c) = \lim_{x \to c} \frac{\Delta y}{\Delta x} = \lim_{x \to c} \frac{f(x) - f(c)}{x - c}$$

provided that limit exists.

For example: Let $f(x) = x^3$. Find the instantaneous rate of change of f at the point, $(2, 8)$. By using the definition of the derivative given above, the point $(2, 8)$ is used as the point $(c, f(c))$. The equation then becomes:

$$f'(2) = \lim_{x \to 2} \frac{f(x) - 8}{x - 2}$$

Given the equation $f(x) = x^3$, the derivative equation becomes:

$$f'(2) = \lim_{x \to 2} \frac{x^3 - 8}{x - 2}$$

Because the objective is to find the derivative as x approaches 2, the equation can be factored and simplified to the following value at $x = 2$:

$$\lim_{x \to 2} \frac{(x-2)(x^2+2x+4)}{x-2} = \lim_{x \to 2} (x^2 + 2x + 4) = (2)^2 + 2(2) + 4 = 12$$

The binomial $(x - 2)$ cancels on the top and bottom of the fraction and the equation that is left is:

$$(x^2 + 2x + 4)$$

Substituting $x = 2$ into the final equation yields the value 12. The following equation gives the value for the instantaneous rate of change for the function $f(x) = x^3$ as x approaches 2.

$$f'(2) = \lim_{x \to 2} \frac{f(x) - f(2)}{x - 2} = \lim_{x \to 2} \frac{x^3 - 8}{x - 2}$$

$$\lim_{x \to 2} \frac{(x - 2)(x^2 + 2x + 4)}{x - 2} = \lim_{x \to 2}(x^2 + 2x + 4) = (2)^2 + 2(2) + 4 = 12$$

The instantaneous rate of change at some point $(c, f(c))$ can also be denoted using the form:

$$f'(c) = \lim_{\Delta x \to 0} \frac{f(c + \Delta x) - f(c)}{\Delta x}$$

For example: Let $f(x) = \frac{1}{x}$. Find the instantaneous rate of change of f at the point where $x = 3$. At a value of $x = 3$, the function f has a value $f(3) = \frac{1}{3}$. For this problem, the value of $f'(3)$ can be found using the definition given above. The equation becomes:

$$\lim_{\Delta x \to 0} \frac{f(3+\Delta x) - f(3)}{\Delta x} = \lim_{\Delta x \to 0} \frac{\frac{1}{3+\Delta x} - \frac{1}{3}}{\Delta x}$$

Simplifying further, as $\Delta x \to 0$, the equation becomes:

$$\lim_{\Delta x \to 0} \frac{-1}{3(3+0)} = \frac{-1}{9}$$

Defining the Derivative of a Function and Using Derivative Notation

Derivatives

The **derivative of a function** is found using the limit of the difference quotient:

$$\lim_{\Delta x \to 0} \frac{f(x + \Delta x) - f(x)}{\Delta x}$$

This finds the slope of the tangent line of the given function at a given point. It is the slope, $\frac{\Delta y}{\Delta x}$, as $\Delta x \to$ 0. The derivative can be denoted in many ways, such as $f'(x)$, y', or $\frac{dy}{dx}$.

The following graph plots a function in black. The gray line represents a secant line, formed between two chosen points on the graph. The slope of this line can be found using rise over run. As these two points get closer to zero, meaning Δx approaches 0, the tangent line is found. The slope of the tangent line is equal to the limit of the slopes of the secant lines as $\Delta x \to 0$.

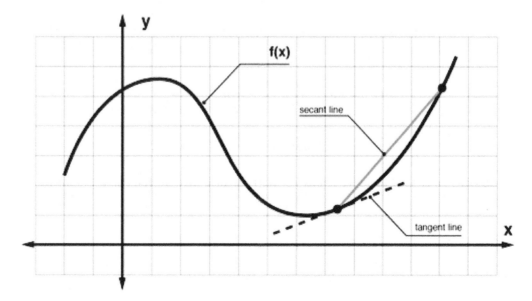

The derivative of a function can be found algebraically using the limit definition. Here is the process for finding the derivative of $f(x) = x^2 - 2$:

$$f'(x) = \lim_{h \to 0} \frac{f(x+h) - f(x)}{h}$$

$$= \lim_{h \to 0} \frac{(x+h)^2 - 2 - (x^2 - 2)}{h}$$

$$= \lim_{h \to 0} \frac{(x+h)(x+h) - 2 - x^2 + 2}{h}$$

$$= \lim_{h \to 0} \frac{x^2 + xh + xh + h^2 - 2 - x^2 + 2}{h}$$

$$= \lim_{h \to 0} \frac{x^2 + 2xh + h^2 - 2 - x^2 + 2}{h}$$

$$= \lim_{h \to 0} \frac{2xh + h^2}{h}$$

$$= \lim_{h \to 0} \frac{h(2x + h)}{h} = \lim_{h \to 0} 2x + h = 2x + 0 = 2x$$

Once the derivative function is found, it can be evaluated at any point by substituting that value in for x. Therefore, in this example, $f'(2) = 4$.

Derivative Notation

The derivative of the function, $y = f(x)$, can be denoted in many ways, including

$$f'(x), y', \frac{dy}{dx}, \text{ and } \frac{d}{dx}y$$

For example, the derivative of the function, $y = x^3 + 5x^2 - 6x + 1$ is $\frac{dy}{dx} = 3x^2 + 10x - 6$.

To denote the value of the derivative of a function, $y = f(x)$, at a particular x-value, say $x = c$, we can write $f'(c)$, $y'(c)$, and $\frac{dy}{dx}_{x=c}$. For example, given the function:

$$f(x) = 4x^5 - 2x^3 + 5x - 8$$

the value $f'(1)$ can be found. The first step is to find the derivative, $f'(x)$. By using the definition found above, the equation becomes:

$$f'(x) = 20x^4 - 6x^2 + 5$$

To find the function value of 1, simply substitute 1 into all values of x. This results in the equation:

$$f'(1) = 20(1)^4 - 6(1)^2 + 5 = 19$$

Representing Derivatives Verbally, Graphically, Numerically, and Analytically

Verbally, the derivative of a function can be described as the value of the slope of the graph at any given point. The steepness at any given point can be described as the **ratio**. This ratio is the comparison of the change in function value to the change in the independent variable. For linear functions, the derivative is a constant because the value of the slope is the same constant value throughout the graph. For a quadratic function, the steepness of the line changes at different points depending on the values of the independent variable for which the derivative is being evaluated.

Graphically, the derivative can be seen as the slope of the tangent line on a graph. For a given function, the derivative can be found and then graphed to show the value of the steepness at any given point. Below are two graphs: the first shows the original equation and the second shows the graph of the derivative. The original equation is a quadratic, where the slope of the line changes constantly. On the right, the graph of the function value of the derivative shows the slope for a given value of x. For example, at the value $x = 0$ the slope is zero because the derivative line crosses the point $(0, 0)$. At a value of $x = 1$, the y-value for the derivative is 2. This shows that the slope of the line is 2 at the value of $x = 1$.

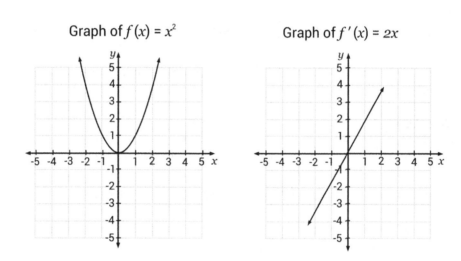

Graph of $f(x) = x^2$ Graph of $f'(x) = 2x$

Numerically, the derivative can be found by using the rules of differentiation of a function and then finding the function value at any given point. In the example above, the function for the derivative is $f'(x) = 2x$. To find the derivative at a given point, a value for the independent variable can be chosen and plugged in to the function. For example, the value of the derivative at $x = 4$ is:

$$f'(4) = 2(4) = 8$$

To interpret the meaning of this number, the slope of the original line $f(x) = x^2$ is 8 when the value of x is 4. To refer back to the method of graphing, the tangent line at the point $(2, 4)$ would be a straight line with a slope of 8.

Analytically, the derivative can be used to find helpful information about the meaning behind functions. One way derivatives share useful information is when the maximum or minimum value on a graph relates to cost or profit. For example, the function:

$$P = 7x - 0.03x^2$$

represents the profit for a company that produces steel. If the value of x is the number of steel beams produced, then the value of P is the profit made by the company. The derivative of this function is $P' = 7 - 0.06x$. If the function for the derivative is set equal to zero, the maximum profit point can be found. This equation has a maximum instead of a minimum because the coefficient of x^2 is negative. The derivative set equal to zero occurs at the maximum because that it where the slope is zero. The equation turns into:

$$P' = 0 = 7 - 0.06(x)$$

By solving for x, the number of steel beams produced to make a maximum profit turns out to be $x = 116.6$. If there are fewer beams produced, then the profit is increasing, but if there are more beams produced, then the profit is decreasing. This example of using the derivative to find the maximum profit point is only one of many uses for derivatives. Mainly they are used to make predictions because by definition it is the rate of change for the function, so it shows the change in value for the different behaviors of functions.

We have seen that the derivative at a point represents the slope of the tangent line at that point. Using this relationship, we can sketch a graph of the derivative function using the graph of the original function. In the graph below, we see that the slope of the tangent line to $f(x)$ is 0 at $x = -1$ and at $x = 2$. (The graph has a horizontal tangent line at these points.) This indicates that the derivative of f, $f'(x)$, at these values of x is 0.

Therefore, we know that $f'(-1) = 0$ and $f'(2) = 0$, as shown on the graph of $f'(x)$. Because the graph of $f(x)$ is increasing for $x < -1$ and $x > 2$, we know that the slope of the line tangent to f is positive in these intervals. This is shown on the graph of $f'(x)$ because the graph is *above* the x-axis. Likewise, since the slope of the line tangent to f is negative for $-1 < x < 2$, the graph of $f'(x)$ is *below* the x-axis.

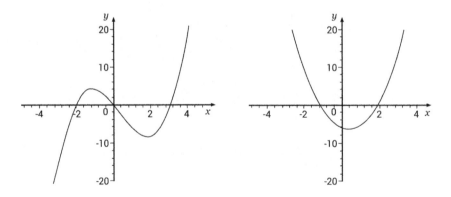

We can remember that if the graph of f has a horizontal tangent line, the slope is 0 at that point so the graph of the derivative touches the x-axis at that value of x. If the graph of f is increasing, the slope

of f is positive, so that graph of $f'(x)$ is above the x-axis. If the graph of f is decreasing on an interval, the slope of f is negative and the graph of $f'(x)$ is below the x-axis.

To represent the derivative of a function numerically, we recall that the derivative of a function at a point is the slope of the tangent line at that point. Applying the definition for slope of a line:

$$m = \frac{y_2 - y_1}{x_2 - x_1}$$

the slope can be estimated at any point by finding a slope of the secant line near that point. The table and graph below represent the equation $y = x^2$.

X	y
-2	4
-1	1
0	0
1	1
2	4

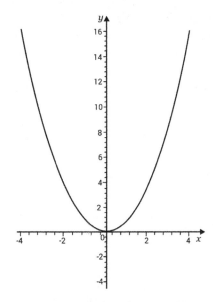

To find the derivative of the function, $y = x^2$, at the point where $x = 1.5$, we can begin by finding the slope of the secant line between the points $(0, 0)$ and $(2, 4)$ to find $\frac{4-0}{2-0} = 2$. This represents an

approximation of the numerical derivative of the function at the given point. As we move closer and closer to the point where $x = 1.5$, though, we will get a better approximation of this numerical derivative.

Try it now with the points $(1.2, 1.44)$ and $(1.8, 3.24)$. We find $\frac{3.24-1.44}{1.8-1.2} = 3$. This is a closer approximation for the derivative, $f'(1.5)$. In fact, using the rules of differentiation we find that this is the exact value for the numerical value of $f'(x)$ because $f'(x) = 2x$ and so:

$$f'(1.5) = 2(1.5) = 3$$

The above example follows from the analytical representation of the derivative, which is found using the formula,

$$f'(x) = \lim_{h \to 0} \frac{f(x + h) - f(x)}{h}$$

called the **difference quotient**. Although this formula can look a little tricky, it is just a representation of what we did above by choosing points near the point of interest to begin. We then chose points that were closer and closer together. As those points moved closer together, our approximation improved. The part of the formula that shows $lim_{h \to 0}$ is indicating to choose points close together (h represents the difference in x-values). The portion of the formula that shows

$$\frac{f(x + h) - f(x)}{h}$$

is a representation of the slope formula $f(x + h) - f(x)$ and represents the difference in y-values. Since the difference in x-values cannot ever reach 0 (because this would be the same point), make use of the concept of the limit to show that difference is getting very, very close to 0. Now use the example with $f(x) = x^2$ to evaluate the derivative analytically.

$$f'(x) = \lim_{h \to 0} \frac{(x + h)^2 - x^2}{h}$$

$$\lim_{h \to 0} \frac{(x)^2 + 2xh + (h)^2 - x^2}{h}$$

$$\lim_{h \to 0} \frac{h(2x + h)}{h} = \lim_{h \to 0} 2x + h = 2x$$

Now confirm analytically that $f'(1.5) = 3$.

Reading through the explanations above, there are many ways to describe the derivative verbally. The derivative is the slope of curve at any point on that curve. It also the slope of the line tangent to the curve at a point, and it is interpreted as a rate of change of the function. Using the example above, the slope of the function, $f(x)$, is $2x$ for any value of x on the curve. Specifically, the slope of the function, $f(x)$, at the point $(1.5, 2.25)$ is 3 because $f'(1.5) = 3$. Likewise, the slope of the line tangent to the curve, $f(x) = x^2$ at the point $(1.5, 2.25)$ is 3.

The Derivative of a Function at a Point

As mentioned, the **derivative of a function** is found using the limit of the difference quotient:

$$\lim_{\Delta x \to 0} \frac{f(x + \Delta x) - f(x)}{\Delta x}$$

This finds the slope of the tangent line of the given function at a given point. It is the slope, $\frac{\Delta y}{\Delta x}$, as $\Delta x \to$ 0. In other words, the derivative of a function at a specific point is equal to the slope of the line tangent to the graph of that function at that specific point.

Estimating Derivatives of a Function at a Point

Estimating Derivatives

Because the derivative is a slope, a table of values can be used to approximate the derivative. The change in y divided by the change in x gives the slope at a point. Using the points in the table, slopes of secant lines can be calculated. Based on the limit of those slopes, the derivative at each point can be approximated. Take the following table for example:

x	$f(x)$
0	0
1	1
4	2
9	3
16	4

To find $f'(4)$ using the table, the slope between $f(4)$ and each of the other points needs to be calculated. The following table shows the slopes between different points. Based on the slopes found from the table, the value of $f'(4)$ is between 0.2 and 0.5.

Given Point	Point to find Secant Line	Slope
(4, 2)	(0, 0)	0.5
(4, 2)	(1, 1)	0.333333
(4, 2)	(9, 3)	0.2
(4, 2)	(16, 4)	0.16667

Using Technology to Calculate or Estimate the Value of a Derivative

The derivative of a function $f(x)$ with respect to x is equal to the following:

$$f'(x) = \lim_{h \to 0} \frac{f(x + h) - f(x)}{h},$$

provided that the limit exists. This function is equal to the limit of the difference quotient, where the difference quotient represents the average rate of change of a function with increment h. The difference quotient is a slope of a secant line, and the derivative is the slope of a tangent line. In order to estimate a derivative instead of calculating it exactly for a given function $f(x)$, small values of h are chosen and the difference quotient is calculated as $h \to 0$. If the limit exists, it can be used to calculate or estimate

42

the value of the derivative at the given point. This information is placed into a table and the value of the limit is estimated. For example, consider the function $f(x) = x^2$. h is chosen to be equal to 0.1, 0.01, 0.001, and 0.001, and the corresponding difference quotients are calculated for $x = 2$. Therefore, the derivative $f'(2)$ is being approximated. The difference quotient when $h = 0.1$ is equal to:

$$\frac{f(2 + .1) - f(2)}{.1} = \frac{2.1^2 - 2^2}{.1} = 4.1$$

Technology can be used to calculate these difference quotients. The following table, which was computed in Excel, shows the calculated difference quotients with their corresponding values of h.

h	Difference Quotient
0.1	4.1
0.01	4.01
0.001	4.001
0.0001	4.0001

Notice that as h gets closer to 0, the difference quotient gets closer to 4. The limit of the difference quotients is being estimated, which are the slopes of the secant line, as $h \to 0$, and it is shown that $f'(2) \approx 4$. This estimation process actually obtained the exact derivative because $f'(2) = 4$. A graphing calculator or **computer algebra system (CAS)** could also have been used to build similar tables that calculate difference quotients in order to estimate derivatives.

Connecting Differentiability and Continuity: Determining When Derivatives Do and Do Not Exist

Differentiability and Continuity

If a function $f(x)$ is continuous at an interior point c inside its domain, then it is true that $\lim_{x \to c} f(x) = f(c)$. Therefore, its limit at that point is equal to the function evaluated at that point. Also, a function is continuous at every point in which it has a derivative. Basically, if $f(x)$ has a derivative at the point c in its domain, then $f(x)$ is continuous at c.

Continuous Functions That Are Not Differentiable

Even though if a function is differentiable at a point, then it has to be continuous at that point; a function does not have to have a derivative at a point in which it is continuous. For instance, consider the absolute value function. The absolute value function is continuous over its entire domain. However, it is not differentiable at $x = 0$. The limit definition fails at this point. Therefore, the absolute value function is only differentiable over $(-\infty, 0)$ and $(0, \infty)$.

The **Intermediate Value Property of Derivatives** is an extension of the Intermediate Value Property of Continuous Functions. It states that if the function $f(x)$ is differentiable on two points a and b in an interval, then $f'(x)$ will take on every value between both $f'(a)$ and $f'(b)$. This theorem further connects the idea of continuity and differentiability.

Applying the Power Rule

Rules of Differentiation

The formal definition of the derivative of any function $f(x)$ with respect to x is the following:

$$f'(x) = \lim_{h \to 0} \frac{f(x+h) - f(x)}{h}$$

provided that the limit exists. The derivative of a constant function $f(x) = c$ is 0 because:

$$f'(x) = \lim_{h \to 0} \frac{c - c}{h} = 0$$

The derivative of a constant multiple of a function is equal to the constant times the derivative of the function because if $f(x) = c \times u(x)$:

$$f'(x) = \lim_{h \to 0} \frac{c \times u(x+h) - u(x)}{h} = c \times \lim_{h \to 0} \frac{u(x+h) - u(x)}{h} = c \times u'(x)$$

Third, it can be shown that $\frac{d}{dx} x^n = n x^{n-1}$. The proof is seen here:

$$f'(a) = \lim_{x \to a} \frac{(x-a)(x^{n-1} + ax^{n-2} + a^2 x^{n-3} + \cdots + a^{n-3} x^2 + a^{n-2} x + a^{n-1})}{x - a}$$

$$\lim_{x \to a} x^{n-1} + ax^{n-2} + a^2 x^{n-3} + \cdots + a^{n-3} x^2 + a^{n-2} x + a^{n-1}$$

$$a^{n-1} + aa^{n-2} + a^2 a^{n-3} + \cdots + a^{n-3} a^2 + a^{n-2} a + a^{n-1}$$

$$na^{n-1}$$

The sum and difference rules of derivatives state that:

$$\frac{d}{dx} [f(x) \pm g(x)] = \frac{d}{dx} f(x) \pm \frac{d}{dx} g(x)$$

Therefore, by combining all of these rules together, a polynomial of any kind can be differentiated. For instance, the derivative of $f(x) = x^4 + 2x^2 + 1$ is:

$$f'(x) = 4x^3 + 4x$$

As the other four trigonometric functions are all derived in terms of sine and cosine, they can be found using the quotient rule. Here are the remaining rules:

$$\frac{d}{dx} (\tan x) = \sec^2 x$$

$$\frac{d}{dx} (\cot x) = -\csc^2 x$$

$$\frac{d}{dx}(\csc x) = -\csc x \cot x$$

$$\frac{d}{dx}(\sec x) = \sec x \tan x$$

The derivative of the natural logarithm function is included in rules for taking derivatives of exponential and logarithmic functions, otherwise known as **transcendental functions**. The other rules are provided below:

$$\frac{d}{dx}(e^x) = e^x$$

$$\frac{d}{dx}(a^x) = a^x \times \ln a$$

$$\frac{d}{dx}(\ln|x|) = \frac{1}{x}, x \neq 0$$

$$\frac{d}{dx}(\log_a x) = \frac{1}{x \times \ln a}, x > 0$$

Differentiation Techniques

Finding the derivative of a function can be done using the definition as described above, but rules proved via the different quotient can also be used. A few are listed below. These rules apply for functions that take the form inside the parenthesis. For example, the function:

$$f(x) = 3x^4$$

would use the **Power Rule** and **Constant Multiple Rule**. To find the derivative, the exponent is brought down to be multiplied by the coefficient, and the new exponent is one less than the original. As an equation, the derivative is:

$$f'(x) = 12x^3$$

$$\frac{d}{dx}(a^b) = 0$$

$$\frac{d}{dx}(x^n) = nx^{n-1}$$

$$\frac{d}{dx}(a^x) = a^x \ln a$$

$$\frac{d}{dx}(x^x) = x^x(1 + \ln x)$$

In relation to real-life problems, the position of a ball that is thrown into the air may be given by the equation:

$$p = 7 + 25t - 16t^2$$

The position, p, can be found for any time, t, after the ball is thrown. To find the initial position, $t = 0$ can be substituted into the equation to find p. That position would be 7 feet above the ground, which is equal to the constant at the end of the equation.

Finding the derivative of the function would use the Power Rule. The derivative is:

$$p' = 25 - 32t$$

The derivative of a position function represents the velocity function. To find the initial velocity, the time $t = 0$ can be substituted into the equation. The initial velocity is found to be 25 ft/s – the same as the coefficient of t in the position equation. Taking the derivative of the velocity equation yields the acceleration equation $p'' = -32$. This value is the acceleration at which a ball is pulled by gravity to the ground in feet per second squared.

Because integration is the inverse operation of finding the derivative, the integral is found by going backward from the derivative. In relation to the ball problem, an acceleration function can be integrated to find the velocity function. That function can then be integrated to find the position function. From velocity, integration finds the position function:

$$p = -16t^2 + 25t + c$$

where c is an unknown constant. More information would need to be given in the original problem to integrate and find the value of c.

Derivative Rules: Constant, Sum, Difference, and Constant Multiple

Differentiating Sums, Differences, Products, and Quotients of Functions

Two functions $f(x)$ and $g(x)$ are differentiable and so are their sums or differences. The following equation shows this definition in function form:

$$\frac{d}{dx}[f(x) \pm g(x)] = f'(x) \pm g'(x)$$

For example, the function $\frac{d}{dx}[5x^3 - 4x^2 + 2]$ can be separated into three terms. The function then becomes:

$$\frac{d}{dx}(5x^3) - \frac{d}{dx}(4x^2) + \frac{d}{dx}(2)$$

By finding the derivative of each term, the function simplifies to $15x^2 - 8x$.

Another example shows the product of two functions, f and g that are differentiable. Multiplying these two functions gives a function that is differentiable. Written in function form, this rule states:

$$\frac{d}{dx}[f(x)g(x)] = f'(x)g(x) + f(x)g'(x)$$

In other words, taking the derivative of the product of these two functions is found by taking the derivative of the first and multiplying by the second. Then add the first function times the derivative of the second function. An example of this rule can be seen using the function:

$$x^3(x^2 - 4)$$

Breaking the process down, differentiation can be done in steps. Taking the derivative of the first function yields:

$$f'(x) = 3x^2$$

The derivative of the second function is:

$$g'(x) = 2x$$

Using the rule, the final function becomes:

$$\frac{d}{dx}[f(x)g(x)] = 3x^2(x^2 - 4) + x^3(2x)$$

This equation can be simplified to:

$$3x^4 - 12x^2 + 2x^4 = 5x^4 - 12x^2$$

The quotient $\frac{f}{g}$ of two differentiable functions f and g is differentiable $g(x) \neq 0$. The following function shows this rule in function form:

$$\frac{d}{dx}\left[\frac{f(x)}{g(x)}\right] = \frac{f'(x)g(x) - f(x)g'(x)}{(g(x))^2}, g(x) \neq 0$$

Take the derivative of the first times the second function. Then subtract the product of the first function and the derivative of the second. Divide this all by the square of the second function.

An example of this is:

$$\frac{2x}{4x^3}$$

To differentiate these functions, the first step is to find $f'(x)$ and $g'(x)$. The derivative of f is $f'(x) = 2$. The derivative of g is:

$$g'(x) = 12x^2$$

Using the function for quotients above, the derived equation becomes:

$$\frac{d}{dx}\left[\frac{f(x)}{g(x)}\right] = \frac{2(4x^3) - 2x(12x^2)}{(4x^3)^2}$$

Simplifying the terms in this function yields the equation:

$$\frac{d}{dx}\left[\frac{f(x)}{g(x)}\right] = \frac{(8x^3) - (24x^3)}{4x^6}$$

$$-\frac{16x^3}{4x^6} = -\frac{4}{x^3}$$

The process of taking a derivative is known as **differentiation**. Many rules exist that allow us to take derivatives without using the limit definition.

For instance, the derivative of a constant function $f(x) = c$ is equal to 0. This rule exists is because the slope of a horizontal line, which is the graph of a constant function, is always 0. For example:

$$\frac{d}{dx}(10) = 0$$

A very important differentiation rule is the **power rule**. The power rule states that if $f(x) = x^n$, then:

$$f'(x) = nx^{n-1}$$

For example, if $f(x) = x^8$, its corresponding derivative function is:

$$f'(x) = 8x^7$$

Also, the power rule can be used to find the derivative of the identity function $f(x) = x$. The power rule with $n = 1$ would be used. Therefore:

$$f'(x) = 1x^{1-1} = x^0 = 1$$

Finally, the power rule can be used for negative powers and powers that are not integers. For example:

$$\frac{d}{dx}x^{-1} = -1x^{-1-1} = -x^{-2}$$

Also:

$$\frac{d}{dx}x^{2.2} = 2.2x^{1.2}$$

Another rule allows us to work with constants when taking derivatives. If $f(x)$ is a differentiable function and c is a constant, then:

$$\frac{d}{dx}\left(c \times f(x)\right) = c \times f'(x)$$

Basically, if a function is multiplied times a constant, the constant can be pulled out front of the expression, and the derivative of that function is multiplied times the constant. For instance:

$$\frac{d}{dx}(5x^2) = 5\frac{d}{dx}(x^2) = 5 \times 2x = 10x$$

This rule is useful when finding the derivative of a negative function. Let $c = -1$ in the constant multiple rule so that:

$$\frac{d}{dx}(-f(x)) = -f'(x)$$

Therefore:

$$\frac{d}{dx}(-5x^2) = -5\frac{d}{dx}(x^2)$$

$$-5 \times 2x = -10x$$

The sum and difference rules are also very important rules in calculus. If $f(x)$ and $g(x)$ are both differentiable functions, then their sum $f(x) + g(x)$ and difference $f(x) - g(x)$ are both differentiable functions. The **sum rule** states that the derivative of the sum of two differentiable functions is equal to the sum of the derivatives of the functions. Therefore:

$$\frac{d}{dx}\big(f(x) + g(x)\big) = f'(x) + g'(x)$$

The **difference rule** states that the derivative of the difference of two differentiable functions is equal to the difference of the derivatives of the functions. Therefore:

$$\frac{d}{dx}\big(f(x) - g(x)\big) = f'(x) - g'(x)$$

For instance:

$$\frac{d}{dx}(x^9 + x^8) = \frac{d}{dx}(x^9) + \frac{d}{dx}(x^8) = 9x^8 + 8x^7$$

Also:

$$\frac{d}{dx}(x^9 - x^8) = \frac{d}{dx}(x^9) - \frac{d}{dx}(x^8) = 9x^8 - 8x^7$$

Finding Derivatives of Polynomial Functions

The power rule, sum rule, difference rule, and constant multiple rules for taking derivatives can be applied when differentiating polynomials. Together, they allow polynomials to be differentiated easily. The reason these differentiation rules can be used on polynomials is that polynomials are composed of sums and differences of constants and constants multiplied times expressions of the form x^n, for positive integers n. The derivative rules allow us to differentiate polynomials term by term. For instance, consider the polynomial function:

$$f(x) = 7x^3 + 5x^2 + 3x + 1$$

Its derivative is:

$$f'(x) = \frac{d}{dx}(7x^3) + \frac{d}{dx}(5x^2) + \frac{d}{dx}(3x) + \frac{d}{dx}(1) = 21x^2 + 10x + 3$$

Derivatives of cos x, sin x, eˣ, and ln x

Finding Derivatives of Trigonometric, Exponential, and Logarithmic Functions

The formal definition of the derivative can also be used to derive the rules for the derivatives of the trigonometric function. Here is the proof for the derivatives of sine and cosine:

$$\frac{d}{dx}\sin x = \lim_{h \to 0} \frac{\sin(x+h) - \sin x}{h}$$

$$\lim_{h \to 0} \frac{\sin x \cos h + \cos x \sin h - \sin x}{h}$$

$$\lim_{h \to 0} \frac{(\sin x)(\cos h - 1) + \cos x \sin h}{h}$$

$$\lim_{h \to 0} \left(\sin x \frac{\cos h - 1}{h} + \cos x \frac{\sin h}{h}\right)$$

$$(\sin x)(0) + (\cos x)(1)$$

$$\cos x$$

$$\frac{d}{dx}\cos x = \lim_{h \to 0} \frac{\cos(x+h) - \cos x}{h}$$

$$\lim_{h \to 0} \frac{\cos x \cos h - \sin x \sin h - \cos x}{h}$$

$$\lim_{h \to 0} \frac{(\cos x)(\cos h - 1) - \sin x \sin h}{h}$$

$$\lim_{h \to 0} \left(\cos x \frac{\cos h - 1}{h} - \sin x \frac{\sin h}{h}\right)$$

$$(1)(0) - (\sin x)(1)$$

$$-\sin x$$

Finally, the formal definition of the derivative can be used to derive the formula for the derivative of logarithmic functions. Here is the proof of the derivative of the natural logarithm function $y = \ln x$:

$$\frac{d}{dx}(\ln x) = \lim_{h \to 0} \frac{\ln(x + h) - \ln x}{h}$$

$$\frac{1}{x} \times \ln(\lim_{n \to \infty}(1 + \frac{1}{n})^n)$$

$$\frac{1}{x} \times \ln e$$

$$\frac{1}{x}$$

The Product Rule

Using the Product Rule

As discussed earlier, it is true that the derivative of the sum and/or difference of two functions is equivalent to the sum and/or difference of their derivatives. However, this is not the case for products. It is not true that the derivative of the product of two functions is equal to the product of the derivatives. The product rule tells us how to differentiate a product of two functions. It states that if two differentiable functions $f(x)$ and $g(x)$ exist, then:

$$\frac{d}{dx}(f(x) \times g(x))$$

$$f'(x) \times g(x) + g'(x) \times f(x)$$

Therefore, the derivative of the product of two functions is equal to the product of the derivative of the first function and the second function plus the product of the first function and the derivative of the second function.

For instance, the power rule would be used to find the derivative of:

$$h(x) = (x^2 + 4x)(x + 1)$$

By setting $f(x) = x^2 + 4x$ and $g(x) = x + 1$, $f'(x) = 2x + 4$ and $g'(x) = 1$.

Therefore:

$$h'(x) = (2x + 4)(x + 1) + 1(x^2 + 4x)$$

$$2x^2 + 2x + 4x + 4 + x^2 + 4x$$

$$3x^2 + 10x + 4$$

Note the same answer would be obtained if the function $h(x)$ was first foiled to obtain a polynomial function and differentiated term by term.

The Quotient Rule

Using the Quotient Rule

Just like with the product rule, the derivative of the quotient of two functions is not equal to the quotient of their corresponding derivative functions. The quotient rule allows one to find the derivative of the quotient of two functions. It states that if there are two differentiable functions $f(x)$ and $g(x)$, where $g(x) \neq 0$, then:

$$\frac{d}{dx}\left(\frac{f(x)}{g(x)}\right) = \frac{f'(x)g(x) - f(x)g'(x)}{(g(x))^2}$$

Therefore, in order to differentiate a quotient, multiply the derivative of the numerator times the denominator, subtract the product of the numerator and the derivative of the denominator, and divide by the denominator squared.

For instance, consider the function:

$$y = \frac{x^2 + 1}{x^4 - 1}$$

The quotient rule can be used with:

$$f(x) = x^2 + 1$$

and

$$g(x) = x^4 - 1$$

to find its derivative.

In this example:

$$f'(x) = 2x$$

and

$$g'(x) = 4x^3$$

The quotient rule results in:

$$y' = \frac{2x(x^4 - 1) - (x^2 + 1)4x^3}{(x^4 - 1)^2}$$

which simplifies using the following steps:

$$\frac{2x^5 - 2x - 4x^5 - 4x^3}{(x^4 - 1)(x^4 - 1)}$$

$$\frac{-2x^5 - 4x^3 - 2x}{(x^2 + 1)(x^2 - 1)(x^2 + 1)(x^2 - 1)}$$

$$\frac{-2x(x^4 + 2x^2 + 1)}{(x^2 + 1)(x^2 - 1)(x^2 + 1)(x^2 - 1)}$$

$$\frac{-2x(x^2 + 1)(x^2 + 1)}{(x^2 + 1)(x^2 - 1)(x^2 + 1)(x^2 - 1)} = -\frac{2x}{(x^2 - 1)^2}$$

Finding the Derivatives of Tangent, Cotangent, Secant, and/or Cosecant Functions

Rearranging Tangent, Cotangent, Secant, and Cosecant Functions

The derivative of the sine function is the cosine function, and therefore:

$$\frac{d}{dx}(\sin x) = \cos x$$

This can be proved by the limit definition of the derivative using the angle sum identity $\sin(x + h) = \sin x \cos h + \cos x \sin h$. Also, the derivative of the cosine function is equal to the negative of the sine function, and therefore:

$$\frac{d}{dx}(\cos x) = -\sin x$$

This can also be proved by the limit definition of the derivative using the angle sum identity $\cos(x + h) = \cos x \cos h - \sin x \sin h$. Both of these rules and the quotient rule can be used to find the derivative of the tangent function. Because:

$$\frac{d}{dx}(\tan x) = \frac{d}{dx}\left(\frac{\sin x}{\cos x}\right)$$

the quotient rule can be used with $f(x) = \sin x$ and $g(x) = \cos x$ to obtain:

$$\frac{d}{dx}(\tan x) = \frac{\cos^2 x + \sin^2 x}{\cos^2 x} = \frac{1}{\cos^2 x} = \sec^2 x$$

The derivatives of the other three trigonometric functions can also be found using the quotient rule. This is because they all can be written as quotients seen here:

$$\cot x = \frac{\cos x}{\sin x}, \sec x = \frac{1}{\cos x}$$

and

$$\csc x = \frac{1}{\sin x}$$

The following derivative rules exist:

$$\frac{d}{dx}(\sec x) = \sec x \tan x$$

$$\frac{d}{dx}(\cot x) = -\csc^2 x$$

and:

$$\frac{d}{dx}(\csc x) = -\csc x \cot x$$

Unit 3: Differentiation: Composite, Implicit, and Inverse Functions

The Chain Rule

Using the Chain Rule to Differentiate Composite Functions

The derivative of a composite function:

$$y = f(g(x))$$

where $f(x)$ and $g(x)$ are two differentiable functions, is given by the following formula:

$$\frac{d}{dx}(f(g(x))) = f'(g(x)) \times g'(x)$$

The derivative of the function value for f when the input value is $g(x)$ is calculated by finding the derivative of the function f and plugging in the $g(x)$ function for all x-values. Then taking that value and multiplying it by the derivative of the $g(x)$ function yields the answer to a differentiated composite function. Another way that this rule can be written using composite functions is:

$$\frac{d}{dx}(f \circ g) = \frac{df}{dg}\frac{dg}{dx}$$

The derivative of $f(g(x))$ is the derivative of $f(x)$ evaluated at $g(x)$ times the derivative of $g(x)$.

A different function representation is:

$$F(g(x)) = F(u)$$

where F is the outside function and u is the inside function. The derivative of $F(u)$ is:

$$F'(u) \times u'$$

An example of this is seen using the functions:

$$f(x) = 2x^3 \text{ and } g(x) = 3x - 4$$

The first step is to find the derivative of the f function. Using the definition of derivative given in the above sections:

$$f'(x) = 6x^2$$

Next the function value for $f'(g(x))$ can be found as

$$6(3x - 4)^2$$

Expanding the work for this function forms the equation:

$$f'(g(x)) = 6(9x^2 - 24x + 16) = 54x^2 - 144x + 96$$

The last step is to find the derivative of the function g. This is found using the definition of the derivative given in the above sections and it comes out to $g'(x) = 3$. Completing the derivative of the composite function of the two functions $f(x)$ and $g(x)$, the equation becomes:

$$\frac{d}{dx}(f(g(x))) = 3(54x^2 - 144x + 96) = 162x^2 - 432x + 288$$

For example, suppose that:

$$h(x) = (2x - 15)^3$$

Notice that this is a composite function because there are two functions that could be defined as $f(x) = x^3$ and:

$$g(x) = 2x - 15$$

then

$$h(x) = f(g(x))$$

so f is the outside function and g is the inside function. To find the derivative of h, or $h'(x)$, the **chain rule** can be used, and it will look like this equation:

$$h'(x) = 3(2x - 15)^2(2) = 6(2x - 15)^2$$

Verbally, this equation can be described as "the derivative of the outside (leave the inside) times the derivative of the inside."

The chain rule can also be used with a trigonometric function. For example, suppose:

$$h(x) = \cos 4x^2$$

In this case $f(x) = \cos x$ and:

$$g(x) = 4x^2$$

Applying the chain rule, the derivative of the first cosine function is found but the angle is left as $4x^2$. Then this is multiplied by the derivative of $4x^2$. It looks like the following function:

$$h'(x) = -\sin 4x^2 * 8x = -8x \sin 4x^2$$

Implicit Differentiation

The Chain Rule is the Basis for Implicit Differentiation

For equations like:

$$y = x^2 + 2x - 7$$

the derivative $\frac{dy}{dx}$, is found by differentiating each term with respect to x. The notation for finding the derivative is

$$\frac{d}{dx}(y) = \frac{d}{dx}(x^2) + \frac{d}{dx}(2x) - \frac{d}{dx}(7)$$

Simplifying the equation leads to the final answer of:

$$\frac{dy}{dx} = 2x + 2$$

Since the derivative is found with respect to x, the coefficient and exponent are both taken into account on the x-value when finding the derivative.

An equation is implicitly defined when one variable is not explicitly defined. For example:

$$x^2 + y^2 = 4$$

is an implicitly defined equation because neither x nor y are explicitly defined. An equation of this type can be differentiated with respect to x, using a special case of the chain rule called implicit differentiation. As before, we can take the derivative of each term. It is most important to realize that we take each derivative with respect to x. This means that we can differentiate a term involving only x terms; we do this exactly as we have before. However, if we differentiate terms with the y variable, we are assuming that y is defined implicitly as a differentiable function of x and so we must use the chain rule.

Applying the chain rule to find the derivative of:

$$x^2 + y^2 = 4$$

with respect to x, the equation is found to be:

$$\frac{d}{dx}(x^2) + \frac{d}{dx}(y^2) = \frac{d}{dx}(4)$$

Simplifying this equation, the variables become

$$2x + 2y\frac{dy}{dx} = 0$$

Solving this function for $\frac{dy}{dx}$ gives the value:

$$\frac{dy}{dx} = \frac{-x}{y}$$

Another example may be given to find $\frac{dy}{dx}$ for:

$$cos(2y) = sin(3x)$$

The derivative notation is

$$\frac{d}{dx}(cos(2y)) = \frac{d}{dx}(sin(3x))$$

Using the chain rule to derive the trigonometric functions, the equation becomes:

$$-sin(2y)\,2\frac{dy}{dx} = 3cos(3x)$$

Solving for the final answer of $\frac{dy}{dx}$, the derivative is:

$$\frac{dy}{dx} = -\frac{3\cos 3x}{2\sin 2y}$$

Another example is to be given the following function: $xy + y^2 = x$, and to find the derivative of y with respect to x. The notation of the derivative with respect to x is:

$$\frac{d}{dx}(xy) + \frac{d}{dx}(y^2) = \frac{d}{dx}(x)$$

Using the product rule, the derivative of xy is found to be:

$$1 \times y + x \times 1\frac{dy}{dx}$$

Completing the work to derive y, the equation becomes:

$$\left(1 \times y + x \times 1\frac{dy}{dx}\right) + 2y\frac{dy}{dx} = 1$$

Using the same logic as solving simple equation in algebra, the derivative $\frac{dy}{dx}$ is found to be:

$$\frac{dy}{dx}(x + 2y) = 1 - y$$

where

$$\frac{dy}{dx} = \frac{1 - y}{x + 2y}$$

Differentiating Inverse Functions

Using the Chain Rule to Find the Derivative of an Inverse Function

Implicit differentiation can be applied to find the derivative of an inverse function. If we have inverse functions so that $y = f(x)$, then:

$$f^{-1}(y) = f^{-1}(f(x)) = x$$

Additionally, it is noted that:

$$f(f^{-1}(x)) = f^{-1}(f(x))$$

Applying the chain rule to use to differentiate implicitly, we can find the derivative of the inverse of f. This rule is shown in the graph below.

$$y = f(x)$$

$$f'(y) = x$$

$$\frac{dy}{dx}(f^{-1}(y))\frac{dy}{dx} = 1$$

$$\frac{d}{dy}(f^{-1}(y)) = \frac{1}{\frac{dy}{dx}}$$

To see what this really means, look at the example below. Suppose $f(x) = x^3$ so that:

$$f^{-1}(x) = \sqrt[3]{x}$$

The graphs of these functions follow.

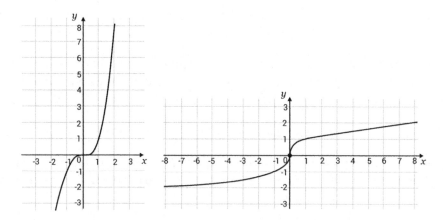

Note that the point $(2, 8)$ is on the graph of $f(x)$ so that $f(2) = 8$. Remember that this means that the point $(8, 2)$ is on the graph of $f^{-1}(x)$ so that:

$$f^{-1}(8) = 2$$

If we find the derivative of f, the equation becomes:

$$f'(x) = 3x^2$$

To find the derivative at the specific point $(2, 8)$, then the equation is:

$$f'(2) = 3(2^2) = 12$$

The value of 12 communicates that the slope of the function f at the point $(2, 8)$ is 12.

Now the derivative of f^{-1} at the point $(8, 2)$ is

$$f^{-1}(x) = \frac{1}{3x^{2/3}}$$

so

$$f^{-1}(8) = \frac{1}{3(8)^{2/3}} = \frac{1}{12}$$

This value of $\frac{1}{12}$ indicates that the slope of $f^{-1}(x)$ at the point $(8, 2)$ is $\frac{1}{12}$.

This example shows that the slope of a function at a point is the reciprocal of the slope of the inverse of that function at the corresponding point.

For example, suppose that,

$$f(x) = 2x^5 + x^4 + 4x - 6$$

and suppose that $g(x)$ is the inverse of f. Find the value of $g'(-6)$. To find the inverse of f would be too difficult algebraically so use the derivatives of inverse functions to find this instead. First, find the point on f where the y-value is –6. In other words, find the function value for a using the following equation:

$$f(a) = 2a^5 + a^4 + 4a - 6 = -6$$

At first glance, this equation is not easily factorable. By observing other characteristics of the equation, the constant is equal to the output value. If the value for a is zero, then the equation is true. Take the following equation as proof:

$$f(0) = 2(0)^5 + (0)^4 + 4(0) - 6 = -6$$

From this equation, there is a point $(0, -6)$ on the graph of $f(x)$. By the definition of inverse functions $(-6, 0)$ is a point on the graph of g. Putting this all together, an example is shown below for the derivative function $f'(x)$. The equation is:

$$f'(x) = 10x^4 + 4x^3 + 4$$

The derivative of the inverse of f is $f'(0) = 4$. This function evaluated at -6 is:

$$g'(-6) = \frac{1}{f'(0)} = \frac{1}{4}$$

Differentiating Inverse Trigonometric Functions

Finding the Derivatives of Inverse Trigonometric Functions

Recall that if a function $f(x)$ is differentiable on every point of an interval I and its derivative is never equal to 0 on that interval, then the function has an inverse $f'(x)$ which is differentiable on every point of the interval $f(I)$. This rule, along with the idea of implicit differentiation, allows for the inverse trigonometric functions to be differentiated. Also, recall that implicit differentiation involves the use of the chain rule, which allows for differentiation of a composite function. The chain rule states that:

$$\frac{d}{dx}(f(g(x))) = f'(g(x))g'(x)$$

Consider the arcsine function. It is true that $x = \sin y$ is differentiable in the interval $\left(-\frac{\pi}{2}, \frac{\pi}{2}\right)$, and the derivative $\cos y$ is never equal to 0 on that interval. Therefore, its inverse function $y = \sin^{-1} x$ is differentiable on the interval $(-1, 1)$. The derivative can be found using $x = \sin y$ and differentiating implicitly both sides with respect to x. Therefore:

$$1 = \cos y \frac{dy}{dx}$$

Notice that the chain rule must be used on the variable y because it is a function of x. Equivalently,

$$\frac{dy}{dx} = \frac{1}{\cos y}$$

From the Pythagorean identity, $\sin^2 y + \cos^2 y = 1$, or $\cos^2 y = 1 - \sin^2 y$, and

$$\cos y = \pm\sqrt{1 - \sin^2 y}$$

It is also known that $\cos y$ is positive over the specified interval, the positive root is chosen, and because:

$$x = \sin y$$

$$\cos y = \sqrt{1 - x^2}$$

Therefore:

$$\frac{dy}{dx} = \frac{1}{\sqrt{1 - x^2}}$$

The differentiation rule for arcsine is:

$$\frac{d}{dx}(\sin^{-1} x) = \frac{1}{\sqrt{1-x^2}} \text{ for } -1 < x < 1$$

Using the chain rule, if f is a differentiable function of x such that:

$$|f| < 1, \frac{d}{dx}\sin^{-1} f = \frac{1}{\sqrt{1-f^2}}\frac{df}{dx}$$

For instance, the derivative of:

$$f(x) = \sin^{-1}(4x) \text{ is } \frac{1}{\sqrt{1-(4x)^2}}(4) = \frac{4}{\sqrt{1-16x^2}}$$

Similar processes allow for differentiation of the other five inverse trigonometric functions.

For $f(x) = \cos^{-1} x$

where $-1 < x < 1$, $f'(x) = -\frac{1}{\sqrt{1-x^2}}$.

For $f(x) = \tan^{-1} x$, $f'(x) = \frac{1}{1+x^2}$.

For $f(x) = \cot^{-1} x$, $f'(x) = -\frac{1}{1+x^2}$.

For $f(x) = \sec^{-1} x$,

where $x \in (-\infty, -1) \cup (1, \infty)$, $f'(x) = \frac{1}{|x|\sqrt{x^2-1}}$.

Finally, for $f(x) = \csc^{-1} x$, where:

$$x \in (-\infty, -1) \cup (1, \infty)$$

$$f'(x) = -\frac{1}{|x|\sqrt{x^2-1}}$$

Calculating Higher-Order Derivatives

Differentiating to Produce the Second Derivative

First-Order Differential Equations
A **first-order differential equation** is said to be separable if the variables can be separated on either side of the equals sign. A separable differential equation can be written as:

$$f(y)dy = g(x)dx$$

In this case, to obtain the solution, both sides can be integrated with respect to their given variables. A constant of integration needs to be added to only one side. For example:

$$\frac{4}{x^2+1}\frac{dy}{dx} = 1$$

is a separable differential equation because it can be written as

$$4dy = (x^2+1)dx$$

Integrating both sides results in:

$$4y = \frac{x^3}{3} + x + c$$

and its explicit solution is:

$$y = \frac{x^3}{12} + \frac{x}{4} + c$$

Models involving growth and decay problems can utilize this method when solving. The first-order differential equation that models growth and decay is: $\frac{dy}{dt} = ky$, where k represents a constant. If $k > 0$, it models exponential growth and if $k > 0$, it models exponential decay. The differential equation is separable, and its solution is:

$$y(t) = ce^{kt}$$

Representing Higher-Order Derivatives with Various Notations

Taking the derivative of a function given by $y = f(x)$ yields another function, $f'(x)$. This can also be noted by $\frac{dy}{dx}$, y', or $D_x[y]$. From this point we can continue the differentiation to obtain the derivative of the first derivative, and we call this the **second derivative**.

The notation for the second derivative can be shown as:

$$f''(x)$$

$$y''$$

$$\frac{d^2y}{dx^2}$$

or

$$D^2{}_x[y]$$

We can define derivatives of any positive integer order. So, if we take the derivative again, we will find the third derivative and denote this using any of these notations: $f'''(x)$, y''', $\frac{d^3y}{dx^3}$, or $D^3{}_x[y]$.

The second and third derivatives are examples of **higher order derivatives**. As we continue finding higher order derivatives, the notation is similar. The fourth derivative is denoted as $f^4(x)$, y^4, $\frac{d^4y}{dx^4}$, or $D^4{}_x[y]$; the fifth derivative is denoted as $f^5(x)$, y^5, $\frac{d^5y}{dx^5}$, or $D^5{}_x[y]$; and the nth derivative is denoted as $f^n(x)$, y^n, $\frac{d^ny}{dx^n}$, or $D^n{}_x[y]$.

Unit 4: Contextual Applications of Differentiation

Interpreting the Meaning of the Derivative in Context

Basic Interpretation of a Derivative

On a basic level, it is possible to interpret the derivative of a function as the instantaneous rate of change of that function with respect to the function's independent variable.

Expressing Rate of Change Information with Derivatives

One of the most important applications of the derivative is the interpretation of the derivative as a rate of change. Prior examples have shown that the derivative can be interpreted as the slope of curve. Essentially, this slope provides the rate of change of the curve. In the same way, suppose we are given a function for the cost of production of a product, for example:

$$C(x) = 5x^4 + 3x^3 - 4x^2 + 3$$

where C is the cost and x is the number of products. The rate at which this cost is changing is found by taking the derivative of $C(x)$. Since the derivative of $C(x)$ is:

$$C'(x) = 20x^3 + 9x^2 - 8x$$

and $C'(2) = 180$, we can say that the cost is increasing at a rate of $180 per item when two items are produced. Furthermore, looking at the graph below, we observe that the cost continues to increase because the slope (or rate of change) is positive on the interval $(.446, \infty)$.

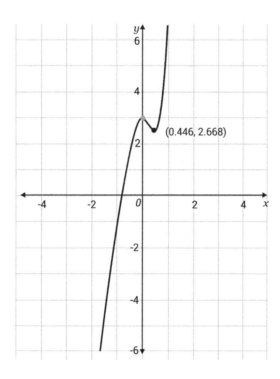

(0.446, 2.668)

64

Motion along a line is another situation where the interpretation of the derivative as a rate of change is often applied. Suppose that a particle moves along a line so that the position is given by the equation:

$$S(t) = t^2 - 6t + 8$$

where s is the distance (in meters) of the particle from the origin at time t (in seconds.) The derivative of s, $\frac{ds}{dt}$, gives the rate of change of the particle at any time, t. This is also known as the velocity of the particle. The second derivative of s, given by $\frac{d^2s}{dt^2}$ or $\frac{dv}{dt}$, gives the rate of change of the velocity, or the acceleration, of the particle at any time, t. Evaluating the derivative of s at $t = 5$, we find that:

$$s'(5) = 2(5) - 6 = 4$$

This is interpreted to show that the velocity of the particle at 5 seconds is 4 meters per second. This indicates that the particle is moving to the right at this rate.

Using the graph of this function, shown below, we find that the slope of s is positive on the interval $(3, \infty)$, indicating that the rate of change, or velocity, is positive on this interval.

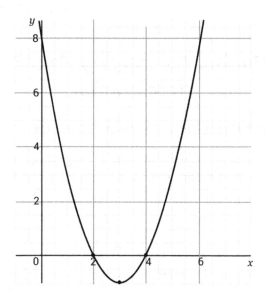

The acceleration of the particle is found using the second derivative of s, $\frac{d^2s}{dt^2} = 2$. Acceleration is the rate of change of the velocity. This value for the second derivative indicates that the velocity is increasing at a rate of 2 meters per second.

Units of Derivatives

The derivative of a function at a point is equivalent to the instantaneous rate of change at that point. Consider an object that is moving along a straight line with position at time t equal to the function $s = f(t)$. Its displacement over a time interval of length Δt is equal to:

$$\Delta s = f(t + \Delta t) - f(t)$$

The average velocity of that object over that time interval is $\frac{\Delta s}{\Delta t}$, which has units of distance over time. The limit of this quotient is taken as the time interval gets smaller and smaller, or $\Delta t \to 0$, to obtain the instantaneous velocity $v(t)$ of the object at time t, which is equal to the derivative at time t.

Therefore:

$$v(t) = s'(t) = \lim_{\Delta t \to 0} \frac{\Delta s}{\Delta t}$$

which also has units of distance over time. The speed of the object at time t is equal to the absolute value of the velocity function, or:

$$|v(t)| = |s'(t)|$$

Also, the acceleration of the object is equal to the derivative of the velocity function with respect to time. Therefore, the acceleration function is equal to the second derivative of the position function, and:

$$a(t) = v'(t) = s''(t)$$

The units of the acceleration function are units of distance over square units of time. Therefore, if the position function has units of meters, and the velocity has units of meters per second, the acceleration function would have units of meters per seconds squared.

Straight-Line Motion: Connecting Position, Velocity, and Acceleration

Using Derivatives to Solve Rectilinear Motion Problems

Rectilinear motion problems involve an object moving in a straight line. Given a position function $s = f(t)$, which outputs the position of an object given a specific time t, the object's velocity can be found by taking the derivative of the position function. Therefore, $v = f'(t)$. Its speed is equal to the absolute value of the velocity function:

$$s = |v| = |f'(t)|$$

Also, the acceleration of the object can be found by taking the second derivative of the position function. Therefore:

$$a = v' = f''(t)$$

Secondly, related rate problems also involve derivatives. Each problem involves both an unknown quantity and known quantities that involve derivatives. The key is to relate the unknown quantity or its rate of change to the known quantities or their rates of change through a known formula or equation. The equation must be differentiated with respect to the independent variable. The functions usually have time as their independent variables, so most derivatives are in respect to time and implicit differentiation needs to be used. Consider an object moving along the path $y = x^3$, and at some time t, its x-coordinate is 8 and this x-coordinate is moving at a rate of 4 units per measurement of time. To

66

find how fast the y-coordinate is moving, a related rates problem must be solved. Using implicit differentiation:

$$\frac{dy}{dt} = 3x^2 \frac{dx}{dt}$$

The problem gives that $x = 8$ and $\frac{dx}{dt} = 4$, so this equation can be used to find that the y-coordinate is moving at a rate of 768 units per measurement of time.

Finally, optimization problems also make use of derivatives. These problems involve finding either the smallest or largest value of a given function. The closed interval method can be used to find absolute extrema of a function on a closed interval. First, the critical values need to be found on the given interval. They are found by setting the derivative equal to zero and solving, and they can also exist where the derivative is undefined. Then the function is evaluated at those points and at the endpoints of the interval. The largest value is the absolute maximum within that interval, and the smallest value is the absolute minimum within that interval.

Integration can be described as an accumulation process because it takes many small areas and adds them up to find a total area over an interval. This process can be used in many real-world problems that deal with volume, area, and distance. Differentiation can also be used in real-world problems. For example, a company may want to maximize the size of the boxes it uses to ship its products. The boxes are to be cut out of a piece of cardboard that measures 8 inches long and 5 inches wide. Since squares must be cut out of the corners to make the boxes, the size of the square needs to be altered to maximize the box volume. The volume of a box can be found using the formula $V = l \times w \times h$. For length, the expression is $(8 - 2x)$ because the initial length is 8, and length x is taken from both sides of the original length to form the box. The width expression is $(5 - 2x)$. The height of the box is x. Therefore, the volume function is:

$$V = (8 - 2x)(5 - 2x)x = 40x - 26x^2 + 4x^3$$

Taking the derivative

$$V' = 40 - 52x + 12x^2$$

and setting it equal to zero will find the potential maximum and minimum points. If a maximum is found, the x-value represents the amount that needs to be cut from the corners of the box to maximize the volume. To find the volume at its max, the x-value can be substituted into the original equation.

Rates of Change in Applied Contexts Other Than Motion

Interpreting Rates of Change

In addition to motion, derivatives can be seen in many other real-world contexts. For instance, derivatives can be used in economics in which rates of changes are referred to as **marginals**. A cost function $c(x)$ in economics is the total cost for producing x units of an item. The cost of producing h more units of that item is equal to $c(x + h) - c(x)$, and the average cost of each of those additional h items is equal to:

$$\frac{c(x + h) - c(x)}{h}$$

The limit of this quantity is taken as $h \to 0$ to obtain the marginal cost of producing one more unit when the current production is at x units. Therefore, the marginal cost function is equal to the derivative of the cost function, and:

$$c'(x) = \lim_{h \to 0} \frac{c(x+h) - c(x)}{h}$$

The **marginal cost** can be thought of as the cost of producing one more item. For example, if it costs:

$$c(x) = x^3 - x^2 + 15x + 100$$

dollars to produce x items, the marginal cost function is:

$$c'(x) = 3x^2 - 2x + 15$$

Plugging $x = 2$ into this function results in:

$$c'(2) = 12 - 4 + 15 = 23$$

Therefore, the cost to produce one more item when 2 have already been produced is \$23.

Other derivatives that exist in the real world are those that deal with rates of change. Some other applications involve derivatives with respect to position in physics, financial derivatives in the financial world, population growth in biology, and rates of reaction in chemistry.

Introduction to Related Rates

Solving Related Rates

Solving related rates is an important application of implicit differentiation. Related rates problems involve discovering a relationship between given quantities by using differentiation to find relationships between the derivatives of those quantities. Once the relationship is found, which is the hardest part of the problem, the unknown quantity can be found. The problems are referred to as related rates because there is a relationship between the derivatives, or rates of change.

When taking the derivative of quantities within these problems, implicit differentiation must be used because the quantities are differentiable functions of t. Usually, t represents time, and the chain rule along with other rules must be applied to find their derivatives. The quantities change over time.

Using Other Differentiation Rules to Differentiate Variables

In addition to using implicit differentiation, other differentiation rules such as the product and quotient rules might be necessary to take the derivative of expressions in related rate problems.

Sometimes it might be helpful to draw a picture of the information given. Many of these problems consist of geometry applications, and pictures can help to determine the relationship between the given quantities. It is very important in these problems to make sure correct units are used as well.

Solving Related Rate Problems

Using Derivatives to Solve Related Rate Problems

Consider the scenario that air is being pumped into a spherical ball, like a basketball, at a rate of 3 cubic centimeters per minute. The technique of related rates can be used to determine the rate at which the radius of the ball is increasing, given a current diameter of 15 centimeters. Both the volume and the radius are changing over time t. It is given that the volume $V(t)$ of the ball is increasing and that its rate of change is 3 cubic centimeters per minute, so:

$$V'(t) = 3$$

Determining the rate at which the radius $r(t)$ is increasing is the goal, so the unknown quantity is $r'(t)$. It is also given that the diameter:

$$d = 2r = 15$$

so the current radius is $r = 7.5$ centimeters. The formula for volume of a sphere is:

$$V(t) = \frac{4}{3}\pi r^3(t)$$

The derivative of both sides is taken with respect to t using implicit differentiation and the chain rule. Therefore'

$$V'(t) = 4\pi r^2(t)r'(t)$$

Plugging in what is already known results in the equation:

$$3 = 4\pi(7.5)^2 r'(t)$$

Then $r'(t)$ is solved for to obtain the rate at which the radius is increasing is;

$$r'(t) = \frac{3}{225\pi} \approx 0.0042$$

centimeters per minute.

In summary, the related rate solution process involved first determining what quantities are known. Then, an equation is determined that relates all of the given quantities. In the given example, the equation relating the quantities was the volume formula. Third, the equation needs to be differentiated with respect to t using implicit differentiation and the chain rule, and then the known quantities need to be plugged in. The last step involves solving for the unknown quantity.

Approximating Values of a Function Using Local Linearity and Linearization

Using the Equation of a Tangent Line

The tangent line to a curve can be used as a good approximation to the y-values on the curve near the specified point. If the curve and its tangent line are both plotted in the same window on a graphing

calculator, zooming in enough will result in the two lines looking almost identical. Therefore, locally, the graphs of all curves look like straight lines. The tangent to the curve $y = f(x)$ at the point $x = a$ has the equation:

$$y = f(a) + f'(a)(x - a)$$

This equation is referred to as the linearization, or a locally linear approximation of the function $f(x)$ near the point $x = a$ and define the linearization function as:

$$L(x) = f(a) + f'(a)(x - a)$$

The point $x = a$ is sometimes referred to as the center of the approximation.

Tangent Line Approximations

For example, consider the function:

$$f(x) = \sqrt{2 + x}$$

Lets find the linearization of $f(x)$ at $x = 2$. The derivative of the function is

$$f'(x) = \frac{1}{2}(2 + x)^{-\frac{1}{2}}$$

and therefore, $f(2) = 2$ and $f'(2) = \frac{1}{4}$. The linearization is:

$$L(x) = 2 + \frac{1}{4}(x - 2) = \frac{1}{4}x + \frac{3}{2}$$

This line gives a locally linear approximation of the function $f(x)$ near the point $x = 2$. Some comparisons of the true value of the function versus the approximation can be performed using the linearization. By letting $x = 2.5$:

$$f(2.5) = \sqrt{4.5} \approx 2.121$$

and

$$L(2.5) = 2.125$$

The difference between the true value and approximate value is approximately −0.004. This is a good approximation. Selecting values further away from $x = 2$, the approximations loses accuracy. In this example, the tangent line value is an overestimate of the function value. Depending on the shape of the original function, the tangent line approximation might be an underestimate or an overestimate of the exact function value.

Using L'Hospital's Rule for Determining Limits of Indeterminate Forms

Indeterminate Forms

An **indeterminate form** is a meaningless expression in mathematics. One example of an indeterminate form is a ratio of the form $\frac{0}{0}$ or $\frac{\pm\infty}{\pm\infty}$. If direct substitution is attempted to evaluate a limit, and an indeterminate form is found, L'Hospital's rule can be used to evaluate the limit. L'Hospital's rule states that:

$$\lim_{x\to a}\frac{f(x)}{g(x)} = \lim_{x\to a}\frac{f'(x)}{g'(x)}$$

In other words, if an indeterminate form is found, take the derivative of the function in the numerator and of the function in the denominator separately to form a new function. Then, take the limit of that new function at the original point. If a limit is reached, you are finished. However, if an indeterminate form is found again, continue the process until a limit is reached. L'Hospital's rule can be used any number of times if necessary.

For example, if direct substitution is attempted to evaluate:

$$\lim_{x\to 2}\frac{x^2-4}{x-2}$$

the indeterminate form $\frac{0}{0}$ is found. Therefore, take the derivative of the function in the numerator and of the function in the denominator, creating the new function $\frac{2x}{1}$. Therefore, from direct substitution:

$$\lim_{x\to 2}\frac{x^2-4}{x-2} = \lim_{x\to 2}\frac{2x}{1} = 4$$

Sometimes indeterminate products, powers, and differences are found. In this case, they could be of the form $0 \times \infty, 0^0, \infty^0$, or $\infty - \infty$. If any of these indeterminate forms are found through direct substitution in a limit calculation, L'Hospital's rule could be applied as long as the expressions are transformed algebraically into an indeterminate form of type $\frac{0}{0}$ or $\frac{\pm\infty}{\pm\infty}$.

Using L'Hospital's Rule to Find Limits of the Indeterminate Forms

L'Hospital's Rule can be used to evaluate limits of the indeterminate forms $\frac{0}{0}$ or $\frac{\pm\infty}{\pm\infty}$. The rule says that the limit can be evaluated by taking the derivative of the numerator and the derivative of the denominator and evaluating the limit by direct substitution. It is necessary to note that the quotient rule is NOT used here, but the derivatives of the numerator and denominator are taken separately.

Take the following cases for example:

$$\lim_{x \to a} \frac{f(x)}{g(x)} = \frac{0}{0}$$

or

$$\lim_{x \to a} \frac{f(x)}{g(x)} = \frac{\pm\infty}{\pm\infty}$$

where a is any real number, infinity or negative infinity. For these cases, the equation becomes:

$$\lim_{x \to a} \frac{f(x)}{g(x)} = \lim_{x \to a} \frac{f'(x)}{g'(x)}$$

Given the limit:

$$\lim_{x \to -4} \frac{x^2 - x - 20}{x + 4}$$

with direct substitution, we find the limit to be:

$$\lim_{x \to -4} \frac{(-4)^2 - (-4) - 20}{(-4) + 4} = \frac{0}{0}$$

an indeterminate form. We could use the method of factoring and simplifying as described above. However, we can also use L'Hospital's Rule. The rule says that the limit can be evaluated by taking the derivative of the numerator and the derivative of the denominator and evaluating the limit by direct substitution. Applying the rule, we will take the derivative of the numerator to get $2x - 1$ and the derivative of the denominator to get 1. Then, we evaluate the new form of this limit:

$$\lim_{x \to -4} \frac{2x-1}{1} = \lim_{x \to -4} \frac{2(-4)-1}{1} = -9$$

Indeterminate forms might look like $\frac{\pm\infty}{\pm\infty}$ as well. Let's look at:

$$\lim_{x \to \infty} \frac{e^{2x}}{x^2}$$

Evaluating this limit, we see that as x approaches infinity, e^{2x} will approach infinity and as x approaches infinity, x^2 will also approach infinity so we have the indeterminate form $\frac{\infty}{\infty}$. Applying L'Hospital's Rule, we take the derivative of e^{2x} to get $2e^{2x}$ in the numerator and the derivative of x^2 to get $2x$ in the denominator; thus, now evaluate:

$$\lim_{x \to \infty} \frac{2e^{2x}}{2x}$$

Now evaluating these limits, it is found that there is still an indeterminate form, $\frac{\infty}{\infty}$. Now apply L'Hospital's Rule again. This time we take the derivative of $2e^{2x}$ to get $4e^{2x}$ and the derivative of $2x$ to get 2. We now have $\lim_{x \to \infty} \frac{4e^{2x}}{2}$ and evaluating finds the limit to be $\frac{\infty}{2}$. The limit is ∞.

Unit 5: Analytical Applications of Differentiation

Using the Mean Value Theorem

The Mean Value Theorem, Rolle's Theorem, and L'Hospital's Rule

The **Mean Value Theorem** states that for any continuous function f, on $[a, b]$ there exists a real number represented by c between a and b, where the derivative at the given point equals the slope of the second line connecting a and b. This value can be found by solving the equation:

$$f'(c) = \frac{f(b) - f(a)}{b - a}$$

Rolle's Theorem is a specific case that states if f is a continuous function on the interval $[a, b]$, f' is differentiable on (a, b), and $f(a) = f(b)$, then then there exists at least one real number c in (a, b) such that $f'(c) = 0$.

The graph below can be used to explain the Mean Value Theorem.

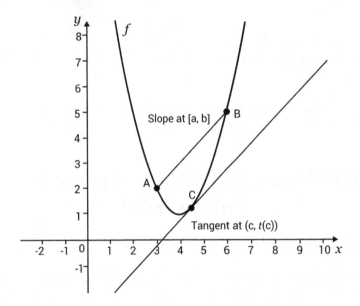

The **Mean Value Theorem** says that if there is a function that is continuous and differentiable on a certain internal, say $[a, b]$, then there is a guaranteed point, $(c, f(c))$ on that interval where the slope of the function is equal to the slope of the secant line between a and b. Essentially, this means that the derivate at c, or we can say the slope of the curve at c or the slope of the tangent line at c, is equal to the slope of the line through points $(a, f(a))$ and $(b, f(b))$. Mathematically it looks like the following function:

$$f'(c) = \frac{f(b) - f(a)}{b - a}$$

For an example, suppose that:

$$f(x) = (x - 2)^2$$

and we are interested in the interval $[1, 5]$. We know that since f is a polynomial function, it is continuous for all values of x so f is continuous on $[1, 5]$. Also:

$$f'(x) = 2(x - 2) = 2x - 4$$

so the function is differentiable on $(1, 5)$. Therefore, the conditions of the Mean Value Theorem are met.

The theorem states then that there is a value of x, the theorem calls it c, in the interval $(1, 5)$ where the derivative of f is equal to the slope of the line between the points $(1, 1)$ and $(5, 9)$ on the curve. To find that value of c, the slope of the line is found first. The slope is found by taking the difference in y-values and dividing it by the difference in x-values. The following calculation shows the value of the slope:

$$\frac{9 - 1}{5 - 1} = 2$$

Now to find the guaranteed c-value, the derivative is set equal to 2. The equation becomes:

$$2c - 4 = 2$$

Solving this equation in two steps can be shown in adding 4 to both sides, then dividing both sides by 2. The resulting equation is $c = 3$.

Now the value of c has been found in the interval (a, b) where the derivative of f (which we know is the instantaneous rate of change), equals the slope of the secant line of f (which we know is the average rate of change of f).

Extreme Value Theorem, Global Versus Local Extrema, and Critical Points

Applying the Extreme Value Theorem

Consider the function defined over its domain D. The value $f(c)$ is an absolute or global maximum value on D if and only if $f(x) \leq f(c)$ for all x values in the domain D. The value $f(c)$ is an absolute or global

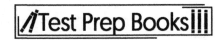

minimum value of D if and only if $f(x) \geq f(c)$ for all x values in the domain D. Absolute maximum and minimum values are also referred to as global extrema. Consider the function:

$$f(x) = x^2$$

whose graph can be seen here:

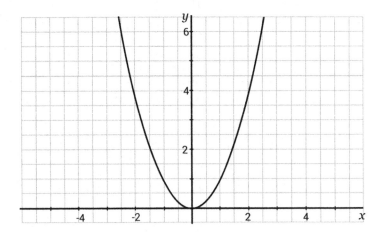

It has an absolute minimum at $x = 0$, and the absolute minimum value is equal to $f(0) = 0$. This example does not have an absolute maximum because its range is $[0, \infty)$. Second, consider the function $f(x) = -x^2$, whose graph can be seen here:

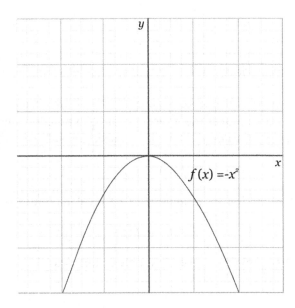

It has an absolute maximum at $x = 0$, and the absolute maximum value is equal to $f(0) = 0$. This example does not have an absolute minimum because its range is $(-\infty, 0]$. These two examples show

that a function does not have to have both types of global extrema. Some functions do not have any extrema. Consider the function $f(x) = x^3$, whose graph is shown here:

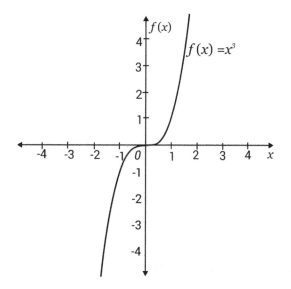

This function has neither an absolute maximum nor an absolute minimum.

The **Extreme Value Theorem** states that if $f(x)$ is continuous over a closed interval $[a, b]$, then the function has both an absolute maximum value and absolute minimum value on that interval. For instance, even though the function:

$$f(x) = x^3$$

does not have an absolute maximum or minimum over its domain, if only the interval $[0, 4]$ is considered, an **absolute minimum** occurs at $x = 0$, and an **absolute maximum** occurs at $x = 4$.

Local, otherwise known as relative, extreme values are different from absolute extreme values. **Absolute extreme values** are defined over the entire domain of a function, and **local extreme values** are defined only nearby a given point. A value $f(c)$ is a local maximum value if and only if:

$$f(x) \leq f(c)$$

for all x in an open interval that contains c. A value $f(c)$ is a local minimum value if and only if:

$$f(x) \geq f(c)$$

for all x in an open interval that contains c. Note that only values close to c are being looked at and not values over the entire domain of the function.

To determine local extreme values of a function, the critical values of a function must be found. A critical point of a function $f(x)$ is a point c that is in the domain of the function and either $f'(c) = 0$ or $f'(c)$ is undefined. Therefore, an interior point of a function's domain can be a relative extreme value if the derivative at that point is either equal to 0 or undefined. Note that it is not true that every critical point is an extreme value. Just because a critical value is found, it does not mean that an extreme value exists at that point.

Determining Intervals on Which a Function Is Increasing or Decreasing

Using the First Derivative of a Function

If $f(x)$ is defined on the interval I, then $f(x)$ increases over the entire interval I if for any two points a and b in the interval where:

$$a \leq b, f(a) \leq f(b)$$

Conversely, $f(x)$ decreases over the entire interval I if for any two points a and b in the interval where:

$$a \leq b$$

$$f(a) \geq f(b)$$

The first derivative test for increasing and decreasing functions allow us to determine over which intervals a function is increasing and decreasing. If a function $f(x)$ is continuous over $[a, b]$ and differentiable over (a, b) and if $f'(x) > 0$ over the entire interval (a, b), then the function $f(x)$ increases over the interval $[a, b]$. If $f'(x) < 0$ over the entire interval (a, b), then the function $f(x)$ decreases over the interval $[a, b]$.

For instance, consider the function:

$$f(x) = x^2$$

Its first derivative is equal to:

$$f'(x) = 2x$$

The first derivative is negative over the interval $(-\infty, 0)$ and is positive over the interval $(0, \infty)$. Therefore, by the first derivative test, the function is decreasing over the interval $(-\infty, 0]$ and increasing over the interval $[0, \infty)$. These properties can be verified by looking at the graph of $f(x)$.

Using the First Derivative Test to Determine Relative (Local) Extrema

Determining the Location of Relative Extrema

A function's first derivative can be used to visualize both the rise and fall of its graph. A function rises, or is increasing, when its first derivative is positive, and function falls, or is decreasing, when its first derivative is negative. Therefore, at some point, the derivative changes sign if the function changes from increasing to decreasing or from decreasing to increasing. The points at which the derivative changes sign are local extreme values.

The first derivative test for local extreme values tests critical points of a function to determine if they are local extrema. If a critical point of $f(x)$ exists at $x = c$, and if $f'(x)$ changes from negative to positive at that point, then the function has a local minimum there. If $f'(x)$ changes from positive to negative at

that critical point, then the function has a local maximum there. Finally, if $f'(x)$ remains the same sign on either side of the critical point, then there is no local extreme value at that point. The function:

$$f(x) = x^2$$

can also be used to visualize this test. The function's derivative changes sign at the critical point $x = 0$. The function's derivative changes from negative to positive at that point, and therefore, a local minimum exists at the critical point $x = 0$.

Using the Candidates Test to Determine Absolute (Global) Extrema

Determining Absolute Extrema

All this information can be put together to find both absolute and local extreme values. Extreme values of a continuous function defined over a closed interval can occur at interior points of the domain where either the derivative is equal to 0 or undefined or at the endpoints of the domain. Therefore, in order to find absolute extrema using the closed interval method, all the critical points must be tested within that interval and the endpoints of the interval. The smallest function value is the absolute minimum value, and the largest function value is the absolute maximum value.

For instance, consider the function:

$$f(x) = x^4$$

defined over the interval $[-2, 2]$. It has a critical point at $x = 0$ because

$$f'(x) = 4x^3$$

at $x = 0$. The absolute minimum value of the function exists at that point, and its minimum value is $f(0) = 0$. The absolute maximum value of the function exists at both endpoints because:

$$f(-2) = f(2) = 16$$

Determining Concavity of Functions Over Their Domains

Determining Concavity Using the Derivative of a Function

A function is **concave up** if it opens upward. For instance, the function:

$$f(x) = x^2$$

is concave up over its entire domain. A function is **concave down** if it opens downward. For instance, the function:

$$f(x) = -x^2$$

is concave down over its entire domain. It is true that the graph of a differentiable function $f(x)$ is concave up on an open interval if its derivative $f'(x)$ is increasing on that interval. Also, the graph of a differentiable function $f(x)$ is concave down on an open interval if its derivative $f'(x)$ is decreasing on that interval.

Determining Concavity Using the Second Derivative of a Function

As the first derivative gives us information about the shape of a graph, the second derivative can also give some information. The second derivative of a function can determine where a graph is concave up or concave down. Because a function is increasing if its derivative is positive and decreasing if its derivative is negative, this information allows us to define the second derivative test for concavity. It states that a function that is twice differentiable is concave up on an interval in which its second derivative is greater than 0 and is concave down on an interval in which its second derivative is less than 0. It is neither concave up nor concave down when its second derivative is equal to 0.

For example, the second derivative of the function:

$$f(x) = x^2$$

is

$$f''(x) = 2$$

which is always greater than 0. This analysis shows why the graph of the function is always concave up. Also, the second derivative of the function:

$$f(x) = -x^2$$

is

$$f''(x) = -2$$

which is always less than 0. This analysis shows why the graph of this function is always concave down.

Using the Second Derivative of a Function to Locate Points of Inflection

Some graphs can have points in the domain in which the function changes from concave up to concave down or from concave down to concave up. A point at which the graph changes concavity is referred to as a point of inflection. The graph of the original function also has a tangent line at that point. Either the second derivative of the original function is equal to 0 or is undefined at a point of inflection, and the graph of the first derivative function $f'(x)$ has either a local maximum or local minimum at an inflection point. Therefore, to find inflection points of functions, the points in which $f''(x)$ is either equal to 0 or undefined must be found.

Using the Second Derivative Test to Determine Extrema

Using the Second Derivative of a Function to Locate Relative Maximum and Minimum

The second derivative test for local extrema uses the second derivative of a function to test critical points in order to determine if those points are local extrema. Consider a point c in the domain of a function $f(x)$.

If $f'(c) = 0$ and $f''(c) < 0$, then the function $f(x)$ has a local maximum at $x = c$. Because that point is a critical point, and the graph is concave down at that point, it is the highest point locally. If $f'(c) = 0$ and $f''(c) > 0$, then the function $f(x)$ has a local minimum at c. Because that point is a critical point,

and the graph is concave up at that point, it is the lowest point locally. Note that if a critical point of a function is found, but the second derivative fails to exist or is equal to 0 at that given point, then the second derivative test cannot be used. The first derivative test would have to be used in such a scenario to determine if it is either a local max or min.

Determining If a Local Extremum Corresponds to an Absolute Extremum

In some scenarios, tests for local extrema lead to classifying absolute extrema. For instance, consider a function that only has one critical point on an interval on its domain, and the second derivative test concludes that it is a local maximum. It might be true that this point is also a global maximum. For instance, consider the function:

$$f(x) = x^6$$

The first derivative of the function is:

$$f'(x) = 6x^5$$

and setting the derivative equal to 0 results in only one critical point $x = 0$. This critical point corresponds to a local minimum over the interval $[-3, 3]$. However, because there is only one critical point over this closed interval, this local minimum is also an absolute minimum. If a continuous function has only one critical point inside a smaller interval that is a subset of its domain, the critical point can be classified as both a local and absolute extreme value over that interval.

Sketching Graphs of Functions and Their Derivatives

Key Features of Functions and Their Derivatives

The first derivative of a function can be used to determine almost everything needed to be known about the shape of a graph of a function that is twice differentiable. It is known where it both rises and falls, based on the sign of the first derivative over specific intervals. Locations of extrema can be determined because local maxima and minima exist at critical points where the first derivative is zero or undefined. Also, if a function bends can be determined based whether the graph is either concave up or concave down, based on where the first derivative is positive or negative. All this information can be summarized together to sketch the graph of a function. Thus, the graphical, numerical, and analytical representations of a graph can all be utilized when sketching a graph of a function by hand. The only information that the derivative does not give is where exactly in the plane the graph lies. The location of the graph can be determined by plugging at least one point into the function of the graph and determining the output to obtain a coordinate pair to plot. A common point to use is the y-intercept.

Consider the function:

$$f(x) = x^4 + 4$$

Its first derivative is:

$$f'(x) = 4x^3$$

Both $f(x)$ and $f'(x)$ have a domain of $(-\infty, \infty)$. The function has one critical point $x = 0$, which is found by setting $f'(x) = 0$. The critical point splits up the domain into two intervals over which the function either rises or falls. The intervals are $(-\infty, 0)$ and $(0, \infty)$. The first derivative is positive over

$(0, \infty)$ and negative over $(-\infty, 0)$. Therefore, the graph rises over $(0, \infty)$ and falls over $(-\infty, 0)$. Because the first derivative changes from negative to positive at $x = 0$, the point is a local maximum. The second derivative of the function is:

$$f''(x) = 12x^2$$

and is equal to 0 at $x = 0$. This point is a potential inflection point, and it splits up the domain into the same two intervals $(-\infty, 0)$ and $(0, \infty)$. The second derivative is positive over both intervals, so the graph is concave up over its entire domain. Therefore, the point $x = 0$ is not an inflection point because the graph does not change concavity there. The y-intercept of the function is $f(0) = 4$. The following figure shows the graph of the function:

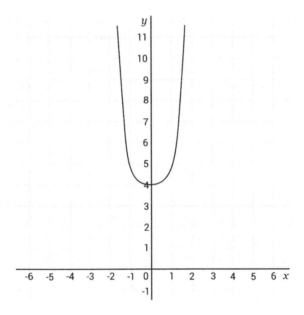

Using Derivatives to Predict and Explain the Behavior of a Function

To sketch a graph by hand, without using technology, analytical information from both the first derivative and second derivative of a function must be summarized. First, where extrema occur must be determined. Then, over which intervals of the domain the function is increasing or decreasing should be found. Finally, inflections points and intervals of the domain over which the function is concave up or concave down must be located.

Consider the function:

$$f(x) = x^3 - 3x + 2$$

It has derivative:

$$f'(x) = 3x^2 - 3$$

Both $f(x)$ and $f'(x)$ have a domain of $(-\infty, \infty)$. The critical points exist where the first derivative either does not exist or is equal to 0. Setting $f'(x) = 0$ results in:

$$3(x^2 - 1) = 3(x + 1)(x - 1) = 0$$

so the critical points exist at $x = \pm 1$. These critical points allow us to split up the domain into three intervals over which the function either rises or falls. The intervals are $(-\infty, -1), (-1, 1)$, and $(1, \infty)$.

The first derivative is positive over $(-\infty, -1)$ and $(1, \infty)$ and negative over $(-1, 1)$. Therefore, the graph rises over $(-\infty, -1)$ and $(1, \infty)$ and falls over $(-1, 1)$. Because the first derivative changes from positive to negative at $x = -1$, a local maximum exists at that ordered pair. Also, because the first derivative changes from negative to positive at $x = 1$, a local minimum exists at that ordered pair. The second derivative of the function is:

$$f''(x) = 6x$$

and is equal to 0 at $x = 0$. This point is a potential inflection point, and it splits up the domain into the two intervals $(-\infty, 0)$ and $(0, \infty)$. The second derivative is negative over the interval $(-\infty, 0)$, so the graph is concave down over this region. The second derivative is positive over the interval $(0, \infty)$, so the graph is concave up over this region. Therefore, the point $x = 0$ is an inflection point because the graph

changes concavity at this ordered pair. The y-intercept of the function is $f(0) = 2$. The following figure shows the graph of the function:

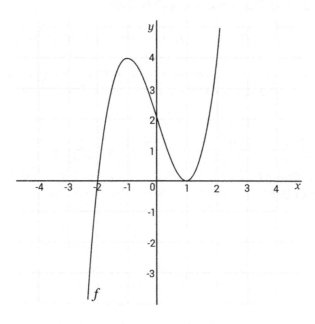

Connecting a Function, Its First Derivative, and Its Second Derivative

Key Features of the Graphs of Functions and Their Derivatives

In summary, the first and second derivative tests show that a function, its first derivative, and its second derivative are all related and can help determine the shape of a graph. If a function $f(x)$ is continuous and differentiable, its first and second derivatives are taken to determine important aspects of the graph. If:

$$f'(x) > 0$$

over a subinterval of the domain, the graph rises over that region. If:

$$f'(x) < 0$$

over a subinterval of the domain, the graph falls over that region. Points at which the graph changes from rising to falling are **local maxima**, and points at which the graph changes from falling to rising are **local minima**. If:

$$f''(x) > 0$$

over a subinterval of the domain, the graph is concave up over that region. If:

$$f''(x) < 0$$

over a subinterval of the domain, the graph is concave down over that region. Points at which the graph changes concavity are inflection points.

Introduction to Optimization Problems

Using Derivatives to Solve Optimization Problems

Optimizing a function means that you are finding either the maximum or minimum value of that function. Mathematically, maximum and minimum values are found by using the first derivative of the given function. First derivatives are used to find and classify critical points of the function over the given domain. Recall that critical points are values for which either the first derivative is equal to zero or undefined.

For instance, consider that you are building a rectangular garden and have 200 feet of fencing. One side of the garden is against your house, so you only must fence three sides. To find the largest possible garden, an optimization process would be used. Let x be length of the side of the garden parallel to the house and y be the length of the other two parallel sides. Therefore, the garden has an area of $a = xy$ and a perimeter of:

$$p = 2x + 2y$$

However, only three sides need to be fenced in, so if all 200 feet of fencing is used:

$$200 = x + 2y$$

Solving this equation for x results in:

$$x = 200 - 2y$$

This equation is plugged into the area formula to obtain:

$$a = (200 - 2y)\, y = 200y - 2y^2$$

which is now a function of only y. This is the function needing to be maximized. Note that its domain is $y > 0$; only positive lengths should be used. Its first derivative is equal to:

$$a'(y) = 200 - 4y$$

Setting this equal to 0 and solving for y gives the critical point $y = 50$. Because this is the only critical point, the maximum value of the function exists at this point. Therefore, one of the sides of the garden of maximum area is 50 feet long. The other side is 100 feet long, which is found by using the equation:

$$x = 200 - 2y$$

These values are plugged in to the formula for area to obtain:

$$a = 50(100) = 5,000$$

Therefore, the largest garden that can be made with the given fencing is 5,000 square feet.

Solving Optimization Problems

Interpreting Minimum and Maximum Values of a Function

Optimization problems are useful in many different scenarios and the maximum and minimum values of a given function can have various meanings. Depending on the situation, either the maximum value or the minimum value might be optimal. For instance, in economics, the minimum value of a cost function would be optimal, but the maximum value of a revenue function would be optimal. Also, in construction, a building that has the maximum area or volume might be the most desirable but would also be the most expensive. It would be up to the builder to determine whether the largest or the smallest was optimal.

Another scenario in which optimization is used is with equations of motion. To determine the maximum height of an object over a given time interval, the maximum value of the given position function would have to be determined. To determine the maximum velocity over a given time interval, the maximum value of the velocity function would have to be determined.

Exploring Behaviors of Implicit Relations

Determining Critical Points of a Function

A function can be given explicitly or implicitly. Either way, the way in which a critical point is defined is still the same. Critical points exist at places in the domain at which either the first derivative equals 0 or does not exist. If a function is not defined explicitly, **implicit differentiation** can be used to find the first derivative. For instance, consider the equation:

$$x^2y + x = 8$$

which is an implicitly defined function. Therefore, $\frac{dy}{dx}$ can be found by using implicit differentiation. It is true that:

$$\frac{d}{dx}(x^2y + x) = \frac{d}{dx}(8)$$

so

$$2xy + x^2\frac{dy}{dx} + 1 = 0$$

Solving this equation for $\frac{dy}{dx}$ results in:

$$\frac{dy}{dx} = \frac{-1 - 2xy}{x^2}$$

It has a critical point at $x = 0$ because the first derivative is undefined at that point.

Implicitly Defined Functions

In addition to explicitly defined functions, applications of derivatives can also be found within implicitly defined functions. As discussed previously, related rate problems involve implicit differentiation of

equations that relate quantities that change over time. These equations include real world quantities such as measurements of length, height, and any other distance. When such quantities are differentiated, the chain rule must be used because the quantities are changing over time. Another important application of implicit differentiation is finding the tangent to a curve at a given point. If the function is defined implicitly, implicit differentiation must be used to find the first derivative of the function, which would then allow the slope of the tangent line to be calculated.

Second Derivatives Involving Implicit Differentiation

Implicit differentiation can also be used to find second derivatives and derivatives of higher order. When calculating the second derivative of an implicitly defined function, implicit differentiation is first used to find the first derivative, and then another differentiation process is used to find the second derivative. The second derivative might be defined in terms of the quantities x, y, and dx. For instance, consider the implicitly defined function:

$$4x^3 - 8y^2 = 2$$

In order to find the second derivative, the first derivative must be calculated. The differential operator $\frac{d}{dx}$ is applied to both sides of the equation to obtain:

$$12x^2 - 16y\frac{dy}{dx} = 0$$

Solving for:

$$\frac{dy}{dx}, \frac{dy}{dx} = \frac{3x^2}{4y}$$

The quotient rule can be used to find the second derivative. Therefore:

$$\frac{d^2y}{dx^2} = \frac{24xy - 12x^2\frac{dy}{dx}}{16y^2}$$

Finally, $\frac{dy}{dx} = \frac{3x^2}{4y}$ is substituted into this equation to obtain:

$$\frac{d^2y}{dx^2} = \frac{24xy - \frac{9x^4}{y}}{16y^2}$$

which is written only in terms of x and y.

Unit 6: Integration and Accumulation of Change

Exploring Accumulations of Change

Finding the Accumulation of Change

Consider a function $f(x)$ that represents the rate of change of a quantity given the independent variable x. If $f(x)$ is restricted over the interval from $x = a$ to $x = b$, the area of the region between the graph of the function and the two vertical lines represents the accumulation of change of the function over the given interval. A common application involves a velocity function. If $f(x)$ represents the velocity of a given object, the area of the region between the graph of the function over the interval $[a, b]$ represents the total distance traveled over that interval. The velocity is a rate of change function, and the distance traveled is an accumulation of change.

Using Geometry to Evaluate Accumulation of Change

If a function $f(x)$ is nonnegative and integrable over the interval $[a, b]$, then the definite integral:

$$\int_a^b f(x)\, dx$$

represents the area under the curve $y = f(x)$ from $x = a$ to $x = b$. If the shape of that region is simple enough to use a geometric formula instead of an integral, only that formula is necessary to calculate the area.

First, consider the definite integral of a horizontal line. For instance, let us determine the integral of $y = 4$ over the interval $[2, 6]$. In other words, we are trying to find the area of the rectangular region under the horizontal line $y = 4$ from $x = 2$ to $x = 6$. Because this region is a rectangle, we need to just use the formula for area of a rectangle and multiply the base times the height of the region.

The height of the region is 4 units because the horizontal line is 4 units above the x-axis. The base of the region is $6 - 2 = 4$ units long. Therefore:

$$\int_2^6 4\, dx = 4(4) = 16$$

square units. In general, for a constant c, the definite integral is:

$$\int_a^b c\, dx = c(b - a)$$

which is merely base times height.

Other regions can involve different types of geometric shapes. Consider the definite integral of the function $y = x$ from $x = 0$ to $x = 3$. The region being discussed is triangular because the graph of the function is a straight line with slope 1 and y-intercept 0. Its base is 3 units long, and its height is found by evaluating the function at its highest point in the interval, which is at $x = 3$. Therefore, its height is 3

units long. The formula for the area of a triangle is $A = \frac{1}{2}bh$, where b = its base and h = its height. For this region, we have:

$$\int_0^3 xdx = \frac{1}{2}(3)(3) = \frac{9}{2}$$

square units.

A region might involve the sum of a few different area calculations if it is made up of a few different types of geometric shapes. Also, if a portion of the given function $y = f(x)$ lies below the x-axis, then we need to adjust for the signed area. The signed area of a region is equal to the area above the x-axis minus the area below the x-axis. Regardless of whether $f(x)$ is positive or negative:

$$\int_a^b f(x)dx$$

is equivalent to the signed area of the region bounded by the graph of $y = f(x)$ from $x = a$ to $x = b$.

Consider the following region:

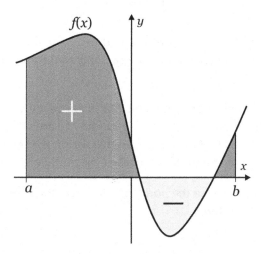

In order to calculate the definite integral of $f(x)$ over $[a, b]$, the areas of both the blue and the yellow regions must be found separately. The nonnegative blue areas are first totaled. Then the yellow area, which is the area below the x-axis, is subtracted from the area of the blue region. Note that this calculation is different than finding the definite integral of $|f(x)|$. In that case, all three regions would have a positive area and would be added together.

Interpreting the Rate of Change

If a rate of change is positive over a given interval, then the accumulation of change will be positive. For instance, if an object always travels with positive velocity, then the accumulation of change, or distance traveled, will be positive. The object will always be traveling in the forward direction. However, if a rate of change is negative, then the accumulation of change will be negative. Therefore, if an object travels with negative velocity over an interval, then the distance traveled during that time interval will be negative.

Determining the Unit for the Area of a Region

It is important to recognize the difference between the units for the rate of change function and the units for the accumulation of change. For example, if the rate of change function is velocity, the units could be meters per second, and the independent variable would have units of meters. In this instance, the accumulation of change would have units of meters, which is equal to the units of the rate of change function times the units of the independent variable. This statement is true regardless of the units of the rate of change function. The units of the accumulation function, or the area of a region, is always equal to the units of the rate of change function times the units of the independent variable.

Approximating Areas with Riemann Sums

Approximating Definite Integrals for Functions

There are many real-life situations that have properties that can be estimated using definite integrals and corresponding approximations with finite sums. A common instance of such a real-world application involves determining distance traveled. Suppose that someone is driving a vehicle and the velocity function:

$$v = \frac{ds}{dt}$$

is known. The units of velocity could be meters per second or miles per hour. Let's say we wanted to determine how far the vehicle traveled in some specific time interval. Because we know that the derivative of a position function is equal to its corresponding velocity function, it is true that the antiderivative of the velocity function is equal to the corresponding position function s. Recall that a position function gives the vehicle's position at some time t.

Because we know the velocity of the vehicle at every time over the given time interval, we can estimate its total distance traveled. Let's say that we want to determine the distance traveled from $t = a$ to $t = b$. We partition the time interval $[a, b]$ into subintervals that have constant, or almost constant, velocity. The distance formula $d = r \times t$ can be used on each subinterval to find the distance traveled over each individual subinterval. For each subinterval the rate is equal to the velocity:

$$r = v = \frac{ds}{dt}$$

and the time is equal to the length of the subinterval Δt. The total distance traveled by the vehicle over the entire interval is equal to the sum of the distances traveled by the vehicle over all subintervals. Note that this scenario works only if the vehicle does not change direction. If the vehicle changes direction, this approximation can be used only to calculate total displacement. If total distance traveled is needed and the vehicle does change direction, we would use $|v|$ in place of v for each distance formula so that speed, the absolute value of velocity, is used. This way negative distances, or moving backwards, would be taken into consideration.

A similar estimation process using finite sums can be used in other real-world scenarios. Consider a ball that is thrown into the air. Its velocity function is:

$$v = v_0 - gt$$

where v_0 is its initial velocity and g represents the gravity constant $9.8\frac{m}{s^2}$. We could use a finite sum to determine how far the ball traveled during a given number of seconds before it hit the ground. The time interval would be partitioned into subintervals, and the distance formula could be applied to each individual subinterval. If the time interval included both the rise and fall of the ball, we use speed instead of velocity over the intervals of descent. Therefore, we would use the absolute value of the velocity function over those intervals. Finally, the individual distances would be totaled to determine how far the ball traveled over the given time interval.

Approximating Definite Integrals with Riemann Sums

Similar to the way in which distance traveled can be approximated, finite sums can be used to approximate definite integrals. Consider a function $f(x)$ defined on the interval $[a, b]$. We can partition that interval into n distinct subintervals so that:

$$a = x_0 < x_1 < \cdots < x_{n-1} < x_n = b$$

In general, the kth subinterval is $[x_{k-1}, x_k]$, and its length is:

$$\Delta x_k = x_{k-1} - x_k$$

We select a value in each subinterval to evaluate the function, called the sample points. The function evaluations at those sample points are equal to the distance from the function to the x-axis at the chosen points. This dimension, along with the length of the subinterval, creates a rectangle for each subinterval. In total, the sum of the rectangles represents an approximation of the area of region between the graph of the function $f(x)$ and the x-axis. The area of each rectangle is equal to the length of the subinterval times the height of the rectangle. The sum of all individual rectangles is known as the Riemann sum of $f(x)$ over the interval $[a, b]$. The smaller the subintervals, the better the approximation to the actual area between the function and the x-axis.

The chosen sample points within in each subinterval can be specified. For instance, if the left endpoints of each subinterval are used, a left Riemann sum is calculated. If the right endpoints of each subinterval are used, a right Riemann sum is calculated. The midpoints of each subinterval can also be used, and a

midpoint Riemann sum would be calculated. Here are drawings of Riemann sums with four subintervals in which a left, a right, and a midpoint Riemann sum are drawn:

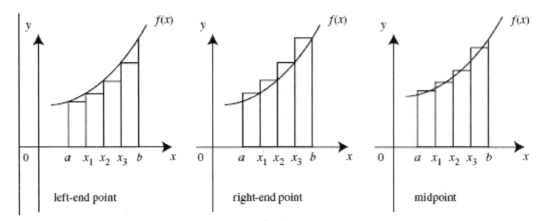

Notice that the left Riemann sum is an underestimate and the right Riemann sum is an overestimate for the actual region between the function and the x-axis. In other words, the actual area is greater than the left Riemann sum approximation, and it is less than the right Riemann sum approximation. This is due to the nature of the function being used; it is not always the case. In each Riemann sum, the length of each subinterval remains uniform. However, this too is not always the case. We could use nonuniform lengths if desired.

Another approximation to the area under a curve is known as the trapezoidal sum. In this case, trapezoids, instead of rectangles, are used to approximate the area between the function and the x-axis. Using a uniform subinterval length of $\frac{b-a}{n}$ and n subintervals, the area of the trapezoid on the kth subinterval is:

$$\Delta x \left(\frac{f(x_{k-1}) + f(x_k)}{2} \right)$$

An example can be seen in the graph shown here:

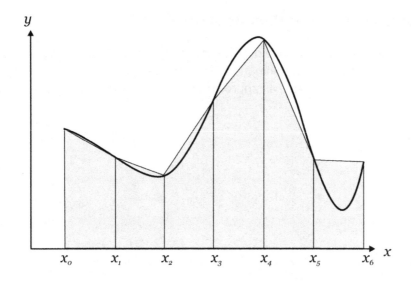

In general, to approximate the integral of $f(x)$ from $x = a$ to $x = b$ by using a trapezoidal sum, use:

$$T = \frac{\Delta x}{2}(x_0 + 2x_1 + 2x_2 + \cdots + 2x_{n-1} + x_n)$$

Where:

$$\Delta x = \frac{b - a}{n}$$

and

$$x_k = x_{k-1} + \Delta x$$

An estimation with a trapezoidal rule tends to be a better approximation than one using left, right, or midpoint sums. Due to the nature of the trapezoids, there is less of a chance for such extreme over- or underestimation.

Approximating Definite Integrals Using Numerical Methods

The sample points selected within each subinterval can be specific. The left endpoints, right endpoints, or midpoints of each subinterval can be used. These finite sums can be calculated with or without technology. Graphing calculators have methods for evaluating finite sums, and **Computer Algebra Systems (CAS)** have built in functionality to calculate finite sums as well. For instance, the Midpoint Rule in a CAS can be used to calculate a finite sum using the midpoints as the sample points.

If a function $f(x)$ is nonnegative and integrable over the interval $[a, b]$, then the definite integral:

$$\int_a^b f(x)\, dx$$

represents the area under the curve $y = f(x)$ from $x = a$ to $x = b$. If the shape of that region is simple enough to use a geometric formula instead of an integral, only that formula is necessary to calculate the area.

Evaluating Approximations of Definite Integrals

Here is a picture of a function $f(x)$ drawn over the interval $[a, b]$ that has been partitioned into four subintervals. In the first graph, an approximation to the definite integral is drawn using left endpoints as the sample points. In the second graph, an approximation to the definite integral is drawn using right

endpoints as the sample points. In the third graph, an approximation to the definite integral is drawn using midpoints as the sample points.

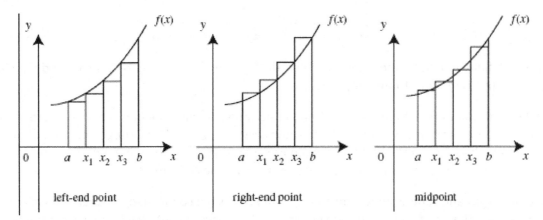

Note that the first graph shows an underestimate to the area, the second graph shows an overestimate to the area, and the third graph shows the best estimate to the area. For the overestimate, the area being calculated is greater than the finite sum approximation. For the underestimate, the area being calculated is less than the finite sum approximation. This is because the function is increasing. If the function was decreasing, the left-endpoints would result in an overestimate, and the right-endpoints would result in an underestimate. The behavior of a function, depending on whether it is increasing over an interval or decreasing over an interval, can help determine whether a finite sum approximation would be an underestimate or an overestimate. If a function is increasing over an interval, a left-endpoint approximation is an underestimate and a right-endpoint approximation is an overestimate. If a function is decreasing over an interval, a left-endpoint approximation is an overestimate and a right-endpoint approximation is an underestimate.

Riemann Sums, Summation Notation, and Definite Integral Notation

The Limit of an Approximating Riemann Sum

We know that the smaller the subintervals used in the Riemann sum calculations, the better they are as an approximation to the definite integral. It is true that the definite integral of the function $f(x)$ over the interval $[a, b]$ is equal to the limit of the Riemann sums as the subintervals get smaller and smaller. Therefore, the number of subintervals used in the calculation gets larger and larger and approaches infinity. As the subintervals get smaller and smaller, the rectangular approximations to the area between the function and the x-axis get closer to the exact region whose area is being calculated.

A Riemann sum is denoted as

$$\sum_{i=1}^{N} f(c_i)\Delta x$$

where N is the number of subintervals used to partition the given interval, Δx is the length of each subinterval, and c_i is the chosen sample point in each ith subinterval that is used to calculate the height of the rectangle.

If we take the limit of the Riemann sum as N approaches infinity, we have:

$$\int_a^b f(x)dx = \lim_{N\to\infty} \sum_{i=1}^N f(c_i)\Delta x$$

Basically, the definite integral is the result of limit of the Riemann sums as we use skinnier and skinnier rectangles for approximations to the area.

Limits of Riemann sums are not typically used when calculating definite integrals. They are more often used from a theoretical point of view in order to show what finding a definite integral involves visually. The fundamental theorem of calculus and other approximations such as the midpoint and trapezoidal rules are preferred methods because they are easier and less time consuming.

The notation of Riemann sums is important to understand, as is the connection between the limit of Riemann sums and the notation of a definite integral. Let's say that the interval $[-2, 4]$ is partitioned into n subintervals of equal length. Therefore, the length of each subinterval has length:

$$\frac{4 - (-2)}{n} = \frac{6}{n}$$

Let c_k represent a sample point chosen for the kth interval:

$$[x_{k-1}, x_k]$$

If we form the following limit:

$$\lim_{n\to\infty} \sum_{k=1}^n (5(c_k)^3 + 2c_k + 1)\left(\frac{6}{n}\right)$$

we have a limit of Riemann sums. The sample points can be any points from each interval, including midpoints, left endpoints, or right endpoints. The function being integrated is:

$$f(x) = 5x^3 + 2x + 1$$

and the definite integral is written as:

$$\int_{-2}^4 (5x^3 + 2x + 1)dx$$

Riemann Sums

Riemann sums can be used to calculate the area under a curve $y = f(x)$ from $x = a$ to $x = b$. In other words, Riemann sums can be used to find:

$$\int_a^b f(x)dx$$

The interval from a to b is divided into n subintervals of equal length Δx, and the function is evaluated at a point x_i^* in each interval. This creates a rectangle over each subinterval, and the area of each rectangle can be found and summed.

The area of each rectangle is:

$$f(x_i^*)\Delta x$$

The total area is:

$$\sum_{i=1}^{n} f(x_i^*)\Delta x$$

If there are infinitely many subintervals, the limit of this expression can be taken as $n \to \infty$ to represent the definite integral.

Definite Integrals

Consider a continuous function $f(x)$ on the interval $a \leq x \leq b$ and divide the interval $[a, b]$ into n equal subintervals of length:

$$\Delta x = \frac{b - a}{n}$$

Each subinterval has a right endpoint x_i, for $i = 1$ to n. For example, the first subinterval has right endpoint x_i and the nth subinterval has right endpoint $x_n = b$. Define $x_0 = a$, and let x_i^* be any point in the ith interval, called the sample points. The definite integral of $y = f(x)$ from $x = a$ to $x = b$ is defined as

$$\int_{a}^{b} f(x)dx = \lim_{n \to \infty} \sum_{i=1}^{n} f(x_i^*)\Delta x$$

The lower limit of integration is a, and the upper limit of integration is b.

In calculus, the area problem involves finding the area under a positive function $y = f(x)$ from $x = a$ to $x = b$, above the x-axis. Such a region Ω is shown in the following graph.

The Definite Integral

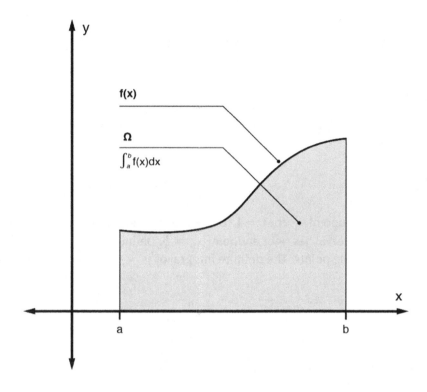

The area is defined as the definite integral of $y = f(x)$ from $x = a$ to $x = b$ and is denoted as:

$$\int_a^b f(x)dx$$

In a similar manner, the area between two curves $y = f(x)$ and $y = g(x)$ from $x = a$ to $x = b$ where:

$$f(x) \geq g(x)$$

over that same interval is given as:

$$\int_a^b \big(f(x) - g(x)\big)dx$$

Using Riemann Sums to Calculate Definite Integrals

Riemann sums can be used to calculate the following definite integral:

$$\int_a^b f(x)dx$$

The interval $[a, b]$ is divided into n subintervals of equal length Δx. Then, $f(x)$ is evaluated at a sample point x_i^* in each subinterval. A rectangle is formed for each subinterval with height $f(x_i^*)$ and width Δx. The area of each rectangle is $f(x_i^*)\Delta x$, and the total area of the region is the sum:

$$\sum_{i=1}^{n} f(x_i^*)\Delta x$$

If n is given as an integer, an approximation to the definite integral exists. However, the limit of this expression is taken as $n \to \infty$, the definite integral is obtained. Therefore:

$$\lim_{n \to \infty} \sum_{i=1}^{n} f(x_i^*)\Delta x = \int_a^b f(x)dx$$

The Fundamental Theorem of Calculus and Accumulation Functions

Using the Definite Integral to Define New Functions

Consider an integrable function $f(x)$ and a lower limit of integration $x = a$. We define the new function:

$$F(x) = \int_a^x f(t)dt$$

as the integral from $x = a$ to another number x. The value of x is the independent variable within the function and is also the upper limit of integration of the definite integral. x exists within the interval (a, b), and therefore, x is between a and b.

For each input of x, there exists an output, which is the dependent variable of the function $F(x)$. If $f(x)$ represents a nonnegative function, then the output of the function is the area between the graph of $f(x)$ and the x-axis over the interval $[a, x]$. For instance, the function:

$$F(x) = \int_2^x t^2 dx$$

represents the area between the graph of x^2 and the x-axis over the interval $[2, x]$. By letting $x = 4$:

$$F(4) = \int_2^4 t^2 dx$$

represents the area between the graph of x^2 and the x-axis over the interval $[2, 4]$.

This process defines new functions, and it also shows the relationship between integration and differentiation. By creating the function:

$$F(x) = \int_a^x f(t)dt$$

from a continuous function $f(x)$, a differentiable function $F(x)$ is created whose derivative is equal to $f(x)$. Therefore, given any value of x, we have:

$$F'(x) = \frac{d}{dx}\int_a^x f(t)dt = f(x)$$

This idea is known as the fundamental theorem of calculus, part 1, and is one of the most important concepts discussed in calculus.

We can use this theorem to construct functions with desired derivatives and specified values. For instance, let us construct a function $y = f(x)$ that has the derivative:

$$\frac{dy}{dx} = \sin x$$

that satisfies $f(2) = 7$. We know by the fundamental theorem of calculus, part 1, that the function:

$$y = \int_2^x \sin t \, dt$$

has a derivative equal to $\sin x$. We also know that $y(2) = 0$ because our limits of integration would be equal. Therefore, we can add 7 to our function to obtain our desired result. The function:

$$f(x) = \int_2^x \sin t \, dt + 7$$

satisfies our specified conditions.

Continuous Functions Equal to the Derivative of Another Function

The fundamental theorem of calculus, part 1, shows the relationship between integration and differentiation. It states that all continuous functions $f(x)$ are equal to the derivative of another function, and that function is always of the form:

$$\int_a^x f(t)dt$$

where x is between a and b. We can apply this theorem to some examples to make it easier to understand.

Previously, we discussed the function:

$$F(x) = \int_2^x t^2 dt$$

Through the fundamental theorem of calculus, part 1, we calculate its derivative as:

$$F'(x) = \frac{d}{dx}\int_2^x t^2 dt = x^2$$

Note that this derivative does not change if the lower limit of integration is changed.

For instance:

$$F'(x) = \frac{d}{dx}\int_3^x t^2 dt = x^2$$

and

$$F'(x) = \frac{d}{dx}\int_5^x t^2 dx = t^2$$

Sometimes the chain rule must be applied alongside the fundamental theorem of calculus, part 1, if the nonconstant limit of integration is a function of x. Consider the function:

$$F(x) = \int_1^{x^3} e^t dx$$

Notice that the upper limit of integration is the function x^3. This limit of integration creates a composite function of the form:

$$F(w) = \int_1^w e^t dt$$

where $w = x^3$. Therefore, the chain rule must be used to find the derivative.

It is true that:

$$F'(x) = F'(w) \times w'(x)$$

So:

$$F'(x) = e^w \times w'(x) = e^{x^3}(3x^2) = 3x^2 e^{x^3}$$

Note that we can also apply the fundamental theorem of calculus, part 1, to an integral with a nonconstant limit of integration as the lower limit of integration. In this case, we would apply the integration rule which allows us to switch the order of the limits. For instance, let's say we want to differentiate the function:

$$y = \int_x^5 \ln t \, dt$$

We know that:

$$y = -\int_5^x \ln t \, dt$$

because switching the order of integration negates the integral. Therefore, the derivative of the function is equal to:

$$\frac{dy}{dx} = -\ln x$$

Interpreting the Behavior of Accumulation Functions Involving Area

Information Provided by Graphical, Numerical, Analytical, and Verbal Representations of a Function

If a function $f(x)$ is nonnegative, the function:

$$g(x) = \frac{d}{dx} \int_a^x f(t) dt$$

represents a geometric concept. The integral from a to x of the given function represents the total area between the graph of the function and the x-axis over the interval $[a, x]$. In this scenario, area is a function of x. We denote the area function as $A(x)$. Therefore, $g(x)$ is equal to the derivative of the area function, meaning $g(x) = A'(x)$. The area function satisfies the initial condition $A(a) = 0$ because the limits of integration would be the same.

Because the derivative of a physical quantity is equal to the rate of change of the quantity, we know $g(x)$ equals the rate at which the area function changes as x changes. Therefore, if we know information about the function being integrated, whether it is graphical, numerical, analytical, or verbal, we know information about the corresponding function $g(x)$ due to its relationship with the area. For instance, the size of the function $f(x)$ determines how fast or slow $A(x)$ changes. Also, the sign of $f(x)$ determines whether the function $A(x)$ increases or decreases, which determines the sign of $A'(x)$. If $f(x)$ is positive, then the area function is increasing. For increasing x, we would be adding more positive area as we move to the right along the x-axis. If $f(x)$ is negative, the opposite occurs. We would be adding more negative area, so the area function would be decreasing. Finally, it is true that the area function has a local maximum at any points where the function $f(x)$ changes sign from positive to negative, and it has a local minimum at any points where the function $f(x)$ changes sign from negative to positive. This idea aligns with the **first derivative test**.

Applying Properties of Definite Integrals

Evaluating Definite Integrals with Geometry

In calculus, the area under the curve of $y = f(x)$ from $x = a$ to $x = b$ is defined as the definite integral:

$$\int_a^b f(x)dx$$

In a similar manner, the area between two curves $y = f(x)$ and $y = g(x)$ from $x = a$ to $x = b$, where $f(x) \geq g(x)$, is given as:

$$\int_a^b \left(f(x) - g(x)\right)dx$$

If the region over which the integral is being calculated is a simple geometric shape, such as a rectangle or square, a geometric formula can be used instead of actual integration.

Properties of Definite Integrals

There are many properties that help simplify the process of finding a definite integral. As shown geometrically, the definite integral of a constant function c is simply:

$$\int_a^b cdx = c(b - a)$$

The definite integral also has some linearity properties, as discussed previously. For instance, a constant multiple times a definite integral does not affect the integral. In other words:

$$\int_a^b cf(x)dx = c\int_a^b f(x)dx$$

Also, the definite integral of a sum or difference of two functions is equal to the sum or difference of two definite integrals, as shown here:

$$\int_a^b [f(x) \pm g(x)]dx = \int_a^b f(x)dx \pm \int_a^b g(x)dx$$

If we know that $\int_0^c x^2\, dx$ is equal to $\frac{c^3}{3}$, the linearity properties can be applied to calculate the definite integral:

$$\int_0^4 (4x^2 + 2)\, dx$$

The integral is split into two separate integrals, and the constant can be pulled out front for simplification purposes. Therefore, this integral is equivalent to:

$$4\int_0^4 x^2 dx + \int_0^4 2dx = (4)\frac{4^3}{3} + 2(4 - 0) = \frac{256}{3} + 8 = \frac{280}{3}$$

Another rule allows us to switch the limits of integration. The limits of integration are the constants that appear above and below the integral symbol; they are what make a definite integral different from an indefinite integral. For limits $a < b$, it is true that:

$$\int_b^a f(x)dx = -\int_a^b f(x)dx$$

Therefore, if we switch the order of the limits of integration, we just have to negate the entire integral. Applying this rule to the previous example, we know easily that:

$$\int_4^0 (4x^2 + 2)dx = -\int_0^4 (4x^2 + 2)dx = -\frac{280}{3}$$

Reversing the limits of integration simply negates the output of the integral.

A simple rule allows us to find the definite integral over an interval of length zero. We use the idea of area to create the following rule:

$$\int_a^a f(x)\, dx = 0$$

Because the definite integral involves calculating the area under the curve over the given interval, if the interval has length 0, the area is 0.

Finally, definite integrals follow an additive property. Consider the interval $a \le b \le c$. It is true that the definite integral of a function $f(x)$ from a to c is equivalent to the sum of the definite integral from a to b and the definite integral from b to c. Symbolically, we have:

$$\int_a^c f(x)dx = \int_a^b f(x)dx + \int_b^c f(x)dx$$

for some interval $a \le b \le c$. The two intervals a to b and b to c are known as adjacent intervals. This rule can be used to calculate the definite integral:

$$\int_0^8 (4x^2 + 2)dx$$

From previous calculations we already know that:

$$\int_0^4 (4x^2 + 2)dx = \frac{280}{3}$$

Therefore, in order to calculate the definite integral over the interval $[0, 8]$ we only need to calculate the definite integral over the remaining portion of the interval $[4, 8]$ and add it to $\frac{280}{3}$. It is true that:

$$\int_4^8 (4x^2 + 2)dx = \frac{1816}{3}$$

Therefore:

$$\int_0^8 (4x^2 + 2)dx = \frac{280}{3} + \frac{1816}{3} = \frac{2096}{3}$$

This additive rule can also allow definite integrals to be calculated as differences if necessary. For instance:

$$\int_4^8 (4x^2 + 2)dx = \int_0^8 (4x^2 + 2)dx - \int_0^4 (4x^2 + 2)dx = \frac{2096}{3} - \frac{280}{3} = \frac{1816}{3}$$

Definite Integrals in Functions with Removable or Jump Discontinuities

We can take the integral of all continuous functions. Therefore, if a function is continuous over the given interval $[a, b]$, then we can always find the definite integral of that function over that interval. However, a function does not always have to be continuous over an interval in order to find a definite integral.

Consider a function that is continuous over the interval $(a, b]$ and discontinuous at the endpoint $x = a$. The definite integral:

$$\int_a^b f(x)dx$$

is equal to:

$$\lim_{t \to a^+} \int_t^b f(x)dx$$

This integral can be evaluated because the function $f(x)$ is continuous over each interval $[t, b]$ for $t > a$.

If the discontinuity existed on the other side of the interval at $x = b$, the function would be continuous only over the interval $[a, b)$. Then, the definite integral:

$$\int_a^b f(x)dx$$

can be computed as:

$$\lim_{t \to b^-} \int_a^t f(x)dx$$

If the discontinuity exists inside the interval $[a, b]$, at a point c which is not equal one of the endpoints, the integral can be split up into two separate definite integrals using the additive property. In this case, we have:

$$\int_a^b f(x)dx = \int_a^c f(x)dx + \int_c^b f(x)dx$$

Therefore, the definite integral is evaluated as:

$$\lim_{t \to c^-} \int_a^t f(x)dx + \lim_{s \to c^+} \int_t^b f(x)dx$$

provided that both integrals exist.

The discontinuities that can appear can be jump or removable discontinuities. A jump discontinuity exists when the one-sided limits are not equal at a given point. Here is a graph of a jump discontinuity at $x = a$.

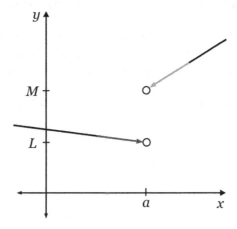

In order to integrate over an interval including $x = a$, the rules described previously must be used, making sure to never use $x = a$ as a limit of integration.

A removable discontinuity, otherwise known as a hole, is a point that is undefined on the graph of a function. There is said to be a gap at that point. Here is the graph of a removable discontinuity:

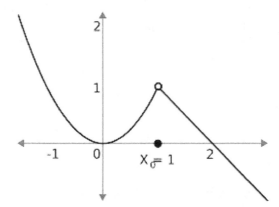

The removable discontinuity in this example exists at $x_0 = 1$. Notice that the one-sided limits are equal; however, the function evaluated at 1 is not equal to the one-sided limits of the function at the same point. Therefore, in order to integrate over the region from $x = 0$ to $x = 2$, the integral would have to be broken up at $x = 1$ and computed as;

$$\lim_{t \to 1^-} \int_0^t f(x)dx + \lim_{s \to 1^+} \int_t^2 f(x)dx$$

Finally, here is an example of a discontinuity at x_0 that is both a jump and a removable discontinuity:

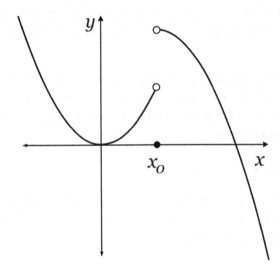

As in the examples above, the point x_0 could never be inserted into a definite integral as a limit of integration. The rules discussed previously would have to be used if we wanted to integrate over this discontinuity.

The Fundamental Theorem of Calculus and Definite Integrals

Antiderivatives

Given a derivative, $f'(x)$, of a function, the process of determining the corresponding function, $f(x)$, includes two steps. The first step involves finding a formula for the function that we are seeking that has its derivative is equal to $f'(x)$. Any function that satisfies this formula is known as an antiderivative, or indefinite integral, of $f(x)$. The second step of the process involves selecting a specific antiderivative from the list of all possible antiderivatives that satisfies a known function value.

Therefore, a function $F(x)$ is an **antiderivative** of the function $f(x)$ if it is true that:

$$F'(x) = f(x)$$

for all x in the domain of $f(x)$. The group of all antiderivatives of $f(x)$ is referred to as the **indefinite integral** of $f(x)$ with respect to the variable x. The integral symbol shown here, $\int f(x)dx$, is used to represent the indefinite integral. The function in the integrand is $f(x)$, and x is referred to as the variable of integration. Once an antiderivative is found for a given function, all other antiderivatives vary only by a constant.

Therefore, it is true that:

$$\int f(x)dx = F(x) + C$$

for an arbitrary constant C. The arbitrary constant is also referred to as the constant of integration. Once the antiderivative is found, the function $f(x)$ is said to have been integrated. Some scenarios might require a specific value to be found in place of the arbitrary constant, and some scenarios might not require that step.

Recall that a function $F(x)$ is said to be an antiderivative of the function $f(x)$ if $F'(x) = f(x)$ for all x in the domain of $f(x)$. Also, the set of all antiderivatives of $f(x)$ is known as the indefinite integral of f and is denoted as $\int f(x)dx$. Antiderivatives can differ by a constant, so, $\int f(x)dx = F(x) + C$ where C is an arbitrary constant of integration.

Evaluating Antiderivatives

Because an antiderivative of a function has the relationship that its derivative is equal to the given function, the function defined by $F(x) = \int_a^x f(t)dt$ is an antiderivative of $f(x)$. This is due to the fundamental theorem of calculus, part 1, because:

$$F'(x) = \frac{d}{dx}\int_a^x f(t)dt = f(x)$$

For instance:

$$F(x) = \int_1^x t^2 dt$$

is an antiderivative of $f(x) = x^2$. Therefore, it is true that $F'(x) = x^2$.

Fundamental Theorem of Calculus, Part 2

The previous discussion brings us now to the fundamental theorem of calculus, part 2. This theorem allows us to calculate definite integrals directly from antiderivatives. Consider a function f that is continuous over the interval $[a, b]$. If F is any antiderivative of f on that interval, then it is true that:

$$\int_a^b f(x)dx = F(b) - F(a)$$

This conclusion is another one of the most important theorems in calculus.

This theorem can be proved by using the fundamental theorem of calculus, part 1, given the idea that derivative of a constant is equal to 0. For example, if it is true that $f'(x) = g'(x)$ over an interval, then there exists a constant C such that:

$$f(x) = g(x) + C$$

over that interval. Therefore, if $F(x)$ is any antiderivative of $f(x)$, then it is true that:

$$F(x) = G(x) + C$$

where $G(x)$ is another antiderivative of $f(x)$ and C is a constant. By evaluating both sides of this equation at the endpoints of the interval $[a, b]$, we have:

$$F(b) - F(a) = G(b) + C - G(a) - C = G(b) - G(a)$$

Therefore, we have:

$$F(b) - F(a) = \int_a^b f(t)dt - \int_a^a f(t)dt = \int_a^b f(t)dt$$

We can use this theorem to evaluate definite integrals without evaluating limits and Riemann sums. The process of using the fundamental theorem of calculus, part 2, is a pleasant alternative to the lengthy process of the other techniques discussed previously. For instance, let us evaluate the definite integral:

$$\int_0^5 (x^5 + 2)dx$$

using this theorem. An antiderivative of:

$$x^5 + 2 \text{ is } \frac{x^6}{6} + 2x + C$$

Therefore, the definite integral is equal to:

$$\left(\frac{x^6}{6} + 2x\right)\Big|_0^5 = \frac{5^6}{6} + 2(5) - 0 = \frac{15625}{6} + 10 = \frac{15685}{6}$$

This theorem also allows us to calculate the area of a region between the graph of a function and the x-axis. For instance, evaluating the definite integral:

$$\int_0^5 (x^5 + 2)dx$$

is equal to finding the area of the region between the function:

$$f(x) = x^5 + 2$$

and the x-axis over the interval $[0, 5]$. Therefore, this region has an area of $\frac{15685}{6}$ square units.

Finding Antiderivatives and Infinite Integrals: Basic Rules and Notation

Adding Constants

As shown previously in the proof of the fundamental theorem of calculus, part 2, antiderivatives can differ with respect to a constant. For instance, if we needed to evaluate the definite integral;

$$\int_1^6 (3x^2 + 5)dx$$

Test Prep Books

we would first need to find an antiderivative of:

$$f(x) = 3x^2 + 5$$

There are infinitely many antiderivatives of this function, just as there are infinitely many antiderivatives of any function. The reason is that adding different constants does not change an antiderivative because the derivative of a constant is equal to 0.

For instance, both:

$$F(x) = x^3 + 5x + 2$$

and

$$G(x) = x^3 + 5x + 22$$

are antiderivatives of the function:

$$f(x) = 3x^2 + 5$$

Therefore, they could both be used in the fundamental theorem of calculus, part 2, to evaluate the definite integral. However, including constants creates more work than necessary. As shown in the proof, the constant cancels out when the antiderivative is evaluated at the endpoints of the interval.

Therefore, it is not necessary to include any constant of integration when using the theorem. The best approach is to use the simplest form of the antiderivative, and that would be when the constant of integration is equal to 0. The best antiderivative to use in this example is:

$$F(x) = x^3 + 5x$$

Therefore, the definite integral is evaluated as:

$$\int_1^6 (3x^2 + 5)dx = x^3 + 5x|_1^6 = 6^3 + 5(6) - 1^3 - 5 = 240$$

Using Differentiation Rules to Find Antiderivatives

There are rules for finding antiderivatives that parallel the rules for finding derivatives. For instance, to find the derivative of a constant multiple of a function, we can just find the derivative of the function and multiply times that constant. For example:

$$\frac{d}{dx}2x = 2\frac{d}{dx}x = 2(1) = 2$$

There is a similar rule with antiderivatives called the **constant multiple rule**:

$$\int cf(x)dx = c\int f(x)dx,$$

where c is a constant.

In order to find the antiderivative of a function multiplied by a constant, just multiply the constant times the antiderivative of the given function. For example:

108

$$\int 2x\,dx = 2\int x\,dx$$

Basically, to make the process easier, we can pull the constant out in front of the integral symbol, ignore it while we find the antiderivative, and multiply it in the final step.

If the constant in the constant multiple rule is equal to -1, we have a similar rule for both differentiation and antidifferentiation. We can pull the -1 out in front of both the derivative and integral symbols, and just incorporate it in the final step. For example, with differentiation:

$$\frac{d}{dx}(-x) = -\frac{d}{dx}x = -1(1) = -1$$

The rule for $c = -1$ in the constant multiple rule for integration is the following:

$$\int -g(x)\,dx = -\int g(x)\,dx.$$

Therefore, $\int -x\,dx = -\int x\,dx$.

Another rule is that the derivative of the sum and/or difference of two or more functions is equal to the sum and/or difference of the derivatives of the individual functions. Basically, this rule enables term-by-term differentiation. We can take the individual derivatives of the given functions and add or subtract them together in the final step. For example:

$$\frac{d}{dx}(2x + 3x^2) = \frac{d}{dx}(2x) + \frac{d}{dx}(3x^2) = 2 + 6x$$

This rule extends to antiderivatives and integration in the following sum and difference rule:

$$\int (f(x) \pm g(x))\,dx = \int f(x)\,dx \pm g(x)\,dx$$

Therefore:

$$\int (2x + 3x^2)\,dx = \int 2x\,dx + \int 3x^2\,dx$$

This rule can be applied to any number of sums and differences. For instance, we can apply the rule to three functions here:

$$\int (5x^4 - 6x^5 + 7x^6)\,dx = \int 5x^4\,dx - \int 6x^5\,dx + \int 7x^6\,dx$$

In both examples, antiderivatives are computed term by term. Note that all functions are integrated separately, and once their antiderivatives are found, they can simply be joined by sums and/or differences in the end.

Another rule that is often used when differentiating functions is the **power rule**. The power rule for differentiation is the following:

$$\frac{d}{dx}(x^n) = nx^{n-1}$$

for a rational number $n \neq -1$.

Attached to the chain rule, the power rule for differentiation is the following:

$$\frac{d}{dx}(u^n) = nu^{n-1}\frac{du}{dx}$$

where u is a function of x and $n \neq -1$ is a rational number.

The chain rule is used when the function is a composite function, and when the power rule is needed, the function is an exponential expression in which the base is a function of x. Both rules, allow for a similar rule for antiderivatives:

$$\int x^n dx = \frac{x^{n+1}}{n+1} + C \text{ and } \int u^n \frac{du}{dx} dx = \frac{u^{n+1}}{n+1} + C, \text{ where } C \text{ is an arbitrary constant.}$$

These rules exist because the following derivatives exist:

$$\frac{d}{dx}\left(\frac{x^{n+1}}{n+1}\right) = x^n$$

and

$$\frac{d}{dx}\left(\frac{u^{n+1}}{n+1}\right) = u^n\frac{du}{dx}$$

Finding the antiderivative of such expressions above involve going in the opposite direction of taking those derivatives.

For example:

$$\int \left(\sqrt{2 + x^2} \times 2x\right) dx$$

can be found by using the power rule for antiderivatives. Notice that it can be written as:

$$\int (2 + x^2)^{1/2} \times 2x\, dx$$

which shows that the exponential portion is a composite function.

It involves a substitution process to place it in the form u^n which will allow us to use the power rule for antiderivatives. Let $u = 2 + x^2$. Therefore:

$$\frac{du}{dx} = 2x$$

We rewrite the problem as:

$$\int u^{\frac{1}{2}} du$$

which we can then apply the power rule to. We have the power rule with $n = \frac{1}{2}$. Therefore:

$$\int u^{\frac{1}{2}} du = \frac{u^{\frac{3}{2}}}{\frac{3}{2}} + C = \frac{2}{3} u^{\frac{3}{2}} + C$$

for an arbitrary constant C. Finally, we need replace u with the function $2 + x^2$ to obtain the antiderivative:

$$\frac{2}{3}(2 + x^2)^{\frac{3}{2}} + C$$

This process of letting u be equal to a function existing within the integrands and making substitutions is known as u-substitution.

In general, u-substitution can be used to find the antiderivative of something in the following form:

$$\int f(g(x))g'(x)dx$$

The integrand contains a composite function with inner function $g(x)$ and outer function $f(x)$. It also contains a form of the derivative of the inner function $g'(x)$. This rule is related to the chain rule for differentiation. We perform the substitutions: $u = g(x)$ and $du = g'(x)dx$ so that the expression turns into the following simpler integral:

$$\int f(u)du$$

Then, we can find the antiderivative using one of the rules previously discussed, making sure to replace u with $g(x)$ in the last step.

Functions that Do Not Have Closed Form Antiderivatives

It should be noted that the fundamental theorem of calculus cannot be used in every instance. In order to use part 2 to determine a definite integral, an antiderivative must be used. Some functions do not have closed form antiderivatives, meaning that a normal functional form of an antiderivative cannot be found. In this case, no explicit formula could be evaluated at the limits of integration. Often, this scenario exists when dealing with real-word applications in science and engineering. A specific example would be when the antiderivative of a given function is an infinite series. Given this situation, a computer algebra system (CAS) would have to be used to calculate the definite integral. One such CAS is MATLAB.

Another example is the following definite integral:

$$\int_0^{\pi} \cos(x^2)\,dx$$

There is no closed form antiderivative of the function $\cos(x^2)$, and in this scenario we would need to evaluate it with a CAS to determine the result.

Integrating Using Substitution

Using Substitution to Find Antiderivatives

An important method of integration, or of finding antiderivatives, is the substitution of variables. Basically, the process involves using the chain rule backwards because the integrand contains a composite function. The substitution formula is the following:

$$\int f(g(x)) \times g'(x)dx = \int f(u)du = F(u) + C = F(g(x)) + C.$$

The substitutions $u = g(x)$ and:

$$du = g'(x)dx$$

are used to turn a complicated function into a simpler version that has a more straightforward antiderivative. Note that the original function is a composite function with inner function $g(x)$ and outer function $f(x)$ that is multiplied times the derivative of the inner function $g(x)$. Here is an example that uses substitution in order to find its antiderivative:

$$\int x^3 \cos(x^4)\,dx.$$

Note that $\cos(x^4)$ is a composite function. We let $u = x^4$ and:

$$du = 4x^3 dx$$

After we make those substitutions, the integral becomes the simpler integral:

$$\int \frac{1}{4}\cos(u)\,du$$

Its antiderivative is:

$$\frac{1}{4}\sin(u) + C$$

Finally, we substitute $u = x^4$ back in to obtain the antiderivative:

$$\frac{1}{4}\sin(x^4) + C$$

Using Substitution to Change the Limits of Integration

Integration by substitution basically involves using the chain rule backward. Recall that the chain rule is how composite functions are differentiated. Consider an integral of the form:

$$\int f(g(x)) \cdot g'(x)dx$$

The integrand, which is the function being integrated, consists of a composite function times the derivative of the inner function. The substitution:

$$u = g(x), du = g'(x)dx$$

is made to turn the integral into the simpler expression:

$$\int f(u)du$$

Therefore, this integral is evaluated by finding the antiderivative $F(u)$ to $f(u)$ and then substituting $g(x)$ back in for u. The result is:

$$F\big(g(x)\big) + C$$

where C is an arbitrary constant.

If a definite integral is given, substitution can be used to change the limits of integration. For instance, consider the definite integral:

$$\int_1^5 2xe^{x^2+1}dx$$

The substitution:

$$u = x^2$$

$$du = 2xdx$$

is made to turn the integrand into a simpler expression. The limits of integration can also be changed using the substitution. It is true that $u(1) = 1$ and $u(5) = 25$. Therefore, the integral turns into;

$$\int_1^{25} e^{u+1}du = e^{u+1}\big|_1^{25} = e^{26} - e^2$$

Integrating Functions Using Long Division and Completing the Square

Finding Antiderivatives Using Long Division and Completing the Square

Computing an antiderivative is less straightforward than computing a derivative, and the process of finding an antiderivative is usually harder than finding a derivative. In many instances, finding an antiderivative does not involve a specific formula or streamlined process, and an alternate method must be used.

If the given function is a rational function, which is a fraction of two polynomials, long division could be helpful in order to find its antiderivative. The division process would place the function in a form in which we know its antiderivative. Dividing the numerator by the denominator, would result in a polynomial function plus a simpler rational function.

For instance, consider the function:

$$f(x) = \frac{x - 6}{-x + 2}$$

We do not have a straightforward formula approach to finding its antiderivative. However, we can divide the numerator by the denominator using long division to obtain:

$$f(x) = -1 - \frac{4}{-x + 2}$$

An antiderivative of the function in this form is:

$$F(x) = -x + 4\ln|-x + 2| + C$$

Completing the square also can be used to find an antiderivative. This process is useful when finding antiderivatives relating to inverse trigonometric functions. We know the following:

- The antiderivative of the function $f(x) = \frac{1}{\sqrt{1-x^2}}$ is $F(x) = \sin^{-1} x + C$.

- The antiderivative of the function $f(x) = -\frac{1}{\sqrt{1-x^2}}$ is $F(x) = \cos^{-1} x + C$.

- The antiderivative of the function $f(x) = \frac{1}{x^2+1}$ is $F(x) = \tan^{-1} x + C$.

- The antiderivative of the function $f(x) = -\frac{1}{x^2+1}$ is $F(x) = \cot^{-1} x + C$.

- The antiderivative of the function $f(x) = \frac{1}{x\sqrt{x^2-1}}$ is $F(x) = \sec^{-1} x + C$.

- The antiderivative of the function $f(x) = -\frac{1}{x\sqrt{x^2-1}}$ is $F(x) = \csc^{-1} x + C$.

Therefore, if we have a rational function of the form $\frac{1}{p(x)}$, we could possibly complete the square in the denominator in order to use one of the antiderivative formulas listed above. For instance, consider the function $f(x) = \frac{1}{\sqrt{2x-x^2}}$. We complete the square in the radicand as follows:

$$2x - x^2 = -(x^2 - 2x) = -(x^2 - 2x + 1 - 1) = -(x^2 - 2x + 1) + 1 = 1 - (x - 1)^2$$

Therefore, our function is equivalent to:

$$f(x) = \frac{1}{\sqrt{1 - (x - 1)^2}}$$

which has an antiderivative of $F(x) = \sin^{-1}(x - 1) + C$.

Integration by parts is a technique that allows one to find antiderivatives of products of functions. It is usually the case that the antiderivative of a product of two functions is not equal to the product of the

two individual antiderivatives. Therefore, we can apply a well-known formula to find the antiderivative of a function of the form $f(x)g(x)$. The formula for integration by parts is the following:

$$\int u\,dv = uv - \int v\,du.$$

Like substitution, this formula takes a more complicated integral and turns it into a simpler integral. The most difficult part of the process is the selection of the parts u and dv. We must select appropriately so that the integral $\int v\,du$ is evaluated easily.

Consider the following integral:

$$\int x \sin x \, dx$$

Notice that the integrand is the product of the two functions x and $\sin x$. We can use the integration by parts formula to evaluate this integral. We let $u = x$ and $dv = \sin x\,dx$. Therefore, we have $du = dx$ and $v = -\cos x$. Plugging these expressions into the formula, we have:

$$\int x \sin x \, dx = -x \cos x + \int \cos x \, dx = -x \cos x + \sin x + C$$

Notice if we had let $u = \sin x$ and $dv = x\,dx$ and tried to use the same formula, we would have been stuck. In this case, $du = \cos x$ and $v = \frac{x^2}{2}$. We would have had to evaluate:

$$\int \frac{x^2}{2} \cos x \, dx$$

which we do not know. This shows why correct selection of both u and dv is so important.

A final alternative technique used to find antiderivatives involves partial fraction decomposition. If we need to find the antiderivative of a rational function that we cannot directly compute or complete the square on, we could rewrite the function into corresponding partial fractions. Then, we could find the corresponding antiderivative of each partial fraction.

The process of partial fraction decomposition involves splitting up the rational function $\frac{P(x)}{Q(x)}$ into the form:

$$\frac{A}{(x-a)} + \frac{B}{(x-b)} + \cdots \frac{N}{(x-n)}$$

where each denominator is a distinct linear factor of $Q(x)$. We will only focus on the case where we do not have any repeating linear factors in the polynomial function in the denominator.

Consider the integral $\int \frac{dx}{x^2 - 5x + 6}$. We do not know the antiderivative of this rational function. However, we can factor the polynomial in the denominator into two linear factors as $(x-3)(x-2)$. Therefore, we will use the partial fraction decomposition:

$$\frac{A}{(x-3)} + \frac{B}{(x-2)} = \frac{1}{x^2 - 5x + 6}$$

115

and solve for the constants A and B. We first multiply both sides of the equation by $(x - 3)(x - 2)$ to clear the fractions. This results in:

$$A(x - 2) + B(x - 3) = 1$$

This equation is considered to be an identity, so we can let x be any real number. Setting $x = 2$ results in $B = -1$. Setting $x = 3$ results in $A = 1$. Therefore, our integral turns into:

$$\int \left[\frac{1}{x - 3} - \frac{1}{x - 2} \right] dx$$

which is equal to:

$$\ln|x - 3| - \ln|x - 2| + C$$

This technique can be used for any number of factors in the denominator. Also, if the degree of the polynomial function in the numerator is greater than or equal to the degree of the polynomial function in the denominator, long division could be used to split up the function into a polynomial plus a rational function, which could then be decomposed into partial fractions.

Unit 7: Differential Equations

Modeling Situations with Differential Equations

Interpreting Differential Equations

A **differential equation** is an equation that describes a relationship between a function and its derivatives. For instance:

$$\frac{dy}{dt} = f(t)$$

is a differential equation that states that the first derivative of an unknown function of y is equal to a given function of t. Note that the independent variable is t. An example could be:

$$\frac{dt}{dt} = \sin t$$

Differential equations tend to model real-life scenarios, and when t is used as the independent variable, it usually represents time. Therefore, the given quantity is changing over time.

Another example of a differential equation is:

$$\frac{dy}{dx} = f(x, y)$$

The unknown function y is a function with independent variable x, and $f(x, y)$ is a given function of two variables that is defined on the plane.

In any case, the goal of solving a differential equation is to determine the equation of the unknown function. A first-order differential equation is one that only involves the first derivative of an unknown function. Higher-order differential equations also exist, and they include higher-order derivatives. For instance, a second-order differential equation can include both second and first derivatives of an unknown function.

Verifying Solutions for Differential Equations

Using Derivatives to Verify Solutions to Differential Equations

Since we have seen that solutions for differential equations are found using antidifferentiation, we can use differentiation to verify the solutions. Suppose we find the solution of the differential equation:

$$\frac{dy}{dx} = 5y$$

Given the differential equation:

$$y' - 5y = 0$$

verify that $y = e^{5t}$ is a solution.

To verify this solution, take the derivative of y. Then the value $y' = 5e^{5t}$, is found to be the derivative. By substituting y for e^{5t} we find that $y' = 5y$ and:

$$y' - 5y = 0$$

The solution has been verified.

General Solutions to Differential Equations

A **solution of a differential equation** is a function that satisfies the given equation. For instance, in order to solve:

$$\frac{dy}{dx} = f(x, y)$$

the function $y = y(x)$ must be found that satisfies:

$$\frac{dy}{dx} = f\big(x, y(x)\big)$$

A differential equation could have infinitely many solutions. In this case, the solution is referred to a **general solution**. If an initial condition is stated that defines the initial point of a solution, a particular solution could be found. For example, the initial condition would be of the form $y(x_0) = y_0$. A differential equation paired with an initial condition is known as an **initial value problem**.

If a differential equation is separable, it can be written as:

$$\frac{dy}{dx} = f(x)g(y)$$

In other words, the function on the right hand side can be separated into a product of a function of x and a function of y. To solve the equation, the variables are separated by moving the y terms to the left and the x terms to the right to obtain:

$$\frac{dy}{g(y)} = f(x)dx$$

Both sides are integrated with respect to the given variable on either side to obtain the general solution, and if an initial condition is given, the particular solution can be obtained through substitution.

An example of a separable differential equation is:

$$\frac{dy}{dx} = x^2 y^2$$

This equation is rewritten as:

$$\frac{dy}{y^2} = x^2 dx$$

Integrating both sides results in:

$$-\frac{1}{y} = \frac{x^3}{3} + c$$

where c is the constant of integration. Note that there are infinitely many solutions because c is arbitrary. A solution to a differential equation can be verified by plugging it back into the original differential as a checking mechanism.

Sketching Slope Fields

Graphical Representations of Differential Equations

For each arbitrary constant, the general solution to a differential equation can be graphed. Therefore, when an initial condition $y(x_0) = y_0$ is specified within an initial value problem that solves:

$$\frac{dy}{dx} = f(x, y)$$

the graph of the solution passes through the point (x_0, y_0). At that initial point, the graph of the curve has slope $f(x_0, y_0)$.

A slope field can be built, which is a graphical representation of small segments of solution curves, using different initial conditions. Given each initial condition (x_0, y_0), a small line segment is drawn at (x_0, y_0) with slope $f(x_0, y_0)$. Many points in the domain of the function $f(x, y)$ are selected in which to draw these line segments. Each line segment has the slope of the solution at the chosen point, and therefore, the line segments are also tangent to the curve at those given points. Together, all the line segments are drawn to create the slope field. Note that slope fields are used only with first-order differential equations and are also referred to as vector fields and direction fields.

Using Slope Fields to Provide Information about Solutions

Because the slope fields consist of tangent lines, they can be used to see how the solution curves behave. They provide visual clues that determine the behavior of the unknown function. Slope fields can be drawn by hand or by using technology such as a slope field generator. Here is an example of a slope field drawn with technology:

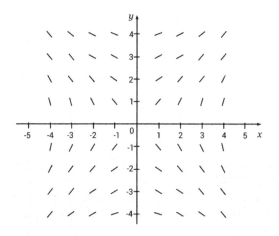

Notice that a small line segment is drawn at each ordered pair in the square region:

$$[-4, 4] \times [-4, 4]$$

Each line segment is drawn with the corresponding slope of the solution curve, and this information provides visual clues to the behavior of the solution. For instance, at the ordered pair $(1, 0)$, the solution curve is vertical because it has infinite slope. Also, at $(0, -1)$, the solution curve is horizontal because it has 0 slope.

Slope fields can help us draw the solution curve given a specific initial condition. For instance, here is a slope field with three solution curves drawn:

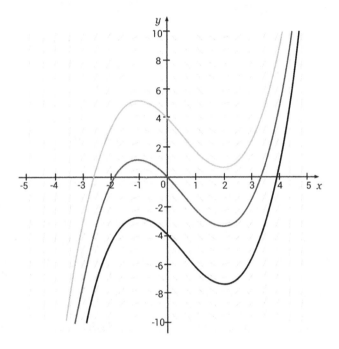

Each curve corresponds to a different initial condition, or ordered pair, within its domain. For example, the curve traveling through the point $(0, 0)$ is drawn by following the directions of the given line segments starting at the origin.

Behavior of a Function

Derivatives can be used to find the behavior of different functions such as the extrema, concavity, and symmetry. Given a function:

$$f(x) = 3x^2$$

the first derivative is:

$$f'(x) = 6x$$

This equation describes the slope of the line. Setting the derivative equal to zero means finding where the slope is zero, and these are potential points in which the function has **extreme values**. If the first derivative is positive over an interval, the function is increasing over that interval. If the first derivative is negative over an interval, the function is decreasing over that interval. Therefore, if the derivative is equal to zero at a point and the function changes from increasing to decreasing, then the function has a

minimum at that point. If the function changes from decreasing to increasing at that point, it is a maximum. The second derivative can be used to define **concavity**. If it is positive over an interval, the graph resembles a U and is concave up over that interval. If the second derivative is negative, the graph is concave down. For this equation, solving:

$$f'(x) = 6x = 0$$

gets $x = 0$, $f(0) = 0$. Also, the second derivative is 6, which is positive. The graph is concave up and, therefore, has a minimum value at $(0, 0)$.

Reasoning Using Slope Fields

Estimating Solutions to Differential Equations

A **differential equation** is an equation involving derivatives. To find the solution to a differential equation means finding the function or functions for which this is the derivative. In other words, we will find the **antiderivative**. For example, take the differential equation:

$$\frac{dy}{dx} = 2x + 8$$

This differential equation is solved by finding the antiderivative:

$$y = x^2 + 8x + C$$

There are an infinite number of values that could be given to C, so there are an infinite number of solutions to this differential equation. The solution to this differential equation is referred to as a **family of functions**. We call the family of functions that satisfy this differential equation the **general solution** for the differential equation.

A particular solution can be found for the differential equation if we are given some condition that is true for the unique solution. For example, suppose we know that the point $(1, 13)$ lies on the curve. This information can show that the following equation makes a true statement:

$$13 = 1^2 + 8(1) + C$$

so $C = 4$. This information gives a particular solution for the differential equation and the equation becomes:

$$y = x^2 + 8x + 4$$

Finding General Solutions Using Separation of Variables

Using Separation of Variables to Solve Differential Equations

Certain types of differential equations that can be solved directly with integration are called separable equations. They are of the form:

$$\frac{dy}{dx} = f(x)g(y)$$

A separable equation can be written as a product of a function of x times a function of y. For instance, the differential equation:

$$\frac{dy}{dx} = e^x \sin y$$

is separable because:

$$f(x) = e^x$$

and

$$g(y) = \sin y$$

The differential equation:

$$\frac{dy}{dx} = e^x + \sin y$$

is not separable because the expression $e^x + \sin y$ cannot be written as a product of a function of x times a function of y.

Separable differential equations can be solved using separation of variables. This process involves moving the y terms to the left side, moving the x terms to the right side, and then integrating both sides with respect to the given variable on either side.

The process in formula form is:

$$\frac{dy}{dx} = f(x)g(y)$$

$$\frac{dy}{g(y)} = f(x)dx$$

$$\int \frac{dy}{g(y)} = \int f(x)dx$$

An example of a differential equation that can be solved using separation of variables is:

$$\frac{dy}{dx} = 5y$$

First, we move the y terms to the left side and the x terms to the right side with algebra laws, resulting in:

$$\frac{dy}{y} = 5dx$$

We integrate both sides with respect to the given variables to obtain:

$$\ln|y| = 5x + C$$

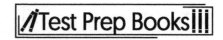

which is an implicit solution. Ideally, we would like an explicit solution in which y is given as a function of x. Therefore, we raise e to both sides of the previous equation, resulting in:

$$e^{\ln|y|} = e^{5x+C}$$

This equation simplifies to:

$$|y| = e^{5x+C}$$

We know that the right-hand side can never be negative, so we drop the absolute value sign. Also, we can rewrite:

$$e^{5x+C} = e^{5x}e^C = C_1 e^{5x}$$

Our general solution to the original differential equation is therefore $y = C_1 e^{5x}$.

This differential equation could also be paired with an initial condition to form an initial value problem. Consider the initial value problem:

$$\frac{dy}{dx} = 5y$$

$$y(0) = 8$$

The first step to solving the initial value problem is to find the general solution, which we have found to be:

$$y = C_1 e^{5x}$$

Then, we apply the initial condition to obtain the particular solution as follows:

$$y(0) = C_1 e^0 = C_1 = 8$$

The solution to the initial value problem is $y = 8e^{5x}$.

Using Antidifferentiation to Find Solutions to Differential Equations

A differential equation is an equation that consists of an unknown function and its derivative, and the derivatives used in the equations can be first-order or higher-order derivatives. The order of a differential equation is equal to the order of the highest derivative shown in the equation. If the derivatives only involve first derivatives, the equation is a first-order differential equation. An example of a first-order differential equation is:

$$y' + 6y = 0$$

If the derivatives involve both first-order and second-order derivatives, the equation is a second-order differential equation. An example of a second-order differential equation is:

$$y'' + y' + y = 0$$

A solution to a differential equation is a function that satisfies the given equation. A general solution involves arbitrary constants, just like the process of finding an indefinite integral does. A general

solution of a differential equation of order n involves n arbitrary constants. If specific values for the arbitrary constants are given, we call those solutions particular solutions.

Differential equations arise in many real-world situations. In these cases, we are more interested in finding particular solutions rather than general solutions. In order to find values for the arbitrary constants, we can use initial conditions. Initial conditions are conditions that specify the value of the missing function $y(x)$ for a given value of x. It is common to have initial conditions that are specified at the initial point $x = 0$. A differential equation paired with initial conditions is known as an initial value problem (IVP).

Some differential equations only need integration to solve them. For instance, $\frac{dy}{dx} = x$ is a simple differential equation that states that the rate at which y changes with respect to x is equal to the expression x. We can integrate both sides with respect to x to obtain:

$$y = \frac{x^2}{2} + C$$

as a general solution. An initial condition would allow us to find the particular solution and solve for the constant of integration.

Differential equations can have a connection to real-world applications because many of them model physical scenarios. Because differential equations involve derivatives, the real-world applications that they model involve rates of change.

The specific relationships between the acceleration, velocity, and position of an object traveling in a straight line can be expressed in differential equations that relate to motion along straight lines. For instance, we have the differential equation:

$$a(t) = \frac{dv}{dt}$$

where $a(t)$ is the acceleration function and $v(t)$ is the velocity function. We also have the differential equation:

$$v(t) = \frac{ds}{dt}$$

where $s(t)$ is the position function. Each of these differential equations could be paired with an initial condition to form initial value problems.

Another application for differential equations is modeling exponential growth and decay. We can work backwards to show these exponential growth and decay relationships with differential equations. Consider the following function of time t, that models exponential growth or decay:

$$y(t) = y_o e^{kt}$$

If $k > 0$, there is exponential growth, and the constant k is referred to as the growth constant. The quantity at time $t = 0$ is y_0 because:

$$y(0) = y_0$$

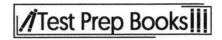

If $k < 0$, there is exponential decay, and in this case, the constant k is referred to as the decay constant. Population is a typical quantity that is modeled by exponential growth. If we take the derivative of this quantity, we have:

$$\frac{dy}{dt} = ky_0 e^{kt} = ky$$

Therefore, the relationship is $\frac{dy}{dt} = ky$, which is a differential equation. By pairing this equation with the initial condition $y(0) = y_0$, we get an initial value problem. Radioactive decay is another typical application for these differential equations because the radioactive material decays exponentially.

The logistic differential equation is the equation:

$$\frac{dy}{dx} = ky\left(1 - \frac{y}{A}\right)$$

where $k > 0$ is the growth constant and $A > 0$ is the carrying capacity. This equation is used to model population growth, but it differs from simple exponential growth because it takes into consideration that realistically, populations cannot increase without limit. There are some limitations that exist in nature that make it difficult for populations to get exponentially large, such as the food chain and disease. Separation of variables, which will be discussed in the next section, can be used to find the general solution to this differential equation. Its general solution is;

$$y = \frac{1}{1 - \frac{e^{-kt}}{C}}$$

and a particular solution can be found using an initial condition.

Finding Particular Solutions Using Initial Conditions and Separation of Variables

General Solutions and Particular Solutions

Consider the function:

$$F(x) = C + \int_a^x f(t)dt$$

for constants C and a. We can use the fundamental theorem of calculus, part 1, to find its derivative. The theorem tells us that the derivative of the integral is equal to the function inside its integrand. We do not have to apply the chain rule to the theorem because the upper limit of integration is just x. Therefore, we have $F'(x) = f(x)$. This equation is actually a differential equation because it contains the derivative of some unknown function $F(x)$. An example of such a function would be the following:

$$F(x) = 5 + \int_2^x e^t dt$$

If we take the derivative, we obtain the differential equation $F'(x) = e^x$. To solve this differential equation we could integrate both sides with respect to x. The antiderivative of e^x is simply e^x, so we have:

$$F(x) = e^x + C$$

This function is equal to our original function of:

$$F(x) = 5 + \int_2^x e^t \, dt$$

In this scenario, we know that our arbitrary constant is equal to 5.

Determining General and Particular Solution

The function:

$$F(x) = C + \int_a^x f(t) \, dt$$

is a general solution to the differential equation $F'(x) = f(x)$. The arbitrary constant has not yet been solved for. If we specify the condition that $F(a) = y_0$, which is an initial condition, we can find the particular solution.

The particular solution is a solution to an initial value problem that is composed of both a differential equation and at least one initial condition. Plugging $x = a$ into:

$$F(x) = C + \int_a^x f(t) \, dt$$

results in $F(a) = C$ because a definite integral with the same upper and lower limits of integration is equal to 0. If we know that $F(a) = y_0$, then we have that $C = y_0$. Therefore, the particular solution is the function:

$$F(x) = y_0 + \int_a^x f(t) \, dt$$

Possible Domain Restrictions of Differential Equations

When determining the solution to a differential equation, it is important to pay attention to its domain. The domain could be restricted due to either an expression in the differential equation or an expression in the solution being undefined across certain intervals, or it could be restricted due to other reasons.

For example, if we have the differential equation:

$$\frac{dy}{dx} = \frac{x}{x+1}$$

we know that x cannot equal -1 because that value would create division by 0. Therefore, the solution to the differential equation would have a restricted domain in which $x \neq -1$. Secondly, if the general solution to a differential equation was a radical like:

$$y(t) = \sqrt{t + 1}$$

its domain is restricted to interval $[-1, \infty)$ since the radicand has to be nonnegative.

Also, consider the differential equation $\frac{dy}{dx} = \frac{3}{\sqrt{y}}$. We can use separation of variables to determine the general solution as:

$$\frac{2}{3}y^{3/2} = 3x + C$$

It has the explicit solution:

$$y = (2x + C_1)^{\frac{2}{3}}$$

This solution is not defined for all values of x. The original differential equation states that the change of y with respect to x is equal to $\frac{3}{\sqrt{y}}$, which is always positive. Therefore, the solution y has to be positive. This means that:

$$2x + C_1 > 0$$

or that the domain is subject to the restriction that $x > \frac{-C_1}{2}$. The value of C_1 can be found with the introduction of an initial condition.

Exponential Models with Differential Equations

Specific Applications of General and Particular Solutions

Differential equations have many real-world applications. For instance, an important application is motion along a line. Consider the position function $s(t)$, which tells the location of an object at time t. The derivative of the position function is equal to the velocity of the object at time t. This relationship gives us a differential equation:

$$v(t) = s'(t)$$

or

$$\frac{ds}{dt} = v(t)$$

If $v(0) = v_0$ is specified as the initial velocity of the object, an initial value problem is given. It is true that the derivative of the velocity function is equal to the acceleration of the object at time t, or $a(t) = v'(t) = s''(t)$. The initial acceleration of the object can be specified as $a_0 = a(0)$. Pairing this initial condition with the differential equation:

$$\frac{dv}{dt} = a(t)$$

127

results in another initial value problem. Recall that the solution to the differential equation alone gives us the general solution, but the application of an initial condition results in a particular solution.

Another important real-world application of differential equations involves exponential growth and decay. Consider the exponential function $y = e^{ct}$, for some arbitrary constant c. Its first derivative is equal to $y' = ce^{ct}$. Therefore, the differential equation is defined $y' = cy$, which tells us the derivative of the unknown function is equal to a constant multiple of a function. This differential equation models exponential growth and decay. If $c > 0$, exponential growth is being modeled, and the constant is known as the growth rate. If $c < 0$, exponential decay is being modeled, and the constant is known as the decay rate. An initial condition $y(0) = y_0$ can be specified, which states the initial amount of the quantity at time $t = 0$. The differential equation can be solved using separation of variables to obtain the general solution $y = Ae^{ct}$ for an arbitrary constant A. Applying the initial condition results in the particular solution $y = y_0 e^{ct}$, which gives the amount of the quantity at any time t.

Exponential Growth and Decay

Previously, we worked backwards to show that the differential equation that models exponential growth is $\frac{dy}{dt} = ky$, for some growth or decay constant k. However, we can begin from a real-life situation in which this differential equation models a physical scenario, and we can thus obtain both the general and the particular solutions. Consider a scenario in which the rate of change of a quantity is proportional to the present amount of the quantity. If the rate of change is proportional and the quantity is increasing, there is exponential growth. Exponential growth in population models exists when each organism helps contribute to the growth through reproduction. In this case, population is proportional to the size of the population. Because there is positive growth, the proportionality constant k is positive, and we have:

$$\frac{dy}{dt} = ky$$

An example of a differential equation that represents growth is:

$$\frac{dy}{dt} = 4y$$

We can use separation of variables to determine the general solution as:

$$y(t) = Ce^{4t}$$

where C is the initial value of the population $y(0)$. The doubling time, or the time it takes a population to double from an initial amount, can be found. We set the solution equal to $2C$, which is double the initial amount, and solve for t. This gives us:

$$2C = Ce^{4t}$$

or

$$2 = e^{4t}$$

Taking the natural logarithm of both sides results in:

$$t = \frac{\ln 2}{4} \approx .173$$

which is the doubling time of the population. In general, for $\frac{dy}{dt} = ky$, the doubling time is $t = \frac{\ln 2}{k}$.

Radioactive substances decay exponentially, and the rate at which the substance decays is proportional to the initial amount of the substance. In this scenario, the proportionality constant k is negative and we have $\frac{dy}{dt} = kt$, which has solution $y(t) = Ce^{kt}$. As discussed previously, this solution can be found by separation of variables. Because the substance is decaying, we can solve for the half-life, which is the time it takes for the initial quantity to decrease by a factor of $\frac{1}{2}$. We set the solution equal to $\frac{1}{2}C$, which is half of the initial amount, and solve for t. This gives us $\frac{1}{2}C = Ce^{kt}$, or $\frac{1}{2} = e^t$. Taking the natural logarithm of both sides results in:

$$t = \frac{\ln \frac{1}{2}}{k} = -\frac{\ln 2}{k}$$

which is the half-life of the substance for a general decay constant k.

Unit 8: Applications of Integration

Finding the Average Value of a Function on an Interval

The Average Value of a Function

The **average value of a function** can be found by the following integral:

$$\frac{1}{b-a}\int_a^b f(x)dx$$

The integral finds the area of the region bounded by the function and the x-axis, while the fraction divides the area to find the average value of the integral. An example of this is shown in the graph below. The function $f(x)$ is the black line. The light gray shading represents the area under the curve, while the rectangle drawn on top with added darker shading represents the same amount of area as the region under the graph of the given function over the interval of a to b. This rectangle has the base $[a, b]$ and height $f(c)$.

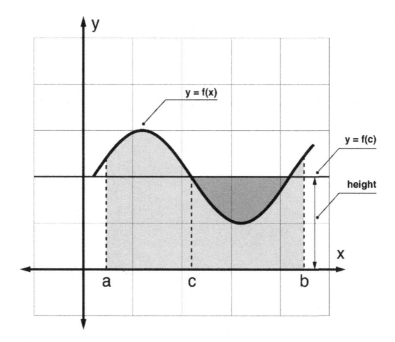

Let's consider the function $f(x) = |x|$ on the interval $[-2, 2]$. We can compute its average value by using the integral formula. The average value of this function over the given interval is:

$$\frac{1}{2-(-2)}\int_{-2}^2 |x|dx = \frac{1}{4}\int_{-2}^2 |x|dx$$

In order to evaluate this definite integral, we must use the fact that the absolute value function is a piecewise-defined function and the integrals have to be divided into two separate integrals. Therefore, the average value is:

$$\frac{1}{4}\left[\int_{-2}^{0} -x\,dx + \int_{0}^{2} x\,dx\right] = \frac{1}{4}\left[-\frac{x^2}{2}\bigg|_{-2}^{0} + \frac{x^2}{2}\bigg|_{0}^{2}\right] = \frac{1}{4}(4) = 1$$

This same result could also be computed using the area definition of the definite integral. Because:

$$\int_{-2}^{2} |x|\,dx$$

is equal to the area under the function $f(x) = |x|$ over the interval $[-2, 2]$, we can calculate the area using a formula from geometry. The region consists of two triangular regions with base 2 and height 2 on either side of the y-axis. Using the formula for area of a triangle, each region has an area of 2 square units. Therefore, the total region over the interval $[-2, 2]$ has an area of 4 square units. Plugging this amount into the average value formula, we have:

$$\frac{1}{2-2}\int_{-2}^{2} |x|\,dx = \frac{1}{4}(4) = 1$$

The average value of the absolute value function over the interval $[-2, 2]$ is 1.

The formula for the average value of a function over an interval is derived from Riemann sums. We know that the formula for average, or mean, of n numbers is equal to the sum of those numbers divided by n. Consider a function $f(x)$ that is continuous over the interval $[a, b]$ and divide the interval into n subintervals of equal length. The length of each subinterval is:

$$\frac{b-a}{n} = \Delta x$$

Also, define c_k to be a sample point in the kth subinterval:

$$[x_{k-1}, x_k]$$

The function $f(x)$ can be evaluated at each of these sample points. Therefore, the average of the function evaluations at all sample points is equal to

$$\frac{f(c_1) + f(c_2) + \cdots f(c_n)}{n}$$

which is the sum of the n function evaluations at the sample points divided by n. In sigma notation, this expression is equivalent to:

$$\sum_{k=1}^{n} \frac{1}{n} f(c_k)$$

Because we have $\frac{b-a}{\Delta x} = n$, this summation is equal to:

$$\sum_{k=1}^{n} \frac{1}{b-a} f(c_k)\Delta x$$

which is a Riemann sum multiplied times $\frac{1}{b-a}$.

This shows that the average value of the function over the interval $[a, b]$ is equal to $\frac{1}{b-a}$ times the Riemann sum of $f(x)$. If we take the limit of the Riemann sums as $n \to \infty$, this expression is equal to:

$$\frac{1}{b-a} \int_a^b f(x)dx$$

Connecting Position, Velocity, and Acceleration of Functions Using Integrals

Solving Rectilinear Motion, Related Rate, and Optimization Problems

Rectilinear motion problems can be solved using integration. If the velocity function of an object moving along a straight line is given, its antiderivative is equal to the position function of the object. Similarly, if the acceleration function of an object moving along a straight line is given, its antiderivative is equal to the velocity function. Initial conditions can be specified in either instance to solve for the constant of integration.

For instance, consider a particle moving along a straight line. Its velocity at time t is equal to $v(t) = 4t^2 - 3t$, and its initial position is $s(0) = 1$. It is true that:

$$\int v(t)dt = s(t)$$

Therefore:

$$s(t) = \int (4t^2 - 3t)dt = \frac{4}{3}t^3 - \frac{3}{2}t^2 + C$$

The initial condition gives us $s(0) = C = 1$. Therefore, the position function of the particle at time t is;

$$s(t) = \frac{4}{3}t^3 - \frac{3}{2}t^2 + 1$$

Secondly, consider a particle moving along a straight line with acceleration $a(t) = 4t$, initial velocity $v(0) = 2$, and initial position $s(0) = 1$. We know that:

$$\int a(t)dt = v(t)$$

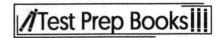

Therefore:

$$v(t) = \int (4t)dt = 2t^2 + C$$

We have $v(0) = C = 2$.

Therefore, the velocity function of the particle at time t is:

$$v(t) = 2t^2 + 2$$

The position function can be found by finding the antiderivative of the velocity function and applying the initial condition of the position function.

Therefore:

$$s(t) = \int (2t^2 + 2)dt = \frac{2}{3}t^3 + 2t + D$$

We have $s(0) = D = 1$, so:

$$s(t) = \frac{2}{3}t^3 + 2t + 1$$

Related rate problems are application problems involving derivatives of unknown functions in which we know information about rates of change. For example, if we know the rate at which air is being pumped into a ball, we can determine the rate at which the radius of the ball is changing. This process involves differentiation and not integration.

Optimization problems are another type of application problem involving derivatives. To optimize a given quantity means to find the best scenario, and in calculus this involves finding either a minimum or maximum value of a given function. Finding a minimum or maximum involves taking derivates and does not involve integration.

Using Accumulation Functions and Definite Integrals in Applied Contexts

Using Integrals to Represent Accumulation of a Rate of Change

A definite integral can be used to describe information regarding accumulation in real-world scenarios. Consider the situation in which water is flowing into an empty container at the constant rate of C liters per second for t seconds. If we want to determine how much water is in the container after a specific number of seconds, we would use the formula that volume is equal to the rate multiplied by elapsed time. Therefore, if water was flowing in at a rate of 2 liters per second, there would be $2(6) = 12$ liters of water in the container after 6 seconds. This idea relates to the definite integral of a constant function. Recall that the definite integral of a constant function is equal to the value of the function times the length of the interval. It is also equal to the area of the rectangle formed from the height of the constant function and the time interval along the horizontal axis.

Now, consider whether the rate $r(t)$ at which water is flowing into the container is not constant. We cannot simply use the multiplication formula used above to find the volume of water after a specific

number of seconds because it is not constant. In this case, we can use the idea of a definite integral. The volume of water after t seconds is equivalent to the area under the graph of $r(t)$ above the t-axis over the interval $[0, t]$.

In both cases, either with a constant or nonconstant rate of change, the definite integral represents an accumulation of those functions. The accumulation totals the amount of water in the empty container. This idea can be applied to many other scenarios that involve the accumulation of quantities.

Finding the Net Change of a Quantity Over an Interval

We can use the idea of a definite integral to compute the net change of a given quantity. Consider a function $f(t)$. The net change of the function over the time interval $[a, b]$ is equal to the integral:

$$\int_a^b f'(t)dt = f(b) - f(a)$$

The derivative function $f'(t)$ is equal to the rate at which the function $f(t)$ changes with respect to time t.

For example, consider a function $p(t)$ representing the population of a city, where the time t represents the number of years after the year 2000. Therefore, the definite integral:

$\int_4^8 p'(t)dt$ represents the net change in population of that city over the years 2004 to 2008. The function in the integrand $p'(t)$ represents the rate at which population changes, and in usual scenarios, it is nonconstant.

For both accumulation and net change contexts, it is important to utilize the correct units. For instance, if the rate of change is given in meters per second, both accumulation and net change is measured in terms of meters. The units relating to the quantity in the numerator are those that will be attached to accumulation and net change.

Also, it is important to pay attention to the limits of integration. If the lower limit of integration is 0 and the upper limit of integration is b, then the definite integral is referring to the first b time units of the given scenario. However, many times the lower limit is nonzero. In this case, the definite integral is referring to a time interval that does not start at the initial point in time. A common mistake is to assume that the interval always starts when time is equal to 0.

Expressing Information About Accumulation and Net Change

The definite integral can be used to express information about accumulation and net change in many real-world scenarios. For instance, consider a car factory that produces cars at a rate of $100 + 6t^2 - 2t$ cars per week, where t is equal to the given week. We could use this expression to determine how many cars were produced from the beginning of the first week to the end of the second week. The corresponding time interval is $[1, 2]$, and we would need to calculate the definite integral:

$$\int_1^2 (100 + 6t^2 - 2t)dt$$

The antiderivative of the rate of change function is:

$$f(t) = 100t + 2t^3 - t^2$$

Therefore, the definite integral is equal to:

$$f(2) - f(1) = 212 - 101 = 111$$

which means that 111 cars were produced from the beginning of the first week to the end of the second week.

The definite integral also applies to linear motion. If the function $s(t)$ represents the position of an object at time t, we know that the velocity of that object is equal to the derivative of the position function, or $s'(t) = v(t)$. The definite integral of the velocity function over a time interval $[a, b]$ is equivalent to the net change of the position of the object over that time. The net change in position is also referred to as displacement. Therefore, the displacement of an object with velocity function $v(t) = s'(t)$ over the time interval $[a, b]$ is equal to:

$$\int_a^b v(t)dt = \int_a^b s'(t)dt = s(b) - s(a)$$

Note that this quantity is different than total distance traveled. If we want to calculate total distance traveled, we calculate the definite integral of the speed $|v(t)|$ as $\int_a^b |v(t)|dt$.

Finally, we can consider the business application of a cost function $C(x)$. A cost function calculates the cost, in dollars, of producing x units of something. The derivative of the cost function, which is the rate of change of the cost function, is referred to as the marginal cost function. It states the cost of producing one more unit. Given two quantities, a and b, the cost of the production between those two given quantities is equal to $C(b) - C(a)$. We also know that this quantity is equal to the definite integral of the marginal cost function over that same interval. Specifically:

$$\int_a^b C'(x)dx = C(b) - C(a)$$

Finding the Area Between Curves Expressed as Functions of x

Calculating Areas in a Plane Using Definite Integrals

As discussed previously, a definite integral can be used to calculate the area between the graph of a function $f(x)$ and the x-axis over the interval $[a, b]$. However, it can also be used to calculate the area between two curves. Suppose that we have two functions $f(x)$ and $g(x)$ where $f(x) \geq g(x)$ over the interval $[a, b]$. Therefore, the graph of $f(x)$ lies above the graph of $g(x)$. The area of the region between the graphs of the function is equal to the integral of $f(x) - g(x)$ over the given interval. Therefore, the area between the graphs of the two curves $f(x)$ and $g(x)$ over the interval $[a, b]$ where $f(x) \geq g(x)$ is equal to

$$\int_a^b \big(f(x) - g(x)\big)dx$$

which can also be evaluated as:

$$\int_a^b f(x)dx - \int_a^b g(x)dx$$

Consider a situation in which we want to determine the area between the graphs of the functions:

$$f(x) = x^2 + 4x + 4$$

And:

$$g(x) = x + 2$$

over the interval $[2, 4]$. By looking at the graphs of each function, we know that:

$$f(x) \geq g(x)$$

over the given interval. Therefore, in order to calculate the area between the two functions, we calculate the following definite integral:

$$\int_2^4 [(x^2 + 4x + 4) - (x + 2)]dx.$$

The integrand can be simplified by collecting like terms. Therefore, we have:

$$\int_2^4 (x^2 + 3x + 2)dx$$

We can use the fundamental theorem of calculus to evaluate this integral. The antiderivative of the integrand is:

$$\frac{x^3}{3} + \frac{3x^2}{2} + 2x$$

Therefore, the area between the two curves over the interval:

$$[2, 4] \text{ is } \frac{x^3}{3} + \frac{3x^2}{2} + 2x \bigg|_2^4 = \frac{160}{3} - \frac{38}{3} = \frac{122}{3}$$

Finding the Area Between Curves Expressed as Functions of y

Calculating Areas in a Plane Using Two Functions

Consider two functions $f(x)$ and $g(x)$ in which $f(x) \geq g(x)$ over the interval $[a, b]$ as seen here:

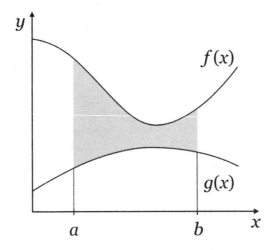

The area of the region between the two curves bounded by the lines $x = a$ and $x = b$ can be determined by using either geometry or calculus. If the area is easily calculated using a geometrical formula such as the area of a circle or rectangular, that approach can be used. If that method is not possible and the region is not simple enough to calculate geometrically, the area is equal to the following integral:

$$\int_a^b [f(x) - g(x)]dx$$

To determine the area between two curves using the integration method, the curves should be graphed to determine which curve is the upper curve and which curve is the lower curve. Then, the limits of integration need to be found. Those limits sometimes are given in the problem. However, if they are not, where the graphs intersect needs to be determined by setting the functions equal to each other and solving for x. Once the limits are determined, the integral:

$$\int_a^b [f(x) - g(x)]dx$$

is calculated.

A similar approach can be used for two functions of y. If two functions $f(y)$ and $g(y)$ are given in which:

$$f(y) \geq g(y)$$

over the interval $[c, d]$ along the y-axis, the area between the two curves is equal to the integral:

$$\int_c^d [f(y) - g(y)]dy$$

Such a region can be seen here:

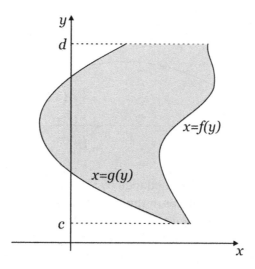

Finding the Area Between Curves That Intersect at More Than Two Points

Using the Sum or Difference of Functions to Find Area in the Plane

If the area between two curves that intersect at more than two points needs to be calculated, it must be taken into consideration which function is larger on each subinterval. For instance, consider the two functions:

$$y = 3x^3 - 10x^2 + 8$$

and

$$y = -x^2 + x + 2$$

The region between the two functions can be seen here:

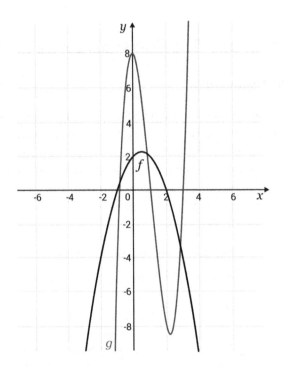

If the area between the two curves from their two outer points of intersection needed to be calculated, it would have to be noted that there is also a third point of intersection. Therefore, two definite integrals would be calculated. The first integral would be calculated from the leftmost point of intersection to the middle point of intersection, and the second integral would be calculated from the

middle point of intersection to the rightmost point of intersection. Note that over each interval, a different function is larger. For this methodology, the area would be equal to:

$$\int_a^b ((3x^3 - 10x^2 + 8) - (-x^2 + x + 2))dx + \int_b^c ((-x^2 + x + 2) - (3x^3 - 10x^2 + 8))dx$$

where a represents the leftmost point of intersection, b represents the middle point of intersection, and c represents the rightmost point of intersection.

Another way to calculate the area between the two functions would be to calculate the absolute value of the difference of the two functions over the entire interval. This method would be simpler. For instance, for the example discussed previously, the area being calculated would be equal to:

$$\int_a^c |(3x^3 - 10x^2 + 8) - (-x^2 + x + 2)|dx$$

where a represents the leftmost point of intersection and c represents the rightmost point of intersection.

Volumes with Cross Sections: Squares and Rectangles

Using Integration to Find Volumes

Integration can be used to find the volume of a solid body. Consider a three-dimensional shape that exists within the Cartesian coordinate system. It extends from lower boundary $y = a$ to upper boundary $y = b$ along the y-axis. Therefore, it has a height of $b - a$. The shape does not have a constant area at each individual cross section at height y, which means that the areas of the cross section change shape as the height changes. We define $A(y)$ to be the area of the horizontal cross section at each height y. We can think of the horizontal cross section as the intersection between the three-dimensional shape and the horizontal plane with height y.

In order to compute the volume of the three-dimensional shape, we use the idea of a Riemann sum. We partition the shape into n horizontal slices with thickness:

$$\frac{b - a}{n} = \Delta y$$

Each of the ith slices exist over the subinterval $[y_{i-1}, y_i]$ and have volume V_i. To have a good approximation, we use a very small thickness of each slice. Each slice approximates the shape of a right cylinder that has a volume of Ah where A is the area of its base and h is its height. Each slice has $A(y_{i-1})$ as the area of its base and has a height of Δy. Therefore, each slice has volume:

$$V_i = A(y_{i-1})\Delta y$$

Adding up all the slices gives us the following sum:

$$V = \sum_{i=1}^{n} V_i \approx \sum_{i=1}^{n} A(y_{i-1})\Delta y$$

This is a Riemann sum that utilizes left endpoints as the sample point in each subinterval. This Riemann sum approximates the definite integral:

$$\int_a^b A(y)dy$$

If we take the limit of the Riemann sum as $n \to \infty$, then the limit is equal to the definite integral. Therefore, if $A(y)$ is equal to the area of the horizonal cross section at the height y of a three-dimensional solid which extends from heights $y = a$ to $y = b$, then the volume of that solid is equal to

$$\int_a^b A(y)dy$$

Let's say that we want to use integration to find the volume of a pyramid whose height is 14 inches and base is a square with sides that are 6 inches long. In order to use integration, we must determine a formula for the horizonal cross section $A(y)$. The horizontal cross section is always a square because the base is a square. We can find a formula for the length of the side of each cross section by using similar triangles. We know that the inside of the pyramid consists of a right triangle with height 14 inches and base 3 inches. We can also create a right triangle inside of the pyramid with a height of $14 - y$ and a base of $0.5s$, where s is the length of the square that creates the cross section. Properties of similar triangles tell us that:

$$\frac{3}{14} = \frac{0.5s}{14 - y}$$

Therefore, we have:

$$7s = 3(14 - y)$$

or

$$s = \frac{3}{7}(14 - y)$$

We know that the area of a square is equal to side squared, so the area of the cross section at height y is:

$$A(y) = \frac{9}{49}(14 - y)^2$$

Therefore, the volume of the pyramid is found by integrating this function over the interval $[0, 14]$ along the y-axis as follows:

$$\int_0^{14} \frac{9}{49}(14 - y)^2 dy = 168$$

Therefore, the volume of this region is 168 cubic inches. Note that this answer agrees with the formula for the volume of a pyramid:

$$V = \frac{1}{3}Ah = \frac{1}{3}(36)(14) = 168$$

where A is the area of the base of the pyramid.

Volumes with Cross Sections: Triangles and Semicircles

Finding the Volume of Solids with Triangular and Semicircular Cross Sections

A **solid of revolution** is a three-dimensional shape formed by rotating a function around an axis. Calculating the volume of a solid of revolution involves integrating the cross-sectional area of the solid. Therefore, the volume of an integrable cross-sectional area $A(x)$ from $x = a$ to $x = b$ is the following integral:

$$\int_a^b A(x)dx$$

The cross-sectional areas can be thought of as slices with thickness dx. The cross-sectional areas can be constant, or nonconstant, depending on the shape of the slice. Geometric formulas, such as the formula for area of a circle, semicircle, and triangle, can be used if the slices are shapes that are studied in geometry. For instance, consider the volume of a sphere with radius r. Each cross-section is a circle with equation:

$$x^2 + y^2 = r^2$$

This equation can rewritten as:

$$y^2 = r^2 - x^2$$

The area of each cross-section in the sphere is πy^2, so we calculate the volume as:

$$\int_{-r}^{r} \pi(r^2 - x^2)dx$$

Volume with Disc Method: Revolving Around the x- or y-Axis

Finding the Volume of Solids Using the Disc Method

A **solid of revolution** can be formed by rotating a function of x about the x-axis. When the disc method is used to calculate such a solid of revolution, the cross section is perpendicular to the axis of revolution, has radius $R(x)$, and area:

$$A(x) = \pi[R(x)]^2$$

For instance, the volume of the region of the solid formed by rotating the curve $y = x^{1/3}$ from $x = 0$ to $x = 1$ is equal to the integral:

$$\int_0^1 \pi \left(x^{\frac{1}{3}}\right)^2 dx$$

This integral is used because for any x, the radius is $R(x) = x^{1/3}$.

A solid of revolution can also be formed by rotating a function of y about the y-axis. In this case, the volume is the integral of integrable cross-sectional area $A(y)$ from $y = c$ to $y = d$:

$$\int_c^d A(y)dy$$

When the disc method is used, the cross section is perpendicular to the axis of revolution, has radius $R(y)$, and area:

$$A(y) = \pi[R(y)]^2$$

Volume with Disc Method: Revolving Around Other Axes

Calculating Volumes of Solids of Revolution Around Any Line

Volumes of solids of revolution can also be formed by rotating functions around lines other than the axes. Any vertical or horizontal line can be used. In this case, it is important to determine the correct radius function if the disc method is used to calculate the volume. Consider the same scenario as above, but instead of rotating the function $y = x^{1/3}$ about the x-axis, it is rotated about the horizontal line $y = 1$. The radius function would now be:

$$R(x) = 1 - x^{\frac{1}{3}}$$

and the integral to compute the volume would be

$$\int_0^1 \pi \left(1 - x^{\frac{1}{3}}\right)^2 dx$$

The function is subtracted from 1 in the radius function because graphically, 1 is larger than $f(x)$ in the discussed region. This method can also be applied to rotating functions of y about vertical lines.

Volume with Washer Method: Revolving Around the x- or y-Axis

Finding the Volume of Solids with Ring Shaped Cross Sections

If a function that is rotated around the x- or y-axis to form a solid of revolution does not border on the chosen axis, the solid will have a hole in it. The cross-sections will be ring shaped, and the **washer method** can be used to find the volume of the region. If the solid is formed by rotating around the x-axis, each cross-sectional ring, or washer, has an outer radius function $R(x)$ and an inner radius function $r(x)$. The area of each ring, or washer, is:

$$A(x) = \pi[R(x)]^2 - \pi[r(x)]^2$$

This area gets integrated with respect to x to determine the volume of the solid.

If the solid is formed by rotating around the y-axis, each cross-sectional ring, or washer, has an outer radius function $R(y)$ and an inner radius function $r(y)$. The area of each ring, or washer, is:

$$A(y) = \pi[R(y)]^2 - \pi[r(y)]^2$$

This area gets integrated with respect to y to determine the volume of the solid.

For example, let's revolve the region between $x = \sqrt{y}$ and $x = \frac{y}{4}$ in the first quadrant around the y-axis. They intersect at $y = 0$ and $y = 16$, so those are the limits of integration. The outer radius is:

$$R(y) = \sqrt{y}$$

and the inner radius is $r(y) = \frac{y}{4}$. Therefore, the volume of the solid is:

$$\int_0^{16} \pi\left(\left[\sqrt{y}\right]^2 - \left[\frac{y}{4}\right]^2\right) dy$$

Volume with Washer Method: Revolving Around Other Axes

Finding the Volume of Solids Around a Line Using the Washer Method

As with the disc method, the **washer method** can also be used to calculate the volume of solids of revolution formed by rotating a curve around any horizontal or vertical line. However, for the washer method to be used, as opposed to the disc method, the cross section must be ring shaped. For example, rotate the region enclosed by the curves $y = x$ and $y = x^2$ about the horizontal line $y = 3$. The curves intersect at both $x = 0$ and $x = 1$, so those are the limits of integration. Note that technically both curves are being rotated around the line $y = 3$ separately, so individual integrals can be used for both curves and the difference from the outermost volume and the innermost integral can be calculated. The radius of the outermost region is $3 - x^2$, and the radius of the innermost region is $3 - x$. Therefore, the volume, calculated by the washer method, is:

$$V(x) = \int_0^1 \pi(3 - x^2)^2 dx - \int_0^1 \pi(3 - x)^2 dx = \int_0^1 \pi((3 - x^2) - (3 - x)^2)) dx$$

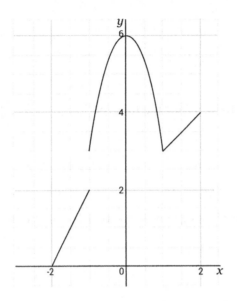

1. The figure above shows the graph of a function f with domain $-2 \leq x \leq 2$. Which of the following statements is/are TRUE?

I. $f(-1) = DNE$

II. $\lim\limits_{x \to -1} f(x) = DNE$

III. $f'(1) = 3$

     a. I only
     b. I and II only
     c. II only
     d. I, II, and III

2. What is $\lim\limits_{x \to \infty} \left(\dfrac{x^3+3x-7}{12x^3-6x+2} \right)$?
     a. $\dfrac{1}{12}$
     b. $\dfrac{1}{8}$
     c. 0
     d. ∞

3. Which of the following is an equation of the line tangent to the graph of $y = sinx + 3x$ at $x = 0$?
     a. $y = 4x$
     b. $y = 2x$
     c. $y = x$
     d. $y = -x$

4. The continuous function, $f(x)$, for all values of x is defined by $f(x) = \begin{cases} 3x^2, & x \neq 0 \\ a, & x = 0 \end{cases}$. What is the value of a?

    a. 2

    b. 0

    c. 6

    d. 5

5. What is the limit as h approaches zero for the function $\lim\limits_{h \to 0} \left(\dfrac{\cos(\frac{-\pi}{2}) + h}{h} \right)$?

    a. 0

    b. 1

    c. -1

    d. Nonexistent

6. The graph of f', the derivative of f, is given below. Which of the following could be the graph of the function, f?

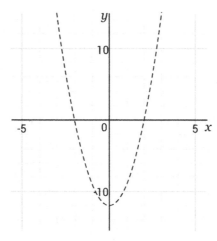

a

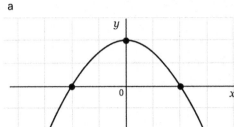

b

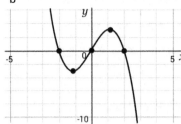

c

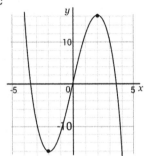

d

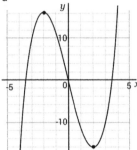

7. Given $F(x) = \int_{-2}^{x^3} (3t + 5)dt$, what is $F'(x)$?
   a. $F^1(x) = 9x^5 + 15x^2$
   b. $F^1(x) = 3x^3 + 5$
   c. $F^1(x) = 9x^5 + 5$
   d. $F^1(x) = 3x + 5$

8. Let f be the function given by $f(x) = \frac{4}{3}x^3 - 100x + 2$. On which of the following intervals is the function f decreasing?
   a. $(-\infty, -5] \, [5, \infty)$
   b. $(-5, 5)$
   c. $(5, \infty)$ only
   d. $(-\infty, -5)$ only

9. If $f(x) = e^{x^2}$, then what is $f'(2)$?
   a. $2e^4$
   b. e^4
   c. $2e^2$
   d. $4e^4$

10. What is the answer when the following integral is evaluated?
$$\int_0^{(\pi)} \frac{\sin(2\theta)}{1 + \cos(2\theta)} d\theta$$

   a. $\ln(2)$
   b. 0
   c. $\ln(\sqrt{2})$
   d. $-\ln(\sqrt{2})$

11. What is the most general antiderivative of the function: $g(x) = \frac{1+x+x^2}{\sqrt{x}}$?

    a. $G(x) = x^{\frac{1}{2}} + x^{\frac{3}{2}} + x^{\frac{5}{2}} + c$

    b. $G(x) = 2x^{\frac{1}{2}} + \frac{2}{3}x^{\frac{3}{2}} + \frac{2}{5}x^{\frac{5}{2}} + c$

    c. $G(x) = 2x^{\frac{1}{2}} + \frac{2}{3}x^{\frac{3}{2}} + \frac{2}{5}x^{\frac{5}{2}}$

    d. $G(x) = x^{\frac{1}{2}} + x^{\frac{3}{2}} + x^{\frac{5}{2}}$

12. What is the $\lim\limits_{x \to 0} \left(\frac{\sin(6x)}{2x} \right) = ?$

    a. $\frac{1}{3}$

    b. 3

    c. $-\frac{1}{3}$

    d. Undefined

13. Integrate the following function: $\int (\sin(x) + 2x + 2)dx$

    a. $\tan(x) + 2 + C$

    b. $\cos(x) + x^2 + 2x + C$

    c. $-\cos(x) + \frac{1}{2}x^2 + 2x + C$

    d. $-\cos(x) + x^2 + 2x + C$

14. Find $\frac{d}{dx} \frac{(x^2+4)}{x}$.

    a. $\frac{x^2-4}{x^2}$

    b. $\frac{x^2+4}{x^2}$

    c. $\frac{x^2-4}{x}$

    d. $\frac{x^2+4}{x}$

15. A particle is moving with acceleration $a(t) = \cos t + \sin t$, $s(0) = 5$, $v(0) = 4$. What is the position of the particle?

    a. $s(t) = -\cos t + \sin t + 5t - 6$

    b. $s(t) = -\cos t + \sin t + 5t + 6$

    c. $s(t) = -\cos t - \sin t + 5t + 6$

    d. $s(t) = -\cos t - \sin t + 5t - 6$

16. If $\int_0^2 f(x) = -5$ and $\int_0^6 f(x) = 8$, what is $\int_2^6 f(x)dx$?

    a. 13

    b. -13

    c. -3

    d. 3

17. The function $f(x) = (x - 2)^3$ satisfies the hypotheses of the Mean Value Theorem on the interval $[0, 2]$. What number c satisfies the theorem?

    a. $2 + \frac{2\sqrt{3}}{3}$

    b. $-2 - \frac{2\sqrt{3}}{3}$

c. 0

d. 2

18. The figure below shows the graph of a piecewise-linear function f. For $-3 \leq x \leq 3$, the function g is defined by $g(x) = \int_{-1}^{x} f(t)dt$. At what value(s) of x does $g(x)$ have a relative minimum?

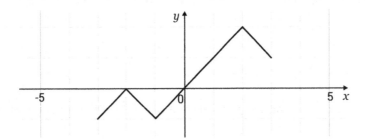

a. 2

b. 2 and 8

c. 0

d. 0 and 3

19. If $f(x) = xe^x$, then at $x = 2$, what is happening to f?

a. Increasing

b. Decreasing

c. Concave up

d. Constant

20. What is the lim as h approaches zero for: $(\frac{\sqrt[3]{27+h}-3}{h})$?

a. 3

b. $\frac{1}{3}$

c. 1

d. Undefined

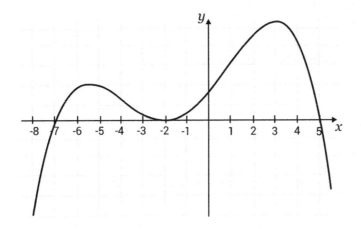

21. The graph of f' is shown above. The graph of f has a point of inflection at $x =$
    a. -7, -2, 3
    b. -7, -4, .3
    c. -7, 5
    d. -5.5, -2, 3

22. What is the area of the region bounded by the graphs of $y = x^3$, $y = 0$, and $x = 3$?
    a. 27
    b. 81
    c. 28.3
    d. $\frac{81}{4}$

23. Use separation of variables to find the general solution to the differential equation $y' + 8xy^2 = 0$.
    a. $y = 4x^2 + C$
    b. $y = (4x^2 + C)^{-1}$
    c. $y = 8x^2 + C$
    d. $y = 4x^{-2} + C$

24. Solve the initial value problem $y' + 4y = 0, y(0) = 8$.
    a. $y = 8\ln x$
    b. $y = e^{-4x}$
    c. $y = 8e^{-4x}$
    d. $y = 8e^{4x}$

25. Evaluate the following using integration by parts: $\int x^3 e^x dx$
    a. $x^3 e^x - 3x^2 e^x + 6e^x x - 6e^x + C$
    b. $x^3 e^x - 3x^2 e^x + 6e^x x + 6e^x + C$
    c. $3x^2 e^x + 6e^x x + 3e^x + C$
    d. $6e^x x + 3e^x + C$

26. Evaluate the following indefinite integral: $\int \frac{4x-9}{(x-2)(x-1)} dx$.
    a. $\ln|x - 1| + \ln|x - 2| + C$
    b. $\ln|(x - 1)(x - 2)| + C$
    c. $-5\ln|x - 1| + \ln|x - 1| + C$
    d. $5\ln|x - 1| - \ln|x - 2| + C$

27. Evaluate the following indefinite integral: $\int \frac{dx}{\sqrt{16x-x^2}}$.
    a. $\sin^{-1}(x - 8) + C$
    b. $\sin^{-1}\left(\frac{x-8}{8}\right) + C$
    c. $\cos^{-1}\left(\frac{x-8}{8}\right) + C$
    d. $\cos^{-1}(x - 1) + C$

28. Find the area of the region bounded by the x-axis and the curve $y = x\ln x$ over the interval $[1, 2]$.
    a. $2\ln 2 - \frac{3}{4}$
    b. $2\ln 3$
    c. $3\ln 2 - \frac{3}{4}$

d. $-\frac{3}{4}$

29. What is the antiderivative of the function $f(\theta) = \sin(8\theta + 4)$?

    a. $\sin(8\theta + 4) + C$

    b. $-\frac{1}{8}\sin(8\theta + 4) + C$

    c. $\cos(8\theta + 4) + C$

    d. $-\frac{1}{8}\cos(8\theta + 4) + C$

30. Determine the net change in velocity over the interval $[2, 5]$ of an object with acceleration $a(t) = 10t - t^2 \frac{m}{s^2}$.

    a. $106 \frac{m}{s}$

    b. $77 \frac{m}{s}$

    c. $66 \frac{m}{s}$

    d. $54 \frac{m}{s}$

31. What is the average value of the function $f(x) = x^{-2}$ over the interval $[1, 6]$?

    a. $\frac{5}{6}$

    b. $\frac{1}{6}$

    c. $\frac{5}{3}$

    d. $\frac{1}{25}$

32. An object is released into the air with an initial velocity of 50 m/s. Therefore, its velocity at time t is $v(t) = 50 - 9.8t$. Determine the distance traveled by the object in the first 10 seconds.

    a. 50 m

    b. 10 m

    c. 100 m

    d. 25 m

33. What is the derivative of $\frac{d}{dx}\int_0^{x^3} \frac{t}{t-1}\,dt$?

    a. $\frac{x}{x-1}$

    b. $\frac{x^3}{x^3-1}$

    c. $\frac{3x^2}{3x^2-1}$

    d. $\frac{3x^5}{x^3-1}$

34. Evaluate $\int \sin^7 x \cos x\,dx$.

    a. $\frac{\sin^8 x}{8} + C$

    b. $\frac{\cos^8 x}{8} + C$

    c. $\frac{\sin x \cos x}{8} + C$

    d. $\sin x \cos x + C$

Test Prep Books

35. Evaluate the definite integral $\int_1^{16} x^{1/4}dx$.

   a. $\frac{64}{5}$

   b. 124

   c. 64

   d. $\frac{124}{5}$

36. If $f(x) = \int_1^{x^2} \frac{e^t}{t}dt$, then what is $f'(3)$?

   a. $\frac{e^3}{3}$

   b. $\frac{2}{3}e^9$

   c. $\frac{e^9}{9}$

   d. $e^9 - e$

37. Which of the following definite integrals is equivalent to $\lim_{N \to \infty} \sum_{i=1}^{N}(c_i^2 - c_i^3)\Delta x$, where $\Delta x = \frac{1}{N}$ is used to partition the interval $[1, 2]$?

   a. $\int_0^2 (x^2 - x^3)dx$

   b. $\int_1^2 (x^3 - x^2)dx$

   c. $\int_1^2 (x^2 - x^3)dx$

   d. $\int_1^2 (x^2)dx$

38. What is the slope of the line tangent to the graph of $y = x^3 - 4$ at the point where $x = 2$?

   a. $3x^2$

   b. 4

   c. -4

   d. 12

39. Let $f(x) = \begin{cases} \frac{x^2-4}{x-2} & if\ x \neq 2 \\ 0 & if\ x = 2 \end{cases}$. Which statement or statements are true?

   I. $\lim_{x \to 2} exists$

   II. $f(2)\ exists$

   III. $f\ is\ continuous\ at\ x = 2$

   a. I only

   b. II only

   c. I and II

   d. I and III

40. What is $\lim_{x \to 4} \frac{x^2-16}{x-4}$?

   a. 0

   b. 1

   c. 8

   d. Nonexistent

152

41. A particle moves along the x-axis so that at any time $t \geq 0$, its velocity is given by $v(t) = \frac{6}{t+3}$. What is the acceleration of the particle at time $t = 5$?

a. $-\frac{2}{3}$

b. $-\frac{3}{32}$

c. $\frac{3}{4}$

d. $\frac{2}{3}$

42. Given the graph of the derivative of $f(x)$, on what interval or intervals is the graph of $f(x)$ increasing?

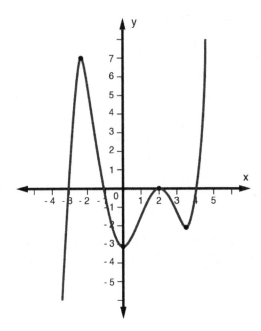

a. $(-3, -1)(4, \infty)$
b. $(-\infty, -2.4)(0, 2)(3.4, \infty)$
c. $(-\infty, -3)(-1, 4)$
d. $(0, \infty)$

43. What is the trapezoidal approximation for the integral $\int_0^4 \sqrt{x}\, dx$, using 4 subintervals?

a. 5.333
b. 12.293
c. 10.293
d. 5.146

44. What is the definite integral that represents the area of the region bounded by the graphs of $y_1 = 5 - x^2$ and $y_2 = -3x - 5$?

  a. $\int_{-\sqrt{5}}^{\sqrt{5}} (5 - x^2)\, dx$

  b. $\int_{-\sqrt{5}}^{\sqrt{5}} (x^2 - 3x - 10)\, dx$

  c. $\int_{-2}^{5} (-x^2 + 3x + 10)\, dx$

  d. $\int_{-2}^{5} [(5 - x^2) + (-3x - 5)]\, dx$

Calculator Permitted

1. What is the doubling time of the following differential equation that models population growth: $\frac{dy}{dt} = 7y$? Round your answer to three decimal places.

  a. 0.693

  b. 0.099

  c. 4.852

  d. 0.710

2. Find the area of the region between the graphs of $f(x) = 4x + 10$ and $g(x) = x^2 + 4x + 4$ over the interval $[0, 2]$. Round your answer to three decimal places.

  a. 19.333

  b. 10.111

  c. 9.333

  d. 12.999

3. The marginal cost of producing x recliners is $C'(x) = 200 - 2x + .005x^2$. If the startup cost is $15,000, what is the cost of producing the first 500 units? Round to the nearest dollar.

  a. $750,000

  b. $73,333

  c. $733,333

  d. $75,000

4. Calculate the Riemann sum for the function $f(x)$ over the interval $[1, 2]$ using a partition with a fixed Δx equal to 0.2 and left endpoints as sample points.

  a. 1.4

  b. 1.6

  c. 1.8

  d. 2

5. A 20-gram quantity of a radioactive isotope decays to 5 grams after 2 years. What is the decay constant of this isotope? Round your answer to three decimal places.

  a. 0.647

  b. -0.693

  c. -1.386

  d. 1.386

6. A rocket leaves the moon with an acceleration of $a(t) = 19.5 + .02t \frac{m}{s^2}$. How fast is the rocket traveling 1.5 minutes later if its initial velocity was $110 \frac{m}{s}$?

  a. $1755 \frac{m}{s}$

b. $1946 \frac{m}{s}$

c. $1865 \frac{m}{s}$

d. $1110 \frac{m}{s}$

7. Calculate the following definite integral: $\int_1^4 \frac{\ln x \, dx}{x^2}$. Round your answer to 3 decimal places.

    a. 0.403

    b. 0.750

    c. 0.806

    d. 0.693

Free Response Questions

1.

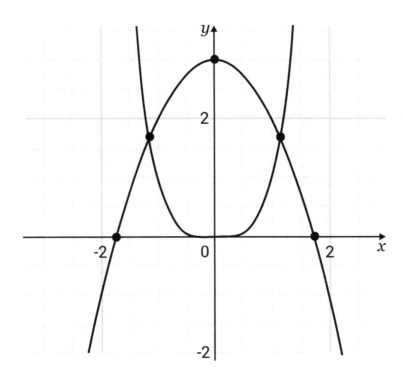

$F(x) = x^4$ and $g(x) = -x^2 + 3$.

    a. Find the area of the region bounded by graphs above.

    b. Find the volume of the solid generated when $f(x)$ is rotated about the x-axis.

    c. Find the volume of the solid generated when the region bounded by the two curves is rotated about the y-axis.

2. Let f be a function with initial condition $f(1) = 1$ such that for all points (x, y) on the graph of f the slope is given by $\frac{2x^2+1}{y}$.

    a. Find the slope of the line tangent to the graph of f at the point where $x = 1$.

    b. Write an equation of the tangent line to the graph at the point where $x = 1$.

c. Find an equation for f using the initial condition given.

3.

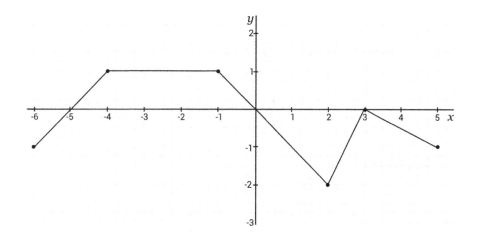

The figure above shows the graph of the piecewise-linear function, $f(x)$. For $-6 < x < 5$, the function g is defined by $g(x) = \int_3^x f(t)dt$.
  a. At what values of x is g increasing?
  b. At what values of x does g have a relative extrema?
  c. For what values of x is the graph of g concave down?

4. A graphing calculator is required for this problem. An object is moving along the x-axis for time $t \geq 0$ seconds. Its velocity is given by the function $v(t) = 2 + 4\cos(5t)$ in meters per seconds.
  a. Where is the initial velocity of the object?
  b. Is the object slowing down or speeding up at 4 seconds?
  c. From 0 to 2 seconds, at what times does the object change directions?
  d. What is the initial position of the object if the initial velocity is 0 meters per seconds?
  e. What is the total distance traveled from 0 to .25 seconds?

A calculator may not be used on these problems.

5. Let $f(x)$ be the continuous piecewise-defined function shown in the following graph:

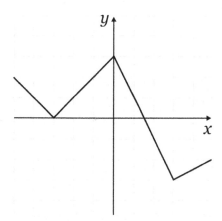

Let $h(x) = \int_0^x f(t)dt$.
   a. Find $h(1.5)$.
   b. Find $h(3)$.
   c. Determine $h'(2)$.
   d. Determine $h''(2)$.

6. Let R be the region bounded by the x-axis, the y-axis, the graph of the function $f(x) = x^2$ and the line $y = 9$.
   a. Sketch this region.
   b. Determine the area of this region.
   c. Determine the volume of this region when it is revolved around the x-axis.
   d. Determine the volume of this region when it is revolved around the y-axis.

Answer Explanations

Answers to No-Calculator Questions

1. C: There is a jump in the graph at $x = -1$, so the limit at that point does not exist. The first statement is false, because the function value can be found at $x = -1$. The third statement is false because the derivative at $x = 1$, or the slope, is not equal to three.

2. A: The numerator and the denominator are polynomials of power 3. Because the highest degree of the independent variable is the same on the top and bottom, the limit for this function is the coefficient of x^3. The coefficient of x^3 is $\frac{1}{12}$.

3. A: To find the value of the slope, take the derivative of the function to get:

$$y' = \cos x + 3$$

Then substitute $x = 0$ to find a slope equal to 4. Find the point on the curve by substituting $x = 0$ in the original equation to get $(0, 0)$. Now use $y = mx + b$ to find the equation of the line. Substitute zero in for x, zero in for y, and 4 in for m, or the slope. By solving for b, the final equation becomes $y = 4x$.

4. B: To be continuous, the limit as x approaches c must equal the value of $f(c)$. Because the function value must fit $f(c)$, find:

$$f(0) = 3(0)^2 = 0$$

5. B: The first step is to plug in zero to yield $\frac{0}{0}$, which means it is indeterminant. Then use L'Hospital's Rule by taking the derivative of the top and the derivative of the bottom. Using this value, substitute zero in place of h.

6. D: The graph has a max and min at $x = \pm 2$. Because the max/min is at these two points, the graph of the derivative, or f', is equal to zero at those points. The value of the f' function is equal to −11 at the x-value of zero. For the graph of d, the slope at $x = 0$ is large and negative. Observing the behavior of the derivative function shows the original function and its parts.

7. C: Apply the second fundamental theorem of calculus. When an integral is evaluated from a constant to a variable, the value is found by substituting the variable into the place of the unknown in the equation, or t. Then take the derivative of the variable. Find the product of these two values.

8. B: Take the derivative of f to get $4x^2 - 100$. Set this equal to 0 and solve for x to get the values 5 and −5. Find the sign of the derivative from negative infinity and −5, between −5 and 5, and between 5 and infinity. If the derivative is negative, then the function is decreasing.

9. D: The derivative of f is $2x(e^{x^2})$. The derivative equation can be written in function form:

$$f'(x) = 2x(e^{x^2})$$

The next step is to substitute $x = 2$ to find the function value:

$$f'(2) = 4e^8$$

10. B: Let $u = 1 + cos(2\theta)$ so:

$$du = -2sin2\theta$$

hen use u substitution to get $\int du/u$. The last step is to integrate to get $-1/2\ ln\ (1 + cos(2\theta))$ then integrate from 0 to π.

11. B: First, the function can be rewritten as:

$$g(x) = x^{-\frac{1}{2}} + x^{\frac{1}{2}} + x^{\frac{3}{2}}$$

The antiderivative is found by using the rule that:

$$\int x^n = \frac{x^{n+1}}{n+1} + c$$

Therefore:

$$G(x) = 2x^{\frac{1}{2}} + \frac{2}{3}x^{\frac{3}{2}} + \frac{2}{5}x^{\frac{5}{2}} + c$$

Only one constant (+c) is necessary for it to be the most general antiderivative.

12. B: The first step is to substitute zero in place of x to yield $\frac{0}{0}$. This is an indeterminant form. Then apply L'Hospital's Rule by taking the derivative of the numerator and denominator to get:

$$\frac{6 \cos 6x}{2}$$

The last step is to substitute zero into this function to get $\frac{6}{2} = 3$.

13. D: Integrate each term separately. The first term, $sin(x)$, is integrated by itself to yield $-cos(x)$. Then the term $2x$ is integrated to yield x^2. The last term is integrated to find $2x$ and the C is added as the constant in integration.

14. A: The derivative can be found by using the quotient rule:

$$\frac{x\frac{d}{dx}(x^2+4) - [(x^2+4)\frac{d}{dx}x]}{x^2} = \frac{x(2x) - (x^2+4)(1)}{x^2}$$

The derivative simplifies to:

$$\frac{x^2 - 4}{x^2}$$

15. C: This problem involves solving an initial value problem. To obtain a position function from acceleration, two antiderivatives must be found, and initial conditions must be applied. The first antiderivative gives velocity:

$$v(t) = \sin t - \cos t + c.$$

$v(0) = 4$ implies that $c = 5$. Therefore:

$$v(0) = 4 = \sin t - \cos t + 5$$

One more antiderivative gives:

$$s(t) = -\cos t - \sin t + 5t + d$$

$s(0) = 5$ implies that $d = 6$.

16. A: This answer is found by integrating using the following equations:

$$\int_0^2 f(x)dx + \int_2^6 f(x)dx = \int_0^6 f(x)dx$$

So:

$$-5 + \int_2^6 f(x)dx = 8$$

17. A: The Mean Value Theorem states that because the function is continuous and differentiable on the given interval, there exists a number, c, in the given interval $[0, 2]$ that satisfies:

$$f'(c) = \frac{f(2) - f(0)}{2 - 0}$$

Therefore:

$$3(c - 2)^2 = 4$$

Placing this quadratic equation in standard form gives:

$$3x^2 - 12x + 8 = 0$$

The quadratic formula yields:

$$c = 2 \pm \frac{2\sqrt{3}}{3}$$

Only the root within the given interval of $[0, 2]$ satisfies the theorem.

18. C: The graph shown is $g'(x)$, which can be interpreted as giving the slope for the original function $g(x)$. This graph changes from positive to negative at $x = 0$ so $g(x)$ has a slope of zero and a maximum value there.

19. C: Find the second derivative of the given function:

$$f(x) = xe^x$$

The next step is to substitute 2 in for the variable x. This answer will yield a positive value.

20. A: First, substitute 0 to get $\frac{0}{0}$. Then use L'Hospital's rule to get:

$$\frac{1}{3}(27 + h)^{\frac{2}{3}}$$

and substitute zero into the equation to yield an answer of 3.

21. D: Find the x values where f' has a relative maximum or relative minimum. If the graph reaches a maximum point, then the slope changes from negative to positive. This point would be an inflection point. Where there is a relative minimum, the slope changes from negative to positive, so there would be a point of inflection here also.

22. D: The answer is found by integrating as follows:

$$\int_0^3 x^3 dx = \frac{81}{4}$$

Integration is used because that shows the area under a curve. The boundaries 0 and 3 are used on the integral because the lines $y = 0$ and $x = 3$ set the limits.

23. B: First, rewrite y' as $\frac{dy}{dx}$. Then move the y terms to the left and the x terms to the right. This results in:

$$y^{-2}dy = -8xdx$$

Integrate both sides to obtain:

$$-y^{-1} = -4x^2 + C$$

This has an equivalent explicit form:

$$y = (4x^2 + C)^{-1}$$

24. C: We first use separation of variables to find the general solution of the differential equation:

$$\frac{dy}{dx} + 4y = 0$$

so

$$\frac{dy}{dx} = -4y$$

or

$$\frac{dy}{-4y} = dx$$

Integrate both sides to obtain:

$$-\frac{1}{4}\ln|y| = x + c$$

This has explicit form:

$$y = e^{-4x+c}$$

which can be written as:

$$y = ke^{-4x}$$

The initial condition says $y(0) = 8$, so $y(0) = k = 8$, so the solution to the initial value problem is:

$$y = 8e^{-4x}$$

25. A: We use integration by parts, first letting $u = x^3$ and:

$$dv = e^x dx$$

Therefore:

$$du = 3x^2 dx$$

and $v = e^x$. Substituting into the formula:

$$uv - \int v \, du$$

we have:

$$x^3 e^x - \int 3x^2 e^x dx$$

We again have to use integration by parts on this second integral. We let $u = 3x^2$ and $dv = e^x dx$. Therefore:

$$du = 6x dx$$

and $v = e^x$. Substituting into the formula $uv - \int v \, du$ we have:

$$3x^2 e^x - \int 6x e^x dx$$

One more round of integration by parts is necessary. We let $u = 6x$ and $dv = e^x dx$. Therefore, $du = 6dx$ and $v = e^x$. Substituting into the formula $uv - \int v \, du$ we have:

$$6x e^x - \int 6 e^x dx = 6x e^x - 6 e^x$$

Putting it all together, we have:

$$x^3 e^x - 3x^2 e^x + 6 e^x x - 6 e^x + C$$

26. D: We use the method of partial fraction decomposition to evaluate this integral. We set:

$$\frac{4x - 9}{(x - 2)(x - 1)} = \frac{A}{x - 2} + \frac{B}{x - 1}$$

Multiplying both sides by $(x - 2)(x - 1)$ gives us the identity:

$$4x - 9 = A(x - 1) + B(x - 2)$$

Setting $x = 1$ results in $B = 5$. Setting $x = 2$ results in $A = -1$. Therefore, the integral is written as:

$$\int \left(\frac{-1}{x - 2} + \frac{5}{x - 1} \right) dx$$

which is equal to:

$$- \ln|x - 2| + 5 \ln|x - 1| + C$$

27. B: We complete the square for the polynomial in the denominator:

$$16x - x^2 = -(x^2 - 16x)$$

$$-(x^2 - 16x + 64 - 64) = -(x^2 - 16x + 64) + 64$$

$$64 - (x - 8)^2$$

Therefore, the integral becomes:

$$\int \frac{dx}{\sqrt{64 - (x - 8)^2}}$$

The antiderivative is:

$$\sin^{-1} \left(\frac{x - 8}{8} \right) + C$$

28. A: To find the area, we need to calculate the definite integral:

$$\int_1^2 x \ln x \, dx$$

Integration by parts is necessary to find the antiderivative. We let $u = \ln x$ and $v' = x$. Therefore:

$$du = \frac{1}{x} dx$$

and $v = \frac{1}{2} x^2$. Using the formula for integration by parts, the antiderivative is equal to:

$$\frac{1}{2} x^2 \ln x - \int \frac{x}{2} dx$$

This expression is equal to:

$$\frac{1}{2} x^2 \ln x - \frac{x^2}{4}$$

Evaluating at the limits of integration, we have:

$$2 \ln 2 - 1 - \left(-\frac{1}{4}\right) = 2 \ln 2 - \frac{3}{4}$$

29. D: This requires a *u*-substitution. Let $u = 8\theta + 4$. Therefore, $du = 8d\theta$. We rewrite the integral as:

$$\int \frac{1}{8} \sin u \, du$$

The corresponding antiderivative is

$$-\frac{1}{8} \cos u + C$$

We back-substitute to obtain:

$$-\frac{1}{8} \cos(8\theta + 4) + C$$

30. C: The net change is found by integrating the acceleration function over the given time interval. Therefore:

$$\int_2^5 (10t - t^2)dt = 5t^2 - \frac{t^3}{3}\Big|_2^5 = 66\frac{m}{s}$$
$$\frac{250}{3} - \frac{52}{3}$$

31. B: The average value is calculated as:

$$\frac{1}{6-1} \int_1^6 x^{-2} dx = \frac{1}{5}(-x^{-1}|_1^6)$$
$$\frac{1}{5}\left(-\frac{1}{6} + 1\right) = \frac{1}{5} \times \frac{5}{6} = \frac{1}{6}$$

32. B: The total distance traveled is found by calculating the definite integral of the velocity function over the interval [0,10]:

$$\int_0^{10} (50 - 9.8t)dt = (50t - 4.9t^2)|_0^{10} = 500 - 490 - 0 = 10m$$

33. D: By the fundamental theorem of calculus, part 1, and the chain rule, we have:

$$\frac{d}{dx}\int_0^{x^3} \frac{t}{t-1} dt = \frac{x^3}{x^3 - 1}\left(\frac{d}{dx}(x^3)\right) = \frac{3x^5}{x^3 - 1}$$

34. A: This integral involves u-substitution because the integral contains a composite function. Let $u = \sin x$. Therefore, $du = \cos x\, dx$. The integral becomes $\int u^7\, du$, which has an antiderivative of $\frac{u^8}{8} + C$. We substitute back in to obtain:

$$\frac{\sin^8 x}{8} + C$$

35. D: We use the fundamental theorem of calculus, Part II:

$$\int_1^{16} x^{1/4}\, dx = \frac{4}{5} x^{5/4}\Big|_1^{16}$$

$$\frac{4}{5}\left(\sqrt[4]{16}\right)^5 - \frac{4}{5} = \frac{128}{5} - \frac{4}{5} = \frac{124}{5}$$

36. B: Using the fundamental theorem of calculus, Part I with the chain rule, we have:

$$f'(x) = \frac{e^{x^2}}{x^2}(2x) = \frac{2e^{x^2}}{x}$$

Therefore:

$$f'(3) = \frac{2}{3}e^9$$

37. C: Because the interval $[1, 2]$ is partitioned, the limits of integration are 1 and 2. The function that should be in the integrand is $x^2 - x^3$. Therefore, the corresponding integral is:

$$\int_1^2 (x^2 - x^3)\, dx$$

38. D: Finding the slope of the line tangent to the given function involves taking the derivative twice. The first derivative gives the line tangent to the graph. The second derivative finds the slope of that line. The line tangent to the graph has an equation $y' = 3x^2$. The slope of this line at $x = 2$ is found by the second derivative, $y = 6x$, or $y = 6(2) = 12$.

39. C: The limit exists because:

$$\lim_{x \to 2} f(x) = 4$$

The limit as x approaches 2 is 4, and the function value $f(2) = 0$; thus, they are not equal. Because they are not the same, the function is not continuous, and the first and second statements are the only ones that are true.

40. C: The numerator can be factored into $(x + 4)(x - 4)$. Since there is a factor of $(x - 4)$ in the numerator and denominator, these factors cancel, leaving the $(x + 4)$. Plugging in $x = 4$ into this function yields $4 + 4 = 8$.

41. B: The acceleration of the particle can be found by taking the derivative of the velocity equation. This equation is:

$$v'(t) = \frac{0 - 6(1)}{(t+3)^2} = \frac{-6}{(t+3)^2}$$

Finding the acceleration at time $t = 5$ can be found by plugging 5 in for the variable t in the derivative. The equation and the answer are:

$$v'(5) = \frac{-6}{(5+3)^2} = \frac{-6}{64} = \frac{-3}{32}$$

42. A: The graph of $f'(x)$ is positive on the intervals $(-3, -1)$ and $(4, \infty)$, meaning that $f(x)$ is increasing on the same intervals.

43. D: The graph of $f(x) = \sqrt{x}$ can be split into 4 trapezoids to approximate the integral. These subintervals can be represented in this expression:

$$\frac{4-0}{2(4)}[f(0) + 2f(1) + 2f(2) + 2f(3) + f(4)]$$

The area of a trapezoid can be calculated using the formula:

$$A = \frac{1}{2} \times h(b_1 + b_2)$$

where h is the height and b_1 and b_2 are the parallel bases of the trapezoid. Each function value in the brackets represents the sum of the bases of the trapezoids. The fraction outside the brackets represents the height of the trapezoids, dividing by two for the $\frac{1}{2}$ in the formula. Finding the function values and simplifying the expression leads to the answer 5.146.

44. C: Setting the y-values of each equation equal to one another finds the point where they meet. The equation:

$$5 - x^2 = -3x - 5$$

can be simplified by solving for 0:

$$0 = x^2 - 3x - 10$$

This equation can be factored into

$$0 = (x + 2)(x - 5)$$

The zeros are $x = -2$ and $x = 5$, between $x = -2$ and $x = 5$, $y_1 > y_2$.

Calculator-Permitted

1. B: The doubling time for a population growth model is $t = \frac{\ln 2}{k}$. For this example, $k = 7$, so we have:

$$t = \frac{\ln 2}{7} \approx 0.099$$

2. C: First, a graphing calculator can be used to see that the graph of $f(x)$ lies above the graph of $g(x)$ over the interval $[0,2]$. To find the area between the curves, we need to calculate the integral:

$$\int_0^2 (f(x) - g(x))dx$$

Therefore, we have:

$$\int_0^2 \left(4x + 10 - (x^2 + 4x + 4)\right)dx$$

$$\int_0^2 (-x^2 + 6)dx = -\frac{x^3}{3} + 6x \Big|_0^2 = \frac{28}{3} - 0 \approx 9.333$$

3. B: The antiderivative of the marginal cost function is the cost function. Therefore:

$$C(x) = \int (200 - 2x + .005x^2)dx$$

$$200x - x^2 + \frac{.005}{3}x^3 + c$$

We know that $C(0) = c = 15000$, the startup cost. Therefore, the cost function is:

$$C(x) = 200x - x^2 + \frac{.005}{3}x^3 + 15000$$

which tells us the cost of producing x units. $C(500) = \$73,333$, which is the cost of producing the first 500 units.

4. A: Because we are using left endpoints, our sample points are 1, 1.2, 1.4, 1.6, and 1.8. Therefore, the Riemann sum is calculated as:

$$\Delta x[f(1) + f(1.2) + f(1.4) + f(1.6) + f(1.8)]$$

$$.2(1 + 1.2 + 1.4 + 1.6 + 1.8) = .2(7) = 1.4$$

5. B: The general solution to the differential equation that models decay is $y(t) = y_0 e^{kt}$ where y_0 is the initial amount and k is the growth constant. In this scenario, after 2 years, the amount has dropped from 20 grams to 5 grams. Therefore, $5 = 20e^{k \cdot 2}$, or $0.25 = e^{2k}$. Taking the natural logarithm of both side results in $\ln 0.25 = 2k$, or:

$$k = \frac{\ln 0.25}{2} \approx -0.693$$

6. B: Because we know the acceleration function, its antiderivative is the velocity of the rocket. Therefore:

$$v(t) = \int (19.5 + .02t)dt = 19.5t + .01t^2 + C$$

Because the initial velocity of the rocket is 110, we have $v(0) = C = 110$. Therefore, the velocity function is:

$$v(t) = 19.5t + .01t^2 + 110$$

We plug 90 seconds in for t to obtain $v(90) = 1946\frac{m}{s}$.

7. A. First, we must use integration by parts to find the antiderivative. We let $u = \ln x$ and $dv = \frac{1}{x^2}dx$. Therefore, $du = \frac{1}{x}dx$ and $v = -\frac{1}{x}$. The integration by parts formula gives us:

$$-\frac{\ln x}{x} - \int -\frac{1}{x^2}dx$$

This expression is equal to:

$$-\frac{\ln x}{x} - \frac{1}{x} + C$$

Therefore:

$$-\frac{\ln x}{x} - \frac{1}{x}\Big|_1^4 = -\frac{\ln 4}{4} - \frac{1}{4} + \ln 1 + 1$$

$$-\frac{\ln 4}{4} + \frac{3}{4} \approx 0.403$$

Free Response Answers

1.

a. $\int_{-1.141}^{1.141} -x^2 + 3 - x^4\, dx = 5.082$

Find the intersection of the graphs at $x = -1.141$ and $x = 1.141$. The next step is to integrate to find the function:

$$-\frac{1}{3}x^3 + 3x - \frac{1}{5}x^5$$

By evaluating this function on the boundaries, −1.141 to 1.141, the answer is found to be 5.082.

b. $\pi \int_{-1.732}^{1.732} (-x^2 + 3)^2 dx = 52.23742$

This problem is solved using the disc method. Start by finding the x-intercepts for the graph of $g(x)$. The intercepts are −1.732 and 1.732. The radius of the disc will be $-x^2 + 3$. Integrate using the calculator for the final answer.

c. $\pi \int_{-1.141}^{1.141} (-x^2 + 3)^2 - (x^4)^2 dx = 45.99727$

This problem is solved using the disc method, which is a strategy that can be used when the cross-sections of the given solid are all circles. Then, the shape can be divided into discs to find the volume.

The large radius is found to be $-x^2 + 3$. The small radius is found to be x^4. Integrate using the calculator for the final answer.

2.

a. The point is given, $(1, 1)$, and can be used to find the slope of the equation of 3. The first step is to substitute the point $(1, 1)$ into the equation for slope.

b. Using the slope of 3, write the equation of the tangent line. The form $y = mx + b$ can be used to substitute values and find the equation. The equation takes the form $1 = 3(1) + b$. By solving for b, the value is $b = -2$. By plugging in the given values, the equation becomes:

$$y = 3x - 2$$

c. The first step is to find:

$$\frac{dy}{dx} = \frac{2x^2 + 1}{y}$$

The next step is to separate the variables by cross-multiplication so that the ys are on one side of the equation and the xs are on the opposite side. This step yields the equation:

$$y\, dy = (2x^2 + 1)dx$$

The next step is to integrate both sides of the equation to yield the equation:

$$\frac{1}{2}y^2 = \frac{2}{3}x^3 + x + C$$

Using the initial condition, find $f(1) = 1$ to find $C = -\frac{7}{6}$.

3.

a. $G'(x) = \frac{d}{dx}\int_3^x f(t)dt = f(x)$, so the graph given is the derivative of g. When the graph of f is positive, or above the x-axis, the derivative of g is positive. Recall that when the derivative is positive, the graph is increasing. Notice that the graph given above is above the x-axis between −5 and 0, which indicates that the graph of g is increasing $(-5, 0)$.

b. Relative extrema occur when the slope of the graph changes from positive to negative or negative to positive in the domain of the function. The graph above is the graph of the slope of g. This graph is below the x-axis $(-6, -5)$, above the x-axis $(-5, 0)$ and below the x-axis $(0, 3)$ and $(3, 5)$. This shows that the slope changes from negative to positive at $x = -5$ and from positive to negative at $x = 0$. There is a relative maximum at $x = -5$ and a relative minimum at $x = 0$.

c. To find the concavity of a function, look at the second derivative. When the second derivative of a function is negative, the graph is concave down. Given that $g'(x) = f(x)$, then $g''(x) = f'(x)$. Now remember that $f'(x)$ is the slope of f, so we will need to consider the slope of the graph given above. When the slope of this graph is negative, then the derivative of f is negative, meaning the second derivative of g is negative. The graph is decreasing on the intervals $(-1, 2)$ and $(3, 5)$ so $f'(x)$ is negative on these intervals, and $g''(x)$ is negative. Because $g''(x)$ is negative, the graph of g is concave downward on the intervals $(-1, 2)$ and $(3, 5)$.

4.

a. The initial velocity is:

$$v(0) = 2 + 4\cos(0) = 6\frac{m}{s}$$

b. Based on the graph of the velocity function, we can see that at time $t = 4$ the velocity curve has a negative slope. Therefore, the object is slowing down at this time.

c. The object changes direction when the velocity function crosses the t-axis and changes sign. From 0 to 2 seconds, this occurs three times at about .42, .84, and 1.68 seconds.

d. The antiderivative of the velocity function is equal to the position function:

$$s(t) = 2t + \frac{4}{5}\sin(5t) + C$$

for an arbitrary constant C. We can let the constant be equal to 0, and evaluate the position function at time $t = 0$. $s(0) = 0\ m$.

e. The total distance traveled from 0 to .25 seconds is equal to the definite integral of the absolute value of the velocity function over the interval $[0, .25]$. Because the velocity function is nonnegative over this interval, we can drop the absolute value. Therefore, we have:

$$\int_0^{.25}(2 + 4\cos(5t))dt = 2t + \frac{4}{5}\sin(5t)\Big|_0^{.25} \approx 1.26\ m$$

5.

a. $h(1.5) = \int_0^{1.5} f(t)dt$ can be calculated as the area under the curve over the interval $[0, 1.5]$. This region is a triangle with a height of 3 and a base of 1.5. Therefore:

$$A = \frac{1}{2}(1.5)(3) = 2.25 \text{ square units}$$

b. $h(3) = \int_0^3 f(t)dt$ can be calculated as the signed area between the curve and the x-axis over the interval $[0, 3]$. The two regions are triangles with a height of 3 and a base of 1.5. Therefore, the height of each triangle is:

$$A = \frac{1}{2}(1.5)(3) = 2.25 \text{ square units}$$

We have to incorporate the signed area. Therefore, we have:

$$h(3) = 2.25 + (-2.25) = 0$$

c. By the fundamental theorem of calculus, part 1, we have $h'(t) = f(x)$. Therefore:

$$h'(2) = f(2) = 0$$

d. Because we know $h'(t) = f(x)$, we have $h''(t) = f'(x)$. The graph of $f(x)$ is a straight line, so its derivative is equal to its slope. We can see that $f'(x) = -2$.

6.

a.

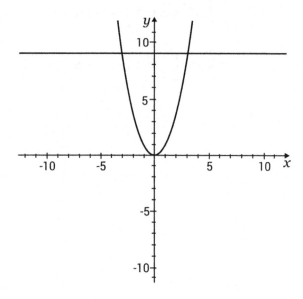

b. The line $y = 9$ lies above the graph of $f(x)$. Also, the line intersects the function at the ordered pair $(3, 9)$. Therefore, the area of this region R is equal to:

$$\int_0^3 (9 - x^2)dx$$

$$9x - \frac{x^3}{3}\Big|_0^3 = 27 - 9 = 18$$

c. The cross-sectional radius of the region is $9 - x^2$. Therefore, the volume of the region rotated around the x-axis is equal to:

$$\pi \int_0^3 (9 - x^2)^2 dx$$

$$\pi \int_0^3 (81 - 18x^2 + x^4)dx$$

$$\pi\left(81x - 6x^3 + \frac{x^5}{5}\Big|_0^3\right) = \pi\left(\frac{648}{5} - 0\right)$$

$$\frac{648\pi}{5} = 129.6\pi \approx 407.15$$

d. The function can be solved for x as $x = \sqrt{y}$, which is also equal to the cross-sectional radius of the region. The volume of the region rotated around the y-axis is equal to:

$$\pi \int_0^9 \sqrt{y}\, dy = \pi \int_0^9 y^{1/2} dy$$

$$\pi \left(\frac{2}{3} y^{3/2} \Big|_0^9 \right) = 18\pi \approx 56.55$$

Dear AP Calculus Test Taker,

We would like to start by thanking you for purchasing this study guide for your AP Calculus exam. We hope that we exceeded your expectations.

Our goal in creating this study guide was to cover all of the topics that you will see on the test. We also strove to make our practice questions as similar as possible to what you will encounter on test day. With that being said, if you found something that you feel was not up to your standards, please send us an email and let us know.

We would also like to let you know about other books in our catalog that may interest you.

AP Chemistry

This can be found on Amazon: amazon.com/dp/1628456914

AP World History

amazon.com/dp/162845671X

We have study guides in a wide variety of fields. If the one you are looking for isn't listed above, then try searching for it on Amazon or send us an email.

Thanks Again and Happy Testing!
Product Development Team
info@studyguideteam.com

FREE Test Taking Tips DVD Offer

To help us better serve you, we have developed a Test Taking Tips DVD that we would like to give you for FREE. **This DVD covers world-class test taking tips that you can use to be even more successful when you are taking your test.**

All that we ask is that you email us your feedback about your study guide. Please let us know what you thought about it – whether that is good, bad or indifferent.

To get your **FREE Test Taking Tips DVD**, email freedvd@studyguideteam.com with "FREE DVD" in the subject line and the following information in the body of the email:

> a. The title of your study guide.

> b. Your product rating on a scale of 1-5, with 5 being the highest rating.

> c. Your feedback about the study guide. What did you think of it?

> d. Your full name and shipping address to send your free DVD.

If you have any questions or concerns, please don't hesitate to contact us at freedvd@studyguideteam.com.

Thanks again!

CPSIA information can be obtained
at www.ICGtesting.com
Printed in the USA
LVHW020211240821
695615LV00009B/88